easyJet

Lois Jones has written about the airline and travel industry for numerous publications, including Bloomberg, the *Sunday Times*, the *Daily Telegraph*, the *European* and *Airline Business* magazine. She has won three prizes for her work: the Reed Business Information Best Newcomer of the Year, the Raytheon Best Aerospace Business Submission, and Transport Journalist of the Year from the Chartered Institute of Transport. This is her second book.

easyJet

easyJet.com

The story of Britain's biggest
low-cost airline

Lois Jones

First published 2005 by
Aurum Press Limited
7 Greenland Street
London NW1 0ND
www.aurumpress.co.uk

This revised and updated paperback edition first
published 2007

A catalogue record for this book is
available from the British Library.

ISBN-10: 1 84513 247 5
ISBN-13: 978 84513 247 7

10 9 8 7 6 5 4 3 2 1
2012 2011 2010 2009 2008 2007

Text design by Roger Hammond

Typeset by SX Composing DTP, Rayleigh, Essex

Printed in the UK by
CPI Bookmarque, Croydon, CR0 4TD

This book is dedicated to
my dear father – thank you
for showing me the way
on the journey through life.

Contents

Acknowledgements

THIS IS AN unauthorised account of easyJet and how the bright orange airline has transformed peoples' lives by making flying affordable for everyone. The story is the result of numerous interviews with key players in the airline industry, people associated with the airline and many passengers.

I would like to thank many for their help in creating this book. Individuals who deserve a particular note of thanks include: David Bryon, managing director of bmibaby; Chris Buckley, senior vice-president Europe at Airbus; Professor Rigas Doganis, industry expert; Tim Jeans, managing director of Monarch Scheduled; Philipa Kane, former easyJet employee; Andrew Lobbenberg, airline analyst at ABN Amro and of course my editor Graham Coster. The biggest thanks of all goes to Barnaby, my wonderful, loving husband, and to my family.

1. How it all started

VISITORS TO LUTON Airport in the autumn of 1995 regularly gawked at two of the Boeing 737s parked outside on the tarmac. Someone had painted human-sized, bright orange digits along the fuselages of the aircraft. A closer look revealed that the digits made up a telephone number. People who dialled it found they could fly between Luton and Glasgow for £29 each way with an airline called easyJet.

EasyJet first took to the skies on 10 November 1995, just five months after its conception, flying to Glasgow with a plane normally used by British Airways. One passenger on flight EZJ 11, on what he described as a 'wet, miserable, lousy day in Luton', was its founder, Stelios Haji-Ioannou; he may not have known it at the time, but his venture would change not only the world of aviation but the culture we live in.

Stelios was a bear-like figure, tall and broad with dark curly hair and a marked Greek accent. He wore a loose, open-necked shirt, slacks and a Swatch watch, even though (as he later admitted) he owned a Patek Philippe. He came from a background of dazzling wealth, with a shipping tycoon father who enjoyed cruising the Mediterranean on a floating gin palace capable of carrying some 180 people. Stelios himself was worth more than £100 million, with homes in London, Athens and Monaco, but he was less interested in showing off his fortune; embarrassed by his vast wealth, he made a conscious effort not to stand out. 'Nobody likes fat cats,' he once commented. 'People are always suspicious of people in grey pinstriped suits with a Rolls-Royce and a chauffeur.'

Stelios's attitudes were key to his imaginative approach to air travel, an approach that was to make him popular with all ranks of society. He realised from the start that it was hard to make short-haul air travel make glamorous, and he had no intention of trying. Instead, the self-proclaimed entrepreneurial Robin Hood wanted to declare the end of 'rip-off Britain' and offer consumers an airline with low-fare flights. The philosophy was simple: cut out the travel agent, the in-flight meals – even the peanuts – and pass on the massive savings to the customer. Instead of wearing a uniform, flight attendants were dressed casually in black jeans and orange polo shirts. 'No frills, no extras,' said Stelios. 'You pay for the flight and nothing less. That's what people want. The so-called freebies that other airline offer aren't freebies at all. They're a rip-off. I look at it like this. If someone came up to me with a plastic tray of airline food and said, "Will you give me a tenner for this shit?" I would say "no". There's no such thing as a free lunch so we don't pretend to provide one.'

It was a strategy that was bound to make Stelios popular with the travelling public. Unsurprisingly, the airline establishment was less enthusiastic, but Stelios was not slow to take up the cudgels. When Swissair opposed easyJet's plans to fly to Barcelona from Geneva, insisting that the airline obey an obscure rule that its cheap flights must come with accommodation attached, Stelios responded by pitching a tent on a rocky hillside north of Barcelona and inviting easyJet passengers to stay there. Stelios was a fierce critic of his rivals, particularly British Airways. When BA launched its own no-frills airline, Go, he tried to hijack the event by booking a seat and turning up in a boilersuit in his company's trademark orange. EasyJet eventually bought Go.

Shrewd business sense accompanied the PR stunts. The essential elements of the easyJet business model have always been fast turnarounds, no free lunch and enticingly low fares that rise as flights fill up. Nine out of ten easyJet seats are now sold via the Internet, a far higher proportion than for any traditional airline. The company squeezes the maximum possible revenue from each flight; even its airsickness bags convert into envelopes to send away camera films for processing. And it differs from the average low-cost airline operators, which fly on routes between secondary airports, by operating competitive routes between major cities.

EasyJet's cost control is legendary, as I learnt during my first interview with Stelios in 1996. At the time, I was a young reporter working for *Airline Business* magazine. I had been swept away by the glamour of the airline industry, the champagne receptions and the luxurious press trips to exciting destinations. EasyJet's larger-than-life chairman soon brought me down to earth. He didn't offer me a sandwich, never mind a lavish lunch when I interviewed him at easyLand, a tin shed at Luton Airport 30 miles north of London which serves as easyJet's headquarters. Instead, I was handed a plastic cup of instant coffee from an automatic machine. The coffee tasted awful and didn't even come with a plastic swivel stick to stir it with.

I hated the coffee but liked Stelios's candour. The tycoon was open about almost everything, even the failure of his diet. The only exception was his love life, which remained off-limits. By the end of the interview, Stelios had given me an excellent set of quotes for my story and fired me up with his vision of how no-frills flying would change the skies over Europe. He was right. The airline led the low-cost revolution in the UK, and Britain, in turn, has spearheaded the introduction of no-frills flights throughout Europe.

Since that first interview, I've watched easyJet grow to become the largest no-frills airline based in Britain, operating 92 aircraft on 89 routes from 36 European airports and beginning to eclipse the traditional carriers who once estimated its survival in days or weeks. 'It's not rocket science,' Stelios is fond of saying. EasyJet flies the same expensive tubes of metal as its competitors, but manages to do it more cheaply, luring passengers away from the established airlines and making travel affordable for everyone, even those who had never flown before.

Thanks to easyJet, the British are flocking to buy second homes in Spain, Italy and France. Fashionistas now refuse to pay retail for Gucci in London when they can fly to Milan for a weekend, buy the real deal at the factory outlet and take in a night of opera for roughly the same price. Prague, Budapest and Amsterdam have replaced Blackpool or Brighton as the most popular destinations for a stag party or hen weekend. For the many young Europeans working abroad, a weekly commute between London and Rome or Barcelona has become possible for the first time. It may not be rocket science but it's still clever stuff. Stelios claims to be redistributing the population of modern-day Europe. 'I meet a lot of people on our flights that don't have to make the stark choice between the sun in the south and business in the north,' he says. 'In the time of my father, this would have been impossible.'

Of course, no boom is all good. Europeans are feeling the effects of commodified travel on the continent's fragile infrastructure. In the clubbing mecca of Ibiza, business people love the budget airlines. Yet years of mass tourism are clearly taking their toll. Much of the tap water tastes salty and has a funny odour: the result of seawater infiltrating the overused wells. Splendid eastern Europe cities such as Prague and Tallinn are having a hard time adjusting to the hordes of English lads who parade through their streets dressed up in women's clothes, screaming and, most of all, getting drunk.

Aimée, the manager of Café Anglais on Tallinn's town hall square, is still struggling to comprehend the behaviour of some of the easyJet passengers who are shipped in each weekend. 'Their behaviour is incredible,' she complains. 'I don't know if they behave like that at home. Maybe they see us as some sort of second-hand, cheap country and think we don't deserve any better because they have money. It seems as if they think they can do whatever they want. They pee on the wall near us or are sick outside and then I have to clean it up. It happens twice a month or even more. For us, it's quite hard to understand.'

But overall the advantages of cheap flights outweigh the disadvantages. Since that first flight in 1995, easyJet, with its lurid orange brand, has become a household name. Nowadays the British flying public has lowered its expectations of on-board service. Sometimes people get on the wrong plane, are stranded for hours at airports or lose their luggage. As for the others, they don't care, as long as they get a cheap deal.

Stelios was born in Athens on Valentine's Day in 1967, the younger son of a wealthy Greek-Cypriot couple, Loucas and Nedi. His father, the eldest of thirteen, left his home village in Cyprus in 1950 with nothing. He made his fortune buying old tankers cheaply when no one wanted them, twice cashing out when there was a shortage of tanker capacity. He called his business Troodos, after the mountains in Cyprus where Stelios's grandfather scraped a living as a poor hill farmer. Talented and ambitious, Loucas made himself the 'Tanker King', the billionaire owner of one of the world's biggest tanker operations.

Shipping, shipping and more shipping was Loucas's philosophy. 'My father was a great advocate of focus,' Stelios has said. 'He decided what he wanted to do in life and stuck with it. He was very disciplined in not investing in anything else. My brother reminds me increasingly of my father. He thinks anything other than shipping is a rubbish business.'

Loucas had a profound influence on his son, and despite their occasional disputes there is no doubt that Stelios recognises his debt to his father. At home in Athens the talk was always business. It was in Stelios's genes. He describes his mother, Nedi, as the 'calming influence in my life' and thanks her for keeping his feet on the ground. She certainly keeps hers there, being so frightened of planes she has not flown for years. At the age of seven, Stelios was also scared of aeroplanes. Fortunately, his phobia didn't last very long.

Stelios enjoyed a privileged childhood: 'It was probably what you would call upper middle class.' As a child, he dreamed of playing football for AEK Athens, and his room, like that of many ten-year-old boys, was full of football posters. He attended private school and learnt English from an early age, later taking private tuition to complete two English A-levels in Mathematics and Economics. He was a 'good student, but not excellent', but his business sense was apparent at an early age. Even in the sixth form Stelios was managing other people's money, when he ran the students' union.

In 1984, aged seventeen, Stelios moved to London for his higher education. He was familiar with the country already: 'I was always coming to England. My father is an Anglophile.' His parents never kept him short of money – by eighteen he owned his own Porsche – but he developed a work ethic very early on: 'I didn't sit on my backside doing nothing. I decided I wanted to make a difference.' He studied at the London School of Economics, graduating in 1987 with a BSc in Economics. The next year, 1988, he also graduated from the City University Business School in London with an MSc in Shipping Trade and Finance.

For years, Stelios's ambition was to take over the family business. He worked for his father in his student holidays, and after graduating in 1988 joined his older brother at Troodos Shipping. Two years later, Loucas made himself chairman and his younger son the chief executive. But it was only on paper. 'Every morning,' said Stelios, 'my father used to wake up, pick up the phone and shout a bit at people, go to lunch and then shout a bit more.' When Stelios tried to move Troodos from old-fashioned typewriters to computers, Loucas interfered with his negotiations with outside suppliers. 'As the son of a father who is active in business, you're never really in charge.'

Stelios was growing more aware of the obstacles to his ambition. His father wasn't ready to retire. His older brother was also involved in the business and he was flanked by what he has described as 'lieutenants of his father', who weren't ready to let a twenty-three-year-old boss them around. Besides, Stelios didn't want to hang around in the shadow of his father and act the Greek playboy. 'Because I had a successful father, I had to prove to myself and the world that I wasn't just the son of a rich father. I was driven by the need to prove myself.'

A tragic event fed Stelios's growing restlessness and marked a turning point in his career. On 11 April 1991, the *Haven*, a Troodos tanker anchored outside Genoa, exploded, the fiery ball killing five crew members and swamping the Italian coast with 35,000 tons of crude oil. Stelios was in the office in Athens when the disaster struck. 'I slept there that night and tried to look after the people and everything else. But once the wreck itself was over, the ship was on the bottom of the sea, pollution was cleared up to the best of our ability, the whole thing became a legal saga instead of a real saga. I was facing criminal charges: a foreigner, a ship owner, and a villain in a foreign country.'

An Italian prosecutor, eagerly backed by the *Haven*'s first officer, went after Stelios and his father on criminal charges that included manslaughter, extortion and attempting to bribe a witness. If the Haji-Ioannous were found negligent they would be personally liable for the $1 billion claims; if human error by the crew was the cause of the accident, the family's liability was limited to $200 million, all paid for by insurance. As it turned out, the *Haven* had been completely refurbished and certificated just prior to the accident, and Stelios and his father were twice cleared of all charges and then finally exonerated.

The traumatic experience shaped the way that Stelios looked at life. He decided that his long-term aspiration was 'to build businesses that people like rather than businesses that people dislike'. He told his father that he was too ambitious to spend his life working for him and persuaded him to help him start his own business. Before he left Troodos, Stelios negotiated a $35 million payout from his father, with the hope that the funds would grant him his longed-for independence: 'If I had to go back and ask for funds every time, he would have been in charge.' Loucas imposed one condition, which Stelios accepted: if he became financially successful, his brother and sister would benefit too. 'My father was hedging his bets,' Stelios has said. 'He had two sons. He wanted to see who would do better.'

In 1992, at the age of twenty-five, Stelios set up Athens-based Stelmar Shipping. 'I had enough of being accused of running an old fleet,' he said later. 'I wanted to run a company with modern ships that focused on operating, not the buying and selling of assets.'

Stelios soon set about proving himself to his father. He built up the shipping line into a multi-million pound business that was comfortably profitable and listed on the New York stock exchange in 2001 at $12 a share. But he still wasn't satisfied. Within three years, he realised that he wasn't the person to run Stelmar. But at least he now knew what he wanted: to be an entrepreneur and start, not run, businesses. 'I was desperately trying to get rid of the "daddy's boy" image. I had to do something away from home, in an industry that my father knew nothing about, where my surname meant nothing to anybody.'

It was on a Virgin Atlantic flight between Athens and London in the early 1990s that Stelios had the idea that launched his empire. He happened to sit next to a friend, who offered him an opportunity to invest in a Virgin franchise. The airline, South East European Airlines, had started flying between London and Athens with just one plane. Stelios researched the deal; in the end he declined the Virgin opportunity, but in the process, he caught the aviation bug. He decided to enter the airline business on his own terms instead. 'Europe was being deregulated and I thought, if anyone is going to do this, it's me,' he recalled. Two years after he founded Stelmar, Stelios once more delegated himself out of a job and directed his attentions towards the airline business.

His first plan, perhaps because it was all he had ever known personally, was to set up something along the lines of Virgin's Upper Class service. Then a trip to the US impressed him with the low-cost business run by Southwest Airlines. 'I saw a winning formula. An internal flights company called Southwest Airlines was carrying 50 per cent more than British Airways with a cheap and cheerful service. I don't mind admitting I copied the idea. But I took it one step further. Southwest give away peanuts – we don't! But you can buy them on board for 50p if you want them.'

Stelios may have spent his privileged youth behind the wheel of a light-blue Porsche and at the helm of a 33-metre yacht by the name of *Gee Whizz*, but he understood the value of a pound. 'The world's biggest companies, such as Wal-Mart and McDonalds, got that way because they sell low-cost products.' His subconscious might have made the additional calculation that the low fares would make him popular. 'The cheaper you can make something, the more people there are who can afford it,' he has said. 'People like you if you give them what they like. And what they like is a low price. As soon as you get into the business of making things cheaper, then you are on the side of the little guy, you become their friend. I enjoy that. I could have chosen many careers. I could have gone into, I dunno, arms dealing or something. But I decided consciously to do something that was likeable.'

As a start-up carrier facing Europe's most highly regarded airline, British Airways, easyJet knew it had to focus on its competitor's soft spot: price. 'I spotted a gap in the market. For many years, BA and the other big airlines conditioned people into believing that air travel had to be expensive. If you give people a good fare they will jump on an aeroplane like they would jump on a bus. You just have to convince them that, if the price is right, they should take the benefit and see other places.'

Whether you're interested in ships, airlines or even stationary objects, having a billionaire shipping magnate as a father always helps when it comes to starting a business, as Stelios is the first to admit. He approached his father again for cash, while starting negotiations with a British Airways franchisee, GB Airways, about leasing aircraft. 'Banks would have laughed at me for trying to set up a low-cost airline with no backing.' He also arranged to operate his new venture under the Air Operating Certificates of GB Airways and the Luton-based Air Foyle, run by the Foyle family of bookshop fame, which flew BAe 146 planes on behalf of passenger airlines before later moving into air cargo and chartering giant Antonov 124s.

The crucial conversation with his father took place over dinner in the family summer house south of Athens, during the summer of 1995. He told his father he wanted the capital to set up a cheap, no-frills airline, designed to attract customers from coaches and trains as well as from other airlines.

'If I set up a marketing organisation and I don't buy the aircraft yet, I think I can make it take off with £5 million,' Stelios told his father. 'That's all I'm asking for at the moment. If it doesn't work, I'll pull the plug.' Stelios's father opened his chequebook, signed a cheque for £5 million and gave his son his blessing.

Loucas had one stipulation: he instructed Stelios not to base the airline in Athens, since he considered the Greek market too small and seasonal. So Stelios started looking around for a suitable base. London was the obvious choice. As a Greek Cypriot, he was born with a British passport, he spoke English and, besides, London served the biggest aviation market in Europe. 'It wouldn't have worked in any other country, with their red tape and state-owned airlines.'

Stelios settled on London Luton Airport. It was the cheapest of the four London airports, the others being Heathrow, Gatwick and Stansted. In June 1995, Stelios turned his back on his luxury yacht and a languid Greek summer and set up shop next to the toilets in a small, prefabricated building in Luton. He believed that offices should be spartan and perks should be banned. The office housed one PC, two desks, three phones and a big round wastepaper bin, with a note from Stelios saying, 'Scan documents, then throw them in the bin. This is a paperless office.' Stelios never relaxed the paperless rule. Finance director Nick Manoudakis, his first colleague and another son of a rich Greek magnate, resorted to keeping a hidden stash of documents in the ladies' toilets, the only place in the airline where they were safe from the boss's eyes.

Stelios worked 100-hour weeks, but his style at work was very relaxed. Colleagues called him by his first name, not least because, as he joked himself, 'the surname is unpronounceable anyway'. His casual approach extended to office attire: 'If anyone turns up for work in a tie, we suspect them of having been for an interview for another job.'

There was one key problem: the airline still didn't have a name. Stelios hired an expensive brand consultancy and offered them £100,000 to come up with one. A month later, the consultants turned up at easyLand with magazine clippings attached to pieces of cardboard. Unimpressed by their efforts, Stelios promptly fired them. In the end, he came up with the airline's name himself. He remembers going to Harry's Bar in Mayfair, London, and scribbling 'CheapJet', 'No-Frillsjet', and other such variations on a napkin. The word 'easy' kept on coming into his head, so he decided to christen the airline easyJet. For the company logo he went to a small local design consultancy, White Knight, which gave the airline its famous shade of orange, known as Pantone 021C, used by no other airline at the time or since. The design consultancy then created a simple set of graphics for the airline's first advertising campaign. EasyJet has always resisted creatives who have wanted to change the original colour and simple design.

The next step was to decide on destinations. The new airline's executives chose Glasgow and Edinburgh as its first routes. The logic was simple: southern Scotland was the biggest domestic market from London for which air was a sensible alternative to road or rail.

The airline opened a telephone reservations centre and took its first booking on 23 October 1995. The phones at the easyJet telephone reservation centre started ringing and never stopped. They were in business.

2. Taking off

EASYJET'S INAUGURAL FLIGHT to Edinburgh roared down the runway at Luton just five days after the airline's maiden flight to Glasgow. There were a few surprises in store for the first passengers on-board, particularly those who had hoped for a celebratory glass of champagne or a few free canapés. There was no free food or drink anywhere to be found. Nor was there a seating plan. Plastic tags handed out to passengers replaced paper tickets.

The whole concept was novel. Ryanair, which would later become easyJet's greatest rival in the no-frills stakes, was still a commuter airline in Ireland; the idea that it would one day sell tickets for as little as £5 and become Europe's most profitable airline would have seemed ludicrous. The other low-cost airlines that fill our skies today hadn't even made it to the drawing board. Stelios was about to change the face of aviation. Of course, it wasn't all down to the larger-than-life

Greek entrepreneur. As well as brains, cheek, charisma and a cheque from Dad, Stelios owes a lot to Sir Freddie Laker, Southwest Airlines and deregulation of the skies.

Laker was probably the first entrepreneur to offer low-cost flights. In 1966, he formed Laker Airways Limited, a charter airline which soon became Britain's first all-jet air carrier. He invented the concept of 'time charters', whereby tour operators bought flight hours, a major factor in the explosive growth of the UK package tour business.

Laker then fought a six-year legal battle in both the UK and the US for the right to fly people cheaply across the Atlantic. At the time, carriers were national emblems and fiercely protected by governments. Laker eventually won his battle to get a licence for a new airline and set up a service he called Skytrain, which allowed passengers to fly between the UK and the US without reservations and at revolutionary cheap fares as low as £32.

On 26 September 1977 the first Skytrain flight left London Gatwick for New York. The service was expanded in 1978 to include a London to Los Angeles service. Miami and Tampa in Florida were added to the route network in 1980 and 1981 respectively, and by 1982 Skytrain was also serving Manchester and Glasgow Prestwick; in all, a total of nine scheduled routes.

By the end of 1981, over two million passengers had travelled on Sir Freddie's planes, and the airline was looking to expand its route network to the Far East, Australia and Japan for what would become Sir Freddie's next venture, Globetrain, a daily, round-the-world air service carrying people from all nations at fares that were substantially lower than anything that had been offered before.

But those plans never materialised. In February 1982, Laker Airways was forced into receivership and subsequently liquidation. Laker filed a $1.5 billion anti-trust action in the US District Court of Washington, claiming that twelve major international and US airlines and others had conspired to put

Skytrain out of business by offering equally low fares, which they could subsidise from more lucrative routes. The action was eventually settled out of court, but it was the end for Laker's innovatory company.

Meanwhile, however, another no-frills airline was already in mid-flight. Southwest started operating in the US in 1971. Stelios and Ryanair boss Michael O'Leary have both dubbed Herb Kelleher, Southwest's founder, their role model. Kelleher eliminated anything superfluous to a safe, cheap and reliable flight: he kept his aircraft in the air for as many hours as possible, ditched pre-assigned seating and served no meals. The airline offered low fares and what is more, it made money in the process, never recording an annual loss in its existing history.

Southwest's concept transformed the US airline industry. 'When Southwest was founded in 1971, only one in four Americans had actually flown,' said Linda Rutherford, head of public relations at Southwest Airlines. 'Air travel was considered a luxury experience, rather than a commodity. Nowadays four out of five Americans have flown. Southwest has democratised the skies in the US. We've made it affordable for people to consider air travel as a choice.'

The US carrier employed a single type of aircraft, the Boeing 737, which meant that maintenance and inventory costs were lower. It kept costs low by high utilisation of aircraft and operating economy class only, making boarding easier and turnarounds quicker. 'As Herb Kelleher says, you're only making money when in the sky,' said Rutherford.

As well as offering low fares, Southwest was favoured by the US flying public for its good service and friendly cabin crew, who were happy to laugh and make jokes with passengers; as Rutherford commented, 'Just because the fares are low, it doesn't mean that customer service shouldn't be high.'

Southwest Airlines was the first carrier to seize upon US airline deregulation in 1978 when it started flying between states, showing that low costs and low fares could stimulate profitable growth in new and existing markets. And its European counterparts were keen to follow its example. Deregulation of the airline industry in Europe became fully effective in April 1997 following a process of reforms which began in 1987. Unrestricted cross-border flying had been permitted since 1993. The deregulation was meant to fell entry barriers and end restrictive practices, which allowed airlines to keep flying despite inefficiency and massive losses. Liberalisation brought about numerous advantages to European travellers, in terms of both higher quality offered by airlines and drastic price reductions.

The free market also permitted any EU airline to operate domestic flights in any other EU country plus Norway and Iceland. Although competition on most major routes was limited by the lack of airport capacity, there were many opportunities for innovative low cost carriers to step in. 'We owe it all to deregulation,' said Tim Jeans, managing director of Monarch Scheduled and previously sales and marketing director at Ryanair. 'There would be no low-cost airlines were it not for deregulation. It would have meant perpetuating flag carriers if deregulation hadn't come about. It is difficult to understate its importance.'

Back in 1995, before deregulation had changed the skies, Stelios was just as unfamiliar with the idea of no-frills flights to Scotland as everyone else. Accustomed to holidaying on Greek islands and flying business class, he had never even been to Glasgow until two weeks before easyJet's first flight there took off. 'My biggest break was shedding my own prejudices and preferences about what an airline should be,' he later commented.

In its first months easyJet was a virtual airline. The carrier contracted in everything, including two leased Boeing 737-200 aircraft, the pilots and check-in staff. It was the fastest way for the airline to get started. Everyone who booked a flight with the airline did so by phone. They could hardly miss the

'0582 445 566' booking number, painted in 20-foot orange letters on the side of the planes. The booking staff prided themselves on picking up the phone after only one ring.

Refusing to sell tickets through travel agents or computer reservation systems allowed easyJet to save 25 per cent on the cost of each ticket. 'I was only capable of cutting out the travel agents because I knew nothing about the travel business,' Stelios has said. 'I had no allegiances, I had no friends in that industry, I just said, "This doesn't make sense, we will not do it."'

The first flights were accompanied by a brash advertising slogan stating that easyJet was as 'affordable as a pair of jeans'. And not even Levi's. Stelios used to walk around carrying a pair of jeans and tell people that they cost £29 at Tesco, exactly the same as a one-way flight with easyJet – and one-tenth of the full fare that British Airways charged from London Heathrow to Scotland.

But it took time for the message to get across to the paying public. Two months after the first easyJet flight, the airline commissioned a survey to see how many people had heard of the company. Only three out of a hundred people surveyed had. Stelios nearly cried. Some of the early flights flew to their destinations with just flight attendants and pilots and without any paying passengers, or with a scant four or five scattered across the cabin. The maximum number of passengers on-board each aircraft was twenty-six out of a possible seventy or so for the first few months.

So Stelios opened his chequebook and spent a million pounds on marketing within three months. The world started to turn orange as easyJet placed full-page ads in the news-papers and paid for wall-to-wall radio advertising as well as a television advertising campaign thrown together in a matter of days.

Lack of awareness wasn't the only problem. Used to high prices, people couldn't understand how they could fly any-where for just £29, and worried that easyJet was compromising on safety. It took time for them to realise that despite its low fares easyJet was as safe as any of its competitors.

But the advertising, and the lack of any accidents, began to take effect. Stelios was perceived by the airline's first passengers as a curious type of folk hero offering value to the masses. 'I don't think people could believe the prices we were charging,' Stelios has said. 'But once they got on to the planes and saw for themselves that they were clean and had the requisite number of wings, they were pleasantly surprised.'

EasyJet's rivals also started to take notice. British Airways had at first treated the new airline with scorn and derision, but before long the flag carrier realised it had a threat on its hands. BA and British Midland, the UK's other large airline, both chose to offer return flights between London and Scotland for £58 – curiously enough, exactly the same price as easyJet's return fare.

Stelios was initially flattered by the established carriers' reactions. 'You can jump up and down as much as you like, but it's only when your opponents recognise you and fight back that you have become a brand. It's a sign you've arrived.' But BA's and British Midland's fare cuts soon placed easyJet under pressure. The company's executives worked long hours as they battled to make easyJet viable. Stelios did everything from greeting customers to dashing out to buy rubbish bins at the local cash-and-carry, and spent flights going up and down the aisle talking to his passengers. This commendable public relations exercise had its drawbacks. As one stewardess said, 'The passengers loved meeting him, but it did mean he was always getting in our way.'

Philipa Kane, née Ripley, was one of easyJet's first twelve flight attendants, whom the airline employed after contracting in crew for the initial weeks of operations. Philipa witnessed Stelios's eagerness to get involved in every aspect of the airline's day-to-day running alongside its fifty-five employees. 'It was like one big family and everyone mucked in and helped each other, including Stelios,' she recalled. 'He would check out everything from the catering to the advertising. He used to man the phones taking bookings in the call-centre if someone was taken ill, or even if they were understaffed. He couldn't fly the plane or act as a flight steward because of safety standards. He would do absolutely everything else though! I've even seen him hoovering the cabin and cleaning the planes in between flights.'

Philipa had applied to the airline after seeing an advert in the local newspaper. The annual starting salary of about £9,000 was a lot lower than those offered by other airlines, which would pay as much as £12,000, but the airline was based near her then home in Stevenage and only operated a couple of aircraft, meaning that flight attendants had to work just four hours a day, two or three times a week, with no stopovers. She would be back at the airport by 9.30 a.m. after the morning flight.

EasyJet was looking for experienced cabin crew who could help boost the airline's reputation. Philipa had gained lots of experience from working for Gulf Air, Saudi Air and Qatar Airways. She knew what to expect from the job. Or so she thought.

British Airways trained the easyJet flight crew, to the same level as their own staff. The surprises started when Philipa discovered that she wouldn't be dressed in high heels, tights and skirts, as she had at previous airlines. Rather than a well-cut designer uniform, Philipa's on-board attire comprised black jeans, an orange polo shirt, an orange bomber jacket and a baseball cap. What's more, she was told she had to shop for her own jeans at Tesco and pay for them herself. She was also asked to buy a pair of plain black boots to wear for work. EasyJet bought a pile of orange polo shirts of various sizes from Benetton and supplied the baseball cap and coat for Philipa and the rest of the crew. Philipa wasn't allowed to keep the duffel coat when she left the airline eight months later to return to the Middle East, although it still evokes fond memories: 'The lettering on the back of the duffel coat said "easy" in big letters, followed by "jet" in small letters and then "cabin crew" in big letters. From a distance it looked like "easy cabin crew" was written on the back, which caused much amusement.'

The easyJet girls and their informal wardrobe were the source of much entertainment at Luton Airport. 'We would turn up at the airport, dressed in our jeans and orange polo shirts. Then the crew for Britannia, a charter airline based at Luton, would turn up dolled up in their skirts and make-up. We were the absolute laughing stock at the airport. EasyJet just wasn't taken seriously at the time.'

After the initial shock, Philipa soon grew to appreciate her unconventional uniform. 'It was a relief to be able to run around and get on with your work in jeans, rather than tottering around in high heels. It was practical too as we were constantly kneeling down or picking things up from the floor. Cabin crew who had worked for other airlines particularly liked it. We all felt very comfortable and had fun and enjoyed our casual uniform. You didn't have to put up any pretence. That was one of the best things about working for easyJet.'

As well as a casual new look, Philipa and the other flight attendants had to adapt to an informal atmosphere on-board. EasyJet was keen to emulate its US role model, Southwest, whose cabin crew would make jokes throughout the flight. The easyJet cabin crew was encouraged to be spontaneous and have fun with the passengers. Flight attendants were encouraged to play games, such as asking which passenger was wearing yellow socks that day, who was the oldest or youngest passenger, or even who had the most points on their driving licence. The winner would normally be rewarded with a free flapjack. A member of the senior cabin crew might read out the *Sun* newspaper to the passengers during the flight and give them an update of the daily news, or ask them to complete that day's crossword with him.

Not all members of the British flying public appreciated the American-style approach. 'Some of the passengers loved it and thought it was funny but others were plain embarrassed,' Philipa recalled. 'The gay flight attendants were best at having fun with the passengers. It wasn't me at all, though, and I didn't make jokes. I had been strictly trained and it was too difficult to switch roles and suddenly become all American. I think nowadays easyJet would probably look for more out-going, bubbly cabin crew to do that kind of thing.'

Philipa's most memorable experience was the run-up to easyJet's first Christmas. 'The flight deck was playing Christmas carols and songs and the crew and the captain ran around wearing flashing Christmas lights. We were diverted to Edinburgh on the Christmas Eve flight back to Luton from Glasgow. But it was like a big party on-board and the atmosphere was absolutely fantastic. The passengers were merry after a few drinks and quite happy. We didn't land in Luton until after midnight but no one cared as we were having such a good time.'

The games and merriment on-board translated into a pleasant working environment. 'It was a lot of fun,' said Philipa. 'Everyone just enjoyed his or her work. I used to look forward to getting up at 4 a.m. and going to work, and I haven't felt like that working anywhere else. We didn't need much motivating, as it was fun to do. We were all really enjoying being part of this exciting new thing.'

Some of easyJet's early employees weren't convinced that the airline would survive six months and few thought that it would last longer than a year. They still wanted to give it their best shot. 'The cabin crew thought easyJet was a good idea but we wouldn't have been that upset if it hadn't worked at the time,' said Philipa. 'There was a big feeling that everyone was making it up as we went along. The head of the cabin crew had a suggestion box which he encouraged us to use. There were suggestions for entertainment for passengers or things that we could sell on the carts.'

Apart from the jokes and on-board comedy acts, the flight crew's day followed a standard routine, which hasn't changed throughout the years. After reaching the airport an hour before the flight took off, the crew would assemble in the briefing room, where they were informed how many people would be flying with them that day and if they had to watch out for any particular passengers, such as celebrities or people with special needs. A safety briefing followed, providing a review of details such as the location of the fire extinguishers on-board.

Once the ground staff had given cabin crew their approval and the safety checks had been carried out on-board, the passengers were allowed to board the aircraft and sit wherever they wanted. There was less of a stampede than normally accompanies easyJet flights today. Next, passengers were shown a safety demonstration and the plane flew to the day's destination, hopefully arriving on time. Approximately thirty minutes after the last passenger left the aircraft, the whole process would start again with the next batch of passengers.

EasyJet threw small parties for cabin crew every time that a new group qualified to join the airline to ensure that staff morale remained high. Stelios often joined in the parties and had fun with his employees. He made sure, however, that he didn't reveal anything about his private life. Even at parties, all he talked about was airlines and business.

The flight attendants were mostly happy to work hard because of the healthy relationship they enjoyed with management. 'The really good thing was that you had the support of the management behind you,' said Philipa. 'You could make decisions on-board and know that you would be backed up by the bosses.'

Stelios made sure that strict rules and operational guidelines accompanied the laughter and games of easyJet's early days. He had strong ideas about how the airline should be run and expected everyone to adhere to them. Nor was he prepared to back down to anyone who challenged his ideas. 'Stelios was very tough on what he wanted,' according to Philipa. 'If Stelios wanted something done a certain way, then you would have to do it that way and not question it. You couldn't have a run-in with him. The head of the cabin crew at the time had a few arguments with him and was fired. There was a personality clash between the two of them. Stelios was very business-minded and strict. That said, none of what he asked for was unreasonable. He was a fair boss. Even though he was a bit over the top sometimes, he was popular with the cabin crew and came across as a genuinely nice guy.'

Not having to serve meals on-board freed up more time for the easyJet flight attendants to help passengers and get to know them. When there were any passengers, that is. It was still taking time for easyJet to get its message across. 'EasyJet didn't seem real to people as the whole concept of budget travel was so new,' said Philipa. 'The cabin crew individually did a lot of advertising. I used to go down to the pub and advertise easyJet myself and tell people to fly with them and reassure them that it was safe! I know that other cabin crew used to do the same. A lot of people learnt about easyJet through word-of-mouth.'

Gradually some business passengers started to realise the economic sense of buying a cheap ticket with the budget carrier. Executives even started to commute to work between London and Glasgow courtesy of the airline. One regular passenger used to take the 6 a.m. flight from Glasgow and be in his office in London by 9 a.m. He and the other passengers started to pay for block bookings of tickets. Flying with easyJet was cheaper than taking a flight with British Airways – and cheaper and much quicker than the train – and Luton was far less busy than London Heathrow, even if it was harder to reach for some people.

EasyJet strove to keep costs as low as possible so that it could continue offering low fares. One of its money-saving strategies was to adopt fast half-an-hour turnarounds of its aircraft between flights. Within thirty minutes, the crew had to ensure that the safety equipment was in place and each passenger seat had its safety card inserted in the back pocket.

The crew had to check the toilets, cupboards and under the seats. Then they had to clean up the cabin before the next passengers came on-board. It was hard work. But easyJet had paid hefty mortgages on its two planes. The only way to pay for the aircraft was to 'sweat the assets', as Stelios liked to say, by keeping them in the air. 'I love planes but, as Sir Freddie Laker said, they're only metal tubes for making money,' he once commented. 'You can only really fall in love with a boat.'

The airline made sure that on-board catering was kept to a minimum to cut back on costs. Drinks were coffee and tea served in plastic cups. The rumour within the airline was that Stelios had bought the cups himself at Tesco. Gone too were the traditional airline's plastic meals. Instead passengers were invited to buy flapjacks or sandwiches, the latter said to be made by an employee before each flight. Passengers were encouraged to bring their own food as well as alcohol on-board, which proved popular. The flight crew intervened if someone was drinking to excess.

Many passengers moaned about the lack of service and huffily pronounced that they weren't prepared to pay fifty pence for a small beaker of coffee. In response, flight attendants reminded them how cheap their ticket was. 'We were trained to communicate to passengers that we weren't putting any costs or money on the tickets for the price of china or meals,' said Philipa. 'We were instructed to tell them that easyJet wasn't cheap but affordable so if people complained, they should just compare their ticket price to the fare charged by BA.'

EasyJet also saved money by operating leased aircraft. The planes were old and the interiors shabby, adding to some passengers' fears about the plane's safety. Their fears were unfounded. The airline didn't make any cutbacks when it came to safety. EasyJet used the same equipment as that used by more traditional airlines and operated to high safety standards. The fledgling carrier was aware that an accident or safety mishap could destroy its reputation and then nobody would fly with it again. EasyJet had a good reference point. It only had to look at the US budget carrier ValuJet, which folded a matter of months after one of its planes plunged vertically into the swamps of the Everglades following a fire on-board on 11 May 1996. The crash destroyed the aircraft, all 105 passengers and five crew, as well as some US travellers' confidence in no-frills aviation. The Florida-based airline was subsequently accused of poor maintenance practices by the National Transportation Safety Board investigation.

Indirect support by famous passengers helped promote easyJet's name to the general public and assuage passengers' mistrust of the airline. The Scottish band Big Country, which was enjoying the height of its popularity at the time, flew to Scotland a few times with easyJet. The airline was quick to advertise the fact, naming one of its aircraft after the group. The pop star Boy George also flew with easyJet in the early days, as did the group Wet Wet Wet. The snooker player Alan McManus was less fortunate in his experience with the airline. He was snowed in at Glasgow airport when he was due to be playing in a snooker tournament in London.

McManus wasn't the only easyJet passenger, famous or not, to be stranded at an airport because of bad weather in the first couple of years. EasyJet's early Boeings weren't equipped with the most up-to-date radar control equipment and Luton's geographical position meant that the airport was often fog-bound.

But those who flew on easyJet's first flights were generally far more tolerant about any delay than passengers today. The novelty factor helped: easyJet was just so different and so cheap. But passengers were still shocked to find out that they wouldn't be given a free night's accommodation when a flight was cancelled. They were told instead that they would be automatically rebooked onto the following morning's flight for free. EasyJet informed passengers that it didn't consider accommodation its responsibility. The company message was that customers wouldn't receive free accommodation if they had been travelling by train, so why should they expect anything different with easyJet?

It wasn't long before passengers' tolerance of mishaps started to weaken as the novelty factor wore off. Tempers were flaring by the time 120 furious passengers landed in Edinburgh more than ten hours late a few days before Christmas in 1997. The plane was forced to turn back to Luton after the pilot couldn't retract the aircraft's nose-gear. Aircraft parts were flown in from Germany as engineers worked on the plane all day. The passengers were told an Airbus 2000 had been laid on to leave at 5 p.m.

Among the disgruntled passengers was Fiona Mulheron, from Bathgate, West Lothian. 'I'm having my family for a Christmas meal tonight, but because of the delay I won't be there when they arrive.' Susan Downie was also angry about the delay. 'I came up to Edinburgh for a holiday with my one-year-old son Craig. He should be in bed now, not being trotted around an airport.'

They were further angered when a luggage mishap caused more delay. 'We got on the plane and after forty minutes, they told us to get off again as there were too many pieces of luggage,' said Neil Blakesly, a Londoner who had planned to spend the weekend Christmas shopping with his Edinburgh girlfriend. 'It turned out to be a nonsense. I don't know why they hauled us off.'

Stelios managed to calm tempers and the bad press generated by the incident by promising to 'personally consider any reasonable claims for compensation' following the 'unacceptable delay'. It wasn't the last time, however, that easyJet would raise tempers and hit the headlines.

3. Going Dutch

EASYJET WELCOMED A new member to the team in March 1996, appointing Ray Webster as managing director. Stelios plucked the fifty-four-year-old Webster from New Zealand and asked him to invest in the start-up.

'This was several times the size of my mortgage to fork out on a business that was unproven,' Webster said at the time. 'It had load factors of about 30 per cent, two planes and £5 million of equity.' Still, it was better than sticking around down under, where the regulators had just forced Air New Zealand to ditch Webster's pioneering plans for a low-cost airline. Until then, he had spent over thirty years working for essentially the same company.

A carpenter's son, he described himself as an electronics buff with a low boredom threshold, who 'was building all sorts of things and blowing things up' as young as nine or ten. He did badly at school and couldn't wait to get out of his small coal-mining town. So he joined New Zealand's National Aircraft Corporation as an apprentice in 1964, largely because the post office and the air force wouldn't employ anyone who was colour-blind (a condition which made easyJet's trademark orange branding 'difficult to see – you spot it by association'). Within a few years he was winning all sorts of scholarships, and in his early thirties he became chief engineer for Air New Zealand before taking a year out to immerse himself in management courses at Stanford.

'Stanford over-delivered against expectations,' he said – a characteristic understatement for a year during which his marriage ended, he met his second wife Brigitte and 'gained a lot more confidence that I could do well outside my field'. ANZ kept him in California as the head of its Americas operation before calling him back to set up the ill-fated no-frills carrier.

Webster's face was lined with deep eye-bags and his measured New Zealand tones matched his relaxed work attire, normally comprising chinos, shirt and no tie. He owned a relatively modest house in Hampstead and his only personal luxury was a brace of Porsches.

EasyJet's focus now was on expansion. In January 1996, the carrier introduced flights from Luton to Aberdeen and started to assess which other routes to add to its network. The airline had started using its own Air Operating Certificate, meaning that it was recognised as a financially viable airline. What is more, easyJet now possessed two wholly owned Boeing aircraft. In April 1996, the airline used the new planes to start flying into Amsterdam, its first international destination; according to Stelios, 'It meets our criteria as a busy route with an overpriced fares structure.' EasyJet had to pay similar fees at Amsterdam and other airports as larger rivals, but planned to offer a cut-price service to Amsterdam with flights at less than half the £150 one-way economy class fare charged by British Airways.

EasyJet promoted the flights to Amsterdam by selling seats for 39 pence on the first day, much to the delight of the British flying public. Viewed by popular consensus as a 'Good Bloke', Stelios liked people to see him as both put-upon and playful. He also enjoyed annoying large multinationals and pulling off publicity stunts, as his next ploy proved. He printed coupons in easyJet's in-flight magazine addressed to the president of KLM, the national carrier of the Netherlands, complaining about the price of KLM flights to and from Amsterdam, then turned up with some easyJet employees at the KLM offices in Amstelveen, on the outskirts of Amsterdam, to present the coupons to Leo van Wijk, the president of KLM. They weren't granted an audience. But the incident did drum up lots of free publicity for easyJet on Dutch television and in the newspapers.

It wasn't the last time that KLM, Europe's fourth largest airline, would hear easyJet's name mentioned. EasyJet's one-way fare of 99 guilders was considerably lower than the return fare of 296 guilders that KLM had been charging between Amsterdam and London, and KLM was forced to reduce its fares dramatically to counter the threat. The no-frills carrier responded to the fare cuts by alleging that KLM was engaged in predatory pricing between London and Amsterdam.

EasyJet's predatory pricing case was significant. If the European Commission's competition arm decided that KLM had abused its position by operating its Amsterdam–London service below cost to force easyJet out of the market, then the Commission could fine KLM up to 10 per cent of the turnover earned on the route. An article from the Dutch press, which was discussed at the hearings, quoted from an alleged internal KLM memo calling for a determined tactical campaign to 'stop the growth and development of easyJet'. 'We didn't do anything which is not in line with EU legislation,' a KLM spokeswoman responded. In the end, a decision was never reached. EasyJet, now focusing on plans by British Airways to set up a no-frills airline, eventually dropped the complaint with the Commission and left KLM alone, at least for the time being.

The Amsterdam route marked a new era for easyJet. It was a prestigious new destination for the carrier and Amsterdam Schiphol, Europe's fourth largest airport, was a key transfer hub. The Amsterdam flights also attracted a new type of passenger, keen to capitalise on easyJet's cheap fares to spend a raucous weekend in the Dutch capital, getting drunk or smoking cannabis. Marijuana was still technically illegal in Amsterdam but the police tolerated coffee shops selling soft drugs, and business was booming. 'Enjoy your visit, have a fat one for me!' declared an easyJet passenger called Wadie on a web chatroom for marijuana users after a trip to Amsterdam. 'I'll be over in the next couple of weeks for some more! Thank the lord for easyJet!'

Of course, drunk, stoned or awkward passengers weren't exclusive to easyJet. But they formed the worst of the new breed of traveller who were lured on trips abroad by affordable fares. Claire Pakes, a twenty-two-year-old easyJet hostess, found the groups of lads on stag weekends the worst. 'They're all off together for the weekend and they are cooped up in a confined space surrounded by women waiting on them while consuming copious amounts of lager. It's never going to be an easy job for us, is it? They are often drunk before they even board the plane. Then we have to make sure all the lockers are shut and so you have to lean over passengers to check everything is secure. These types of guys always leave their lockers open and then make comments about your boobs or your bum. It's pretty predictable, but unfortunately you just have to do it.'

Fortunately, Claire never had to cope with proper abuse from any passengers, although some of her colleagues weren't so fortunate. 'I've heard of girls getting seriously groped but no one has ever gone that far with me. You just have to grit your teeth and smile nicely, which is the worst bit. Underneath, you seriously want to just punch one of them. A colleague of mine was kicked in the shin by a passenger because he got so annoyed with her. She had been having some problems with him since the start of the flight. After an hour, she started to ignore him a bit because he was being such a pain. Then as she was walking past, saying she would be right back to get him whatever he was demanding, he lurched awkwardly out of his seat and did a sort of rugby kick at her as she was walking past. She went down and the two drinks she was carrying went flying up in the air all over the other passengers. She just had to get up, smooth down her uniform and carry on as if nothing had happened. That's the lot of an air hostess, I'm afraid.'

In June 1996, five weeks after introducing flights to Amsterdam, easyJet added Nice to its network. To publicise the new route, Stelios invited the press to fly out with him and watch the Monaco Grand Prix from his flat in nearby Monte Carlo. This wasn't Stelios' sole bachelor pad. He also owned homes in St Katherine's Dock in London, and in Athens. His frequent business trips, however, meant that he slept mostly in hotels.

In the following months, easyJet added more international destinations within two hours' flying time of Luton, including flights from Luton to Geneva in December 1997. At the same time the company started to increase its number of aircraft. In July 1998, the airline placed an order for fifteen of Boeing's new next generation 737s, with a list price in excess of $500 million, to increase its fleet sixfold over the next five years. This was on top of an existing order for twelve Boeing 737-300s, which were due for delivery by 2000. EasyJet knew that a fleet of shiny new planes would enhance its safety reputation to potential customers. 'We're building Europe's leading low-cost airline with what will be one of the world's youngest fleets,' boasted Stelios.

Stelios was characteristically bullish about his ability to fill the new capacity as he expanded into Europe. But easyJet was not alone in attempting to win the lion's share of a new market that analysts believed could grow by 300 per cent over the next few years. Ryanair, which had by now converted itself into a no-frills carrier and the largest of the low-cost contenders, signed up for twenty-five new 737s with the option of another twenty, in a deal priced at more than $2 billion. Richard Branson had ambitious plans for his Virgin Express operation based at Brussels; and Debonair, easyJet's rival at Luton, was in talks to lease ten of Boeing's new 717 regional jets.

Debonair had started operations in June 1996 and linked Rome with Barcelona, Munich, Munchen-Gladbach and Copenhagen, and Madrid with Barcelona. The airline's fares were amazingly cheap. How about Munich to Rome for a mere Dm161 ($104) one-way, as against the regular air fare of Dm793? Or Copenhagen-Rome for Dkr920 ($155) compared with Dkr5,265?

Debonair's chairman was Franco Mancassala, whose twenty-seven-year airline career had begun with Luton-based Court Line Aviation and also included stints with Continental Airlines, World Airways and Mid Pacific Airlines. Mancassola fronted Debonair's own advertising campaigns, normally the preserve of used car salesmen and furniture magnates. Unusually, Mancassala's appearances were actually funny; showing Debonair's (real) finance director crouched at his feet in tears, begging his boss not to offer passengers such low fares.

Then British Airways entered the fray. In November 1996, Bob Ayling, British Airways' then chief executive, had invited Stelios for tea and discussed buying a stake in easyJet. 'He was very flattering,' Stelios recalled. 'He said, "I think you've cracked it."' Stelios took the older man's interest as external confirmation of what he was doing. Talks continued into the spring. Then BA abruptly announced that regulators wouldn't approve the deal. Shortly thereafter, in October 1997, when easyJet was starting to pose a serious threat, BA announced that it would launch an easyJet look-alike, Go Fly Airways, the following year.

Stelios was furious. As soon as he heard of BA's plans, Stelios brought an immediate writ 'to prevent BA illegally cross-subsidising its low-cost subsidiary', arguing, 'There is no point in waiting until you are out of business. Sue – and sue early.' The writ alleged that BA was guaranteeing the leases on Go's initial eight aircraft and that it was supporting other aspects of Go's business, including maintenance, insurance and advertising, and not accepting an adequate return on the £50 million it was investing in the project. It also said that Go benefited from the 'halo' or 'brand image' effect because customers would believe that a company associated with BA would have higher standards of reliability and safety. EasyJet pointed out that cross-subsidies by dominant companies were illegal under Article 86 of the European Community Treaty. 'We believe in fair competition and we asked BA to give an undertaking they would play fair, but they refused,' said Stelios.

BA denied doing anything unlawful, arguing that giving such advantages to a subsidiary was part of normal business for most companies and insisting that Go would be a standalone operation. A BA spokesman said: 'We established our subsidiary Go in response to the growing market for low-cost travel. We are confident the new airline will add to consumer choice and all of Go's operations will be lawful.' Stelios lost the battle. In May 1998, a High Court judge dismissed the injunction sought by easyJet against Go and easyJet was forced to accept that BA would go ahead with its low-cost ambitions.

Franco Mancassola, the flamboyant chairman of Debonair, was, like Stelios, suspicious about BA's motivation. 'Go is like a ten-year-old kid thrown into the ring with Mike Tyson,' he said. 'It should never be allowed to operate. It is a wolf in sheep's clothing, simply a way for BA to eliminate competition. BA can't do it themselves because they are too fat and they don't want to go to Weight Watchers.'

O'Leary, the baseball-capped chief executive of Ryanair, seemed more relaxed than Mancassola about the challenge presented by Go. 'BA has no idea how to run a low-fare airline,' he said dismissively. 'I know more about flying on Concorde than Bob Ayling does about running a low-cost airline and I've never flown on Concorde.' O'Leary predicted that Go would be a 'disaster' and would take passengers away from BA's mainline services.

'Look at Ryanair on London–Stockholm,' said O'Leary. 'Our midweek return fare is £99, while BA's is £500. BA screws you if you don't spend a Saturday night away. If Go were to start on that route, for example, it would have to pitch its pricing somewhere in the middle. Traffic would move from economy cabins to BA and SAS. There's no doubt that Go is going to cannibalise BA's economy passengers over London.'

It was a scene to make all bar a boxing promoter blush as two of the executives holding the key to the future of the European airline industry met for the first time at an industry event in March 1998. Stelios, normally a public relations dream – young, dynamic and always ready to take on and use the media – was strangely subdued as he joined the cream of Europe's airline industry in London to hear a speech by Karel Van Miert, the EU competition commissioner. Asked how easyJet was faring, all Stelios could manage was a barbed comment aimed at Barbara Cassani, Go's chief executive officer: 'Everything's fine apart from that woman over there.'

Cassani, a forty-one-year-old wisecracking American in a miniskirt, shook up the conservative, male-dominated airline industry. A master's graduate from Princeton University, she started out as a management consultant at Coopers and Lybrand (now PricewaterhouseCoopers) in Washington and moved to the company's London offices with her husband, Guy, a British investment banker. Soon after arriving in London, she answered a British Airways advertisement for a job in sales and marketing and thereafter rose swiftly through the airline's management ranks. She helped to buy the airline's Galileo computer reservation system, was part of a negotiating team for BA's long-running alliance talks with American Airlines and became the airline's first general manager in the US.

Cassani became a protégée of Bob Ayling, the airline's former CEO, and it was no surprise to BA employees when she was appointed as head of the airline's new no-frills subsidiary. Cassani said that Ayling told her: 'You've got £25 million – goodbye and good luck', recalling, 'And so there I was with a bagful of money in one hand and a bag of ideas in the other.' After retreating into the cotton wool confines of the BA corporate machine for a few months, Cassani quickly put together a team and secured eight aircraft for Go's launch in May 1998. She declined to divulge any more details about the new airline: 'I haven't even told my mother where Go will be operating to.'

She was determined to make Go work. One thing, however, that she hadn't counted on was a surprise appearance by easyJet's orange army on Go's inaugural flight from London Stansted to Rome in May 1998. Stelios and six of his employees showed up, dressed in orange boiler suits, clashing with Go's purple and green colour scheme. Before boarding at Stansted, Stelios declared: 'Go has been given permission by BA to lose £29 million and then close in three years, having put its rivals out of business.' He added: 'You have only to look at BA's track record to see how predatory they are.' Go denied the claims. 'The low-cost market is set to quadruple in the next five years and there is huge potential,' said Go sales and marketing director David Magliano.

Stelios and his team turned the spotlight away from Go and on to his own venture by handing out 150 letters promising free flights on easyJet. Cassani, travelling among the 147 passengers with her husband Guy and five-year-old daughter Lauren, found herself alone at the front of the plane while journalists piled into the back to interview the garrulous Greek. But she pointed out that Stelios's appearance in an orange boiler suit brought Go far more publicity than it otherwise would have earned, and asserted, 'People don't feel comfortable with the orange brashness of easyJet.'

After its dramatic launch day, Go started operations with twice-daily services from Stansted to Rome, Milan and Copenhagen, none of which was served by easyJet. It hoped to fly to six destinations by the end of its first year. Passengers could buy tickets up to one hour before take-off, with all fares set at £100 return.

Go adopted a more conventional approach than easyJet and was accordingly perceived as slightly more upmarket. The new airline believed in allocating seats rather than the first-come-first-served principle of easyJet, and dressed its flight stewards in proper shirts as opposed to the easyJet crew's polo shirts. Before long it was flying to a larger number of destinations, less frequently than easyJet and with a more fixed discount tariff structure. Food, such as bacon, lettuce and tomato sandwiches or a breakfast box comprising Cornflakes, a muffin and a cereal bar, was available on flights but as on easyJet, passengers had to pay extra for it. The airline also offered the world's first gift vouchers for flights.

In theory, there was plenty of room for growth in the sector. Fewer than 10 million European passengers flew on low-cost carriers in the late 1990s, representing a modest 5 per cent of the region's traffic. That compared with close to 30 per cent in the US, where the no-frills experiment had begun and which provided the inspiration for the new European airline entrepreneurs.

But making a success of the low-fares strategy was less easy. Debonair's ads showing the airline's financial director in tears proved to be a little close to the bone when Debonair missed revenue and profit targets, being put into administration in October 1999. The airline blamed competition from Go for its demise. Mancassola claimed Go was an 'artificial' low-cost airline because it had the wealth of British Airways behind it. 'I believe in competition and I admire easyJet,' he stated. 'What the company has achieved, it has earned. What is not fair is having a parent company that will benefit from the downfall of another airline.'

Industry experts put Debonair's failure down to an inappropriate strategy. The airline had offered low fares but had high costs: it flew to expensive airports; offered business class, which meant frills, and operated the thirsty BAe 146, which meant high fuel costs. To be successful, budget carriers needed low unit costs and high loads. EasyJet didn't break even until loads reached 70 per cent, and Debonair's loads were much lower. Unlike easyJet, which presented a clear no-frills message, Debonair seemed unsure of its own identity, attempting to appeal to both backpackers with low fares and to executive passengers by offering business class.

As Debonair faltered, easyJet was going from strength to strength. The airline used some of its new aircraft to expand its base in Glasgow, creating 150 new jobs and two new routes out of Glasgow, to Palma in Majorca and Geneva in Switzerland. The decision was seen as a vote of confidence in Scotland by the Luton-based airline. EasyJet was already operating daily flights to Glasgow, Edinburgh and Inverness, the latter traditionally expensive to fly to and very time-consuming to reach by train. And Glasgow to Luton services were running at a healthy 75 per cent capacity.

EasyJet then turned its expansion to Northern Ireland, introducing new flights between Luton and Belfast in September 1998 at a special promotional single fare of £9 plus tax of £10 for the first two weeks. The low fares were well received by Belfast residents. One incident, however, helped cool easyJet's popularity with some people in Northern Ireland. Passengers aboard a Belfast-bound easyJet plane were left freezing after a door seal gave way. Dozens of people put on coats and covered their eardrums as wind whistled through the plane. The plane's pilot was forced to do a quick U-turn and fly back to Luton.

Passenger Stephen Whiteman said, 'It was so noisy you couldn't hear a thing. And it was so cold people were putting their coats back on. It was very uncomfortable. They should call themselves Breezy Jet rather than easyJet.' Another passenger, John Earl, complained: 'My ear drums were throbbing. And when the pilot told us that he was returning to Luton I was delighted. When we got there, we ended up in a hangar where a guy with a toolbox spent an hour and a half fixing a seal on the passenger door. I'm nervous flying at the best of times so I was over the moon when we finally got into Belfast International. A lot of people were very annoyed because they were going to be late for business meetings. But the crew did apologise for the delay over and over again.'

EasyJet reassured passengers that there had been no risk to the plane or its passengers at any time during the alert. 'A slight leak in the seal was identified shortly after take-off and the captain was informed. The captain felt that because of the noise level inside the aircraft it was easier to return to Luton to have the problem corrected. This resulted in a 90-minute delay. The leak did not affect the cabin pressure and there was no risk whatsoever to passengers.'

Meanwhile, Go was making it clear that it wasn't afraid of competition. In August 1998, just three months after its launch, the BA subsidiary announced its first route in direct competition with easyJet, pitching its London to Edinburgh services at £70 return – just £2 more than easyJet's lowest fare on the same route. Then, in October 1998, Go introduced a £15 one-way fare on the same route. Stelios was outraged; EasyJet's lowest single fare to Edinburgh at that time was £29 from Luton.

Stelios decided to fly to the European Commission to make a complaint against Go. Never one to miss a public relations stunt, he took with him 150 friends and staff clad in orange boiler suits. The Boeing 737-300 carrying the orange army to Brussels advertised Stelios's message: 'Stop BA, stop Go,' it screamed in giant orange letters on the side of the plane. Stelios alleged that Go's £15 fare was a 'cheap trick' designed to crush the opposition. He claimed that the below-cost fare was subsidised by BA and amounted to unfair competition in breach of EU trade laws.

'I am sure BA/Go is losing a fortune with such prices,' said Stelios. 'I was forced to match that fare since easyJet will never be knowingly undersold, but the BA/Go fare is predatory. A dominant company like British Airways is prohibited by law from operating at a loss in order to eliminate competition.' Stelios admitted that easyJet couldn't afford to keep matching Go's low Edinburgh fare before plunging into 'heavy losses'. He said: 'Consumers must understand that this short-term bonanza of low fares to many destinations will end if we stop flying on the Edinburgh route. Go has the financial strength behind it to squeeze us out.'

BA denied the claims, saying the new rate was simply a promotional fare available for midweek travel until early December, and the European Commission took no action. But the intense rivalry between the two budget carriers provided British tabloids with colourful copy throughout the ensuing seasons. When Luton Airport closed for several days because of a dusting of snow, Go ran advertisements asking, 'Would you rather fly with a) the airline most likely to get you there on time, or b) the airline with a generous refund policy because they don't?' When Go was voted best low-cost airline, Cassani rented a billboard outside Luton Airport on which to proclaim victory – for a year.

The airline even resorted to taking out a full-page advert in the *Evening Standard* newspaper, reprinting press clippings about cancellations and delays at easyJet. In response, easyJet ran an ad listing the six accolades it had won over the past six months. The ad's headline ran: 'BA is wasting shareholders' cash to rubbish easyJet. If their own low-cost airline is so bloody brilliant why does easyJet win all the customer awards?' 'Stelios is a spirited competitor,' Go's sales director, Magliano, commented cheerfully. 'We enjoy our little spats.'

In the meantime, easyJet was working on a project that would help set it apart from other new low-cost operators: the

Internet. Stelios first became aware of the Internet in 1995, when he was setting up easyJet and the world wide web was commercially in its infancy. He learned that there was something called the global distribution system, a computer system where all travel agents log on and sell you tickets. However, in 1995, Stelios still thought that the Internet was something 'for nerds', he later admitted to the *Guardian* newspaper.

He started to change his mind when he began travelling to the US to see Boeing and noticed that the Internet was becoming more commercially available. In April 1997, easyJet decided to launch its own website, easyJet.com, to provide information about the airline. Like that of many businesses at the time, the easyJet website was little more than an invitation to phone the company.

But Stelios decided to experiment with the new tool. He instructed his team to put a separate number on the website and was startled to find so many people using it. As more and more people found easyJet's number online, he realised that here was a perfect business opportunity: instead of paying call-centre staff about £1 for each seat sold, passengers booking online reduced the marginal cost of distribution to almost zero. The airline started its transformation from a telephone business into a web business.

In April 1998, easyJet sold its first seat online at easyJet.com. Web bookings grew from zero to 26 per cent of business within a year. On the first day of trading during one promotion, 13,000 seats were sold, believed to be a record for the most commercial transactions carried out on the Internet in a twenty-four-hour period. By mid-1999, when its Internet sales represented 58 per cent of the total, easyJet became the first airline to make more sales on the Internet than through normal telephone reservations. Stelios was so pleased that he announced that whoever bought the one-millionth seat online would win a prize of unlimited free travel on easyJet for a year. The carrier reached the one-million-seat mark in October 1999. Five months later, in March 2000, easyJet reached two million seats, and it took only another three months to reach the three million mark. By 2001, online bookings regularly reached 80 per cent, the highest proportion of online sales for any airline in the world.

'The Internet is the kind of tool that becomes available to people once in a generation,' Stelios commented. 'The Internet has probably had a bigger effect on people's ability to fly than the jet engine. The jet engine was an improvement on the propeller, but what really made it a mass market was the ability to fly someone for £1. You can only do that with the Internet.' EasyJet pioneered the concept of offering a discount to Internet customers, offering £5 off for each leg of a journey, and the fuselage of each plane proudly proclaimed it to be 'The Web's Favourite Airline' – a claim that was designed to annoy BA, 'The World's Favourite Airline'.

An analysis by Schroder Salomon Smith Barney pronounced that easyJet's embrace of the Internet was 'already enhancing earnings, in the form of higher load factors, lower marketing costs, a leaner organisation structure and better management information'. According to the investment house, easyJet was becoming a paperless company with a powerful electronic infrastructure. The results were lower administration costs, better management information and more responsive decision-making. The major airlines were far behind easyJet, 'encumbered by historical travel agency relationships', the analysis stated.

EasyJet's decision to champion the Internet was, unsurprisingly, not appreciated by travel agents, including those in Stelios's homeland. Greek travel agents took offence at an easyJet advert which posed the question 'Who needs travel agents?', highlighting online booking for the airline's budget Athens–Luton service. The travel agents took easyJet to court in Athens, alleging that the airline's policy of issuing tickets directly to travellers violated fair play.

Representatives of easyJet pledged more than 800 tickets for people who turned up at court to support the company, and hundreds of people accordingly converged on the Athens court hearing in July 1998. The court decided to ban the ads for offending the integrity of travel agents, who insisted that easyJet's budget prices were misleading, offering no in-flight refreshments or refunds for cancellations. Stelios lost his case but – inevitably – gained more publicity.

The success of online ticket sales encouraged Stelios to set up a chain of Internet cafés called easyEverything, allowing travellers cheap and straightforward access to the web. Month after month, a new cavern packed with computer terminals would open in a big city: Amsterdam, Munich, New York. The rate of expansion proved so unsustainable that the value of easyEverything was written down by 99 per cent, forcing Stelios to make an emergency cash injection of £15 million.

The cafés, which charged £1 an hour for internet access, burnt through £40 million since the first outlet was opened in London during the dot.com boom. Stelios admitted that the chain had made a string of elementary retail mistakes, such as having its shops too widely dispersed geographically, and wasting money on expensive shopfronts. EasyEverything's lacklustre start took the sheen off Stelios's reputation as it became clear that his magic touch with easyJet wouldn't necessarily transfer to new ventures.

EasyJet's next publicity coup wasn't self-generated. In January 1999, the UK television channel ITV decided to air a reality TV series called *Airline*, based around the passengers and staff at easyJet. The airline was first approached about the possibility of filming during mid-1998 after an earlier series with Britannia Airways was discontinued; ITV staff had heard about Stelios's colourful publicity stunts and hoped that the airline's fresh approach would translate to screen. The first series on easyJet consisted of ten thirty-minute programmes, giving a 'warts and all' account of goings-on at easyJet's Luton operation. The viewing public watched irate late arrivals, overreacting staff and moaning C-list celebrities at the airport and witnessed Stelios personally go to Seattle to kick the tyres of the new Boeing planes that he had ordered.

It was a surprise hit. Soon 10 million people a week were tuning in to watch what was to become the most popular fly-on-the-wall documentary of all time. For several weeks, it was almost the third national soap opera, beaten in the ratings only by *Coronation Street* and *EastEnders*. The format never varied. Every week, a group of easyJet passengers went berserk before being subdued by staff with basilisk stares and excuses that verged on the brilliant. The cameras have been with easyJet almost constantly ever since. In 2003 *Airline* was ITV's most popular factual programme, with a total of 75 million viewers worldwide; it has been sold to countries including New Zealand, Australia and Japan.

One night's episode illustrated World Cup fever at Luton Airport. Disaster struck for one group of football fans with tickets for the semi-final between Brazil and Holland. Their plane developed a technical fault and they were desperately trying to change their flights. Frustration grew as kick-off time approached. The cameras then focused on Bruno Taylor. Bruno may have hitchhiked all around the world but getting out of Luton was proving to be his greatest challenge yet, as he had come away without his passport. Good old Mum came to the rescue, sending a courier to the airport with the vital document. The series made supervisor Leo Jones and broad Scouser Leanne Cheung favourites with the viewing public. It also helped reinforce the importance of arriving at the airport on time with a valid passport if you wanted to be allowed on to an easyJet flight; and though it occasionally showed the airline at less than its best, the publicity was a gift.

Meanwhile the company continued its domestic expansion. In January 1999, easyJet officially established Liverpool's Speke Airport as a hub airport, with aircraft and crews based in the north-west. The airline started four new scheduled services from Liverpool to Geneva, Barcelona, Belfast and Malaga. 'This is the beginning of the easyJet masterplan to turn Liverpool into an easyAirport,' said Stelios. 'The north-west has been neglected. People are fed up with having to travel to London airports or go via Manchester. Speke is a wonderful, uncongested airport and the routes we're offering will give people new holiday choices. Geneva will be for skiers, Barcelona for city breaks, Malaga for sun seekers and Belfast for people visiting friends and family.'

Keen to encourage short-break travel, easyJet started to plan overseas expansion alongside its burgeoning domestic operations. In April 1999, the airline rebranded a Swiss charter operation, TEA Basel AG, as 'easyJet Switzerland' and moved it from Basle to Geneva. EasyJet had bought a 40 per cent stake in the ailing Swiss carrier in March 1998 for three million Swiss francs. In June 1999, the company increased its stake in easyJet Switzerland to 49 per cent and acquired an option for the remaining 51 per cent. It set about making Geneva its third hub airport, planning services for easyJet Switzerland from Geneva to Nice, Amsterdam and Barcelona – the first easyJet services wholly outside the UK.

Stelios was about to celebrate easyJet's inaugural flight from Geneva to Barcelona on 29 July 1999 when word came through the captain that the Swiss authorities had withdrawn easyJet's commercial licence to fly the route after alleged objections by Swissair, the national carrier. Swissair, which didn't welcome easyJet's approach, claimed that national laws gave it a de facto monopoly over the Barcelona route. The decision lay with the Federal Office for Civil Aviation, an industry watchdog in Switzerland. EasyJet said it was pre-pared to go to court if FOCA ruled against them. The company had already sold 6,500 seats on the disputed route and vowed to fly via London if necessary. To the airline's fury, a spokesman for FOCA stated that as long as Swissair 'flies this route, it has the right to maintain an exclusive concession until 2008 at the latest or until the bilateral accords with the EU take effect'.

Rather than accept defeat, Stelios pulled off a masterstroke.

Announcing the bad news to passengers, he then explained: 'We can however still fly you to Barcelona as a private flight. So, I'm pleased to refund all your money in cash, and welcome you aboard the plane as my guests.' Never one to miss a trick, he then walked up and down the aisle with a bucket, saying: 'Collection for the pilot.' He managed to recoup 40 per cent of the fares in cash.

EasyJet went ahead with its plans to fly passengers from Geneva to Barcelona despite Swissair's objections, operating the flight as a tour operator rather than an airline, which entitled it to a different licence, and ran a free bus from Barcelona airport to the city centre to conform with tour operator requirements. Swissair insisted that the rival airline obey an obscure rule that the only way to operate flights on the Geneva–Barcelona route was to sell a package that included accommodation. So easyJet bought five tents and erected them at a campsite 60 miles outside Barcelona. 'We got them from Argos for £29.99 each,' Stelios announced proudly, explaining that anyone who booked a cheap flight to the Catalan capital from Geneva was welcome to camp out at his expense. Not surprisingly, only a few people took up his offer.

4. Turbulence over Luton

STELIOS CONTINUED TO lose no opportunity of getting his voice heard. He took out a full-page advert in *The Times* when catering employees at British Airways were about to go on strike. It read: 'Our catering staff will never vote for a strike . . . we don't have any!'

He placed another *Times* advert asking UK Chancellor Gordon Brown to review airport tax as he launched a campaign against the government's proposed changes to Air Passenger Duty – a tax on airline passengers introduced by the Conservative Party in 1994. 'The Tories doubled it to £10 on all flights, which is ridiculous if you're only paying £29 to fly to London,' Stelios complained. 'It should be proportional to the cost of the fare. That would reduce the tax for the low-budget individual traveller and increase it for the long-haul business traveller who is on an expense account and doesn't care anyway.' EasyJet's lobbying efforts proved successful. The government decided to reduce taxes on flights within Europe to £5.

More people continued to climb aboard easyJet's tangerine aircraft. EasyJet welcomed its 10 millionth passenger and in June 2000 celebrated the sale of 3 million seats online. Every Friday evening some 40 per cent of the viewing public tuned in to watch the fourth series of *Airline* on ITV, which attracted twice as many viewers as the new series of the US sitcom *Friends*.

EasyJet was determined to cater for its growing passenger numbers. In March 2000 the airline placed a firm order with Boeing for a further seventeen next-generation 737-700s. Deliveries were scheduled to begin in July 2001, increasing easyJet's fleet size to forty-four aircraft by 2004.

Meanwhile the airline's relationship with Luton Airport was growing sour. Immortalised by Lorraine Chase's 'No, Luton Airport' catchphrase, the airport was managed by a consortium of Barclays Private Equity and Airports Group International, and Luton's chief executive Graham Roberts wanted to raise take-off and landing charges from £1.60 to £8 per passenger when a five-year agreement with the airline ended in February 2001. The airport claimed that it needed to increase fees following an annual loss of £5 million, which it attributed to the end of EU duty-free sales and low landing fees. But easyJet said £40 million lavished on a new terminal was behind the loss. 'The airport has built an over-sized new terminal and seems to expect our passengers to pay for their mistake,' Stelios complained.

In June 2000, Stelios cut up his own Barclaycard and led a protest outside the Luton branch of Barclays Bank against the increase, which he described as 'absurd and greedy'. He stressed that easyJet was responsible for about 60 per cent of the 5 million passengers passing through Luton each year. 'Luton Airport was in decline before easyJet started operations in late 1995. The fact that it has turned £1.3 million profit into £330,000 in the past year and is on course for such big losses endorses everything I've said about the company and its management.'

EasyJet urged Deputy Prime Minister John Prescott to regulate fees at Luton to stop the airport 'ripping off' passengers. The airline took out full-page adverts in most of the national press, claiming that low-cost airline services would be under threat if Barclays were successful in raising landing charges. 'That is a huge increase which would wipe out our profits at Luton because we would not be able to pass the charge on to our passengers,' said easyJet PR spokesman Toby Nicol. EasyJet also enlisted passengers' support in an Internet campaign against the increase and threatened to take the case to the European Union.

Stelios and his staff even boycotted the royal opening of the airport's new terminal, snubbing the Queen. A spokesman for easyJet announced: 'We do not mean any disrespect to the Queen but we are protesting at the airport management being hell bent on a suicidal route to wrecking Luton Airport and returning it to the days of Lorraine Chase.' The airline threatened to reduce its Luton operations – even to pull out of Luton altogether – unless something was done about the take-off fees. A spokeswoman for the airport replied, 'If easyJet left Luton of course it would be a blow to the local economy and jobs in the area. But we can no longer keep up with the increasing number of passengers at Luton and at £40 million the new terminal is not expensive.'

EasyJet decided to cap its development at Luton in favour of expansion at other airports where it operated. EasyJet's flights from Geneva had already increased four-fold in the previous twelve months. It also signed a twenty-year deal at Liverpool Airport to base up to seven aircraft there from the following April. The airline was keen to develop Amsterdam Schiphol airport into its fourth European hub. Stelios wanted to operate flights to destinations already served from the UK and make use of the 'Open Skies' bilateral agreement, which allowed airlines to operate between countries they did not have their headquarters in. The company said it would start twice-daily services to Edinburgh and daily flights to Belfast and Nice from Amsterdam from 5 January 2001, on top of its existing flights between Amsterdam and Luton, Liverpool and Geneva.

Stelios had been eager to get established in the Netherlands for some time, having twice failed to acquire bankrupt charter carrier Air Holland. The airline was eventually snapped up in January 2000 by local investors. KLM, the Dutch operator, with its low-cost carrier, Buzz, was meanwhile cutting 2,700 jobs. To rub salt into KLM's wounds, Stelios said he intended easyJet to 'become the Dutch low-cost carrier'.

Hiccups inevitably accompanied easyJet's expansion. Like every airline, it experienced mishaps. More flights meant that more delays, incidents and cancellations plagued passengers, even as more punctual, problem-free flights took off each day. In May 2000, easyJet had to pay over £1 million in compensation after fog at Luton Airport delayed over sixty flights for longer than four hours. In June it paid out another £600,000 following an incident earlier in the year when snow closed Luton for twelve hours. Spokesman Toby Nicol took advantage of the situation to point out that compensation was a crucial part of easyJet's customer service contract.

Another public-relations problem awaited easyJet. In October 2000, charges of manslaughter and shipwreck were brought against Stelios in an Italian court following the explosion of the *Haven* oil tanker in April 1991. The charges had been dismissed twice in the lower courts, but a Genoa prosecutor filed an appeal with the Supreme Court alleging Stelios's responsibility for the disaster. At the time of the sinking, Stelios, then twenty-four, had been a director of the company that owned the ship, and as such could be pursued for manslaughter under Italian law.

Stelios dismissed the new appeal, pointing out that the earlier trials, which acquitted him, had placed the blame on human error, not on company negligence. 'In typical Italian fashion, however, they have gone after the wealthiest man they could find, and his son. It's a joke. This is a politically motivated attack – the prosecutor, having lost at the first and second degrees, has to be seen to be taking the case to the third and final degree. The only consequence for me is that I will have to pay more money to my lawyers.'

It was bad timing for easyJet: the trial took place just before the budget airline's planned £600 million flotation on the London stockmarket in November 2000, with Donaldson, Lufkin & Jenrette and UBS Warburg as joint co-ordinators. People still weren't sure whether Stelios was a proper businessman or just a playboy having a bit of fun on Dad's account. 'I think whether I am a proper businessman or not will be judged by the results. EasyJet will open its books in a few months and people will have to judge for themselves. As for me being a playboy, I don't have the time!' he laughed. 'Look, I'm not a suit, that's for sure. I enjoy starting companies, starting dreams. Maybe a proper businessman would have stayed in Greece in the family firm.'

Stelios divided his time between his home in Monaco, where he still had the requisite yacht, his family in Athens, the airline at Luton and easyGroup headquarters in Camden, north London, where he devised new companies to add to easyGroup, the umbrella organisation he had set up in 1998. His plan for his easyGroup companies was to follow the route he was taking with the airline and float them. Which is why he considered the flotation of easyJet as his biggest test to date. 'I don't know how I'll like running a public company, I've never done it,' he admitted. 'I'm adaptable and a fast learner but it is like asking me how I'd like being an astronaut. I just don't know.'

EasyJet appointed managing director Ray Webster as chief executive to help prepare it for the listing, while Stelios was to act as non-executive chairman. To the outside world, Stelios remained the public face of easyJet but Webster was the brains behind the operation. It was his customer yield management system, which he brought with him from Air New Zealand, that made easyJet tick. Yield management explains why the passenger sitting next to you has always paid less than you have. The key is to find the trade-off between selling discounted ticketing in order to fill up the plane completely, and selling full fare tickets and only filling up a portion of the plane.

EasyJet's yield management system was a complicated animal but worked on the basic principle that the later you booked the more you paid. EasyJet fares increased up to threefold as the plane filled up. The idea was that fares rose with demand – the antithesis of classical airline yield management. Webster finessed the technique and introduced a sophisticated system at the airline.

Webster helped easyJet motor towards its stockmarket lift-off at the same time as other airlines, including British Airways, were starting to suffer from a downturn in the industry amid heightened competition from their low-fares rivals. 'We're in a different business,' Stelios declared. 'It is a sign of the times that a company like BA, that in the past has made money from charging its customers a fortune, has discovered that the world has become more cost-conscious. The number of people prepared to pay £500 to £600 to fly to Europe is diminishing and at the same time they are stuck with high fixed costs. We've designed our business to have a very low cost base.'

EasyJet opened its books before its listing and showed the world that it was profitable and should be taken seriously. In the year to September 2000, the airline reported pre-tax profits of £22.1 million on sales of £263.7 million. This followed annual pre-tax profits of £1.3 million on sales of £139.8 million in 1999, and profits of £5.9 million on sales of £77 million in 1998.

EasyJet shares were formally admitted to the London Stock Exchange on 15 November 2000 at an offer price of 310p, in the middle of the 280p–340p target range. EasyJet spread its wings in early trading, ending its first day on the stockmarket with a price tag of £860 million. The shares, which closed the day's trading up 10 per cent at 341p, were almost six times oversubscribed.

The float raised £195 million, which the company planned to use to buy thirty-two new Boeing 737s as it expanded its European operations. 'The IPO is a significant milestone for easyJet and will allow us to maximise our growth potential by helping fund our planned new Boeing 737-700 purchases,' said Stelios. The airline's flamboyant founder and his family retained a 64 per cent chunk in the company, worth roughly £550 million, with Stelios's stake worth nearly £280 million.

The float enabled the company to reward its 1,400 executives and staff with share options worth about £90 million. Webster owned options giving him the right to buy 4.3 million shares at 182p each. Amir Eilon, a former Barclays and CSFB banker who had acted as easyGroup's in-house corporate finance adviser, had options to buy 3.2 million shares at the same price.

The flotation also boosted easyJet's confidence, and it declared that it could continue to expand at 25 per cent per year. Seat sales were continuing to grow strongly, with October proving to be a record month.

Of course, growth at easyJet, as at all airlines, continued to be accompanied by calamities, such as the one at the end of December 2000, when easyJet passengers were stranded by the freezing weather. Police were called to two airports as passengers staged furious protests. Liverpool's airport was closed for most of one day because of icy conditions and freezing fog, and easyJet staff were reduced to tears at Luton as the airline cancelled flights at both airports.

More than 200 people were forced to spend the night sleeping on the floor at Luton Airport, the scene of a sit-down protest by 100 passengers, and others took a whole two days to get from Belfast to Liverpool. Passengers flying from Glasgow also faced marathon journeys, with some taking fifty-six hours to complete what should have been a one-hour trip.

Passengers reported scenes of chaos and fury. Lucy

O'Neill, a technical manager for Tesco who was travelling from Luton to Belfast, said she should have flown at 7 p.m. on Friday but heard at 9.30 p.m. that her flight was cancelled. She said, 'One lady was flying to Barcelona to get married and was very upset because she couldn't get hold of her husband-to-be to tell him what was happening. One guy got very irate with one of the check-in girls. She just walked off in tears.' Karen Kemmett, from Brighton, who was forced to spend the night at Luton, said, 'The main problem was a complete lack of information. There was no concern, no cups of coffee, no nothing. A few people had had enough.'

Merseyside Police were called to Liverpool's airport when a forty-three-year-old man who had been waiting three days for an easyJet flight to Amsterdam started hurling abuse. Witness Matthew Marks, one of 450 passengers affected, said travellers were angry at poor communication from easyJet. 'A crowd of well over fifty gathered around one easyJet employee,' he said. 'He was trying to talk to the crowd but was constantly interrupted. The police intervened and hauled away one man who was particularly vocal but we could all understand his frustration.'

Problems with de-icing on easyJet aircraft were responsible for the most serious delays. EasyJet blamed a sub-contractor employed to de-ice its aircraft. 'Because they were not de-iced we could not fly and therefore had to cancel flights,' said a spokesman. 'We have said we will refund fares for anyone delayed over four hours and we will look at all claims for compensation.' Mike Goodman, easyJet's commercial director, said: 'This is very embarrassing; it's tragic during the holiday season and we apologise wholeheartedly. We have been let down badly by our de-icing supplier who has had problems with their fluid and machines. But we would not compromise safety.'

EasyJet never recorded a fatality or a crash. The carrier may have been stringent about cost-control but money was not an issue when it came to safety. Like other low-cost operators, however, easyJet was subject to delays, cancellations and mishaps which inevitably resulted in frustrated passengers.

The New Year saw relations with Luton put under further strain. In January 2001, Barclays sold its 65 per cent stake in Luton Airport to the airports operator TBI for £82 million. The deal raised TBI's holding in Luton to 90 per cent, strengthening its position as a regional airports operator. TBI funded the purchase with £50 million of new borrowings and £31.7 million from an underwritten share placing.

Negotiations between Luton and easyJet broke down and until August the airline had to accept the increase of passenger charges to £8. EasyJet said that the higher fees it was now being forced to pay would henceforth appear as a 'Barclays legacy charge' on passenger booking confirmations. Webster announced that easyJet would absorb half of the increase and pass on the other half, meaning passengers would pay an extra £4 per ticket. 'The Barclays legacy at London Luton is that it has negotiated an obscene return on its initial investment which will have to be carried by users of the airport,' he added. The carrier also warned that TBI might not get any easier a ride, pointing out that, as an existing shareholder in Luton, it had been party to all the negotiations over landing charges at the airport.

Keith Brooks, the chief executive of TBI, said he had some sympathy with easyJet but claimed that Barclays had 'called all the shots and made all the running'. He added that TBI had always enjoyed a good relationship with easyJet at Belfast Airport, which it also owned. 'EasyJet is looking for a long-term agreement and we want to help the growth of the airline so I would hope that in a few months we can come to a reasonable agreement,' Brooks said.

In March 2001, easyJet joined a consortium of UK airlines, called the 'The Airline Group', which was awarded the contract to run NATS, the UK's air traffic control system, under a public-private partnership for a thirty-year term. The group's other members were Airtours, Britannia, British Airways,

British Midland, JMC, Monarch and Virgin Atlantic.

The budget carrier continued to add routes to its network. In March, easyJet started operating scheduled flights between Geneva and Barcelona after ailing Swissair abandoned its services on the route. EasyJet must have felt some satisfaction in taking over the service from the carrier that had battled so hard to keep it away. In April 2001, easyJet announced the launch of five new services in the next few months: Amsterdam to Barcelona and Glasgow, Belfast to Edinburgh and Glasgow and London Gatwick to Nice, and started its Amsterdam to London Gatwick service. By July, easyJet had sold 10 million seats through its website.

In August, easyJet's attention was diverted back to the landing-fee row at Luton when the French group Vinci made a hostile £516 million bid, at 90p a share, for airports operator TBI. One of the conditions of the Vinci offer was that the Luton landing fees did not come down. The 'no reductions' clause was in the original cash bid and remained in the formal offer documents.

But easyJet was not prepared to back down and accept higher landing fees. The company vowed that it would not increase the number of its 737 aircraft at the airport, currently standing at eighteen, unless either prices came down or the access and airport infrastructure were improved. It was stalemate.

5. Crisis control

EASYJET'S CAREER AS a public company started badly, with losses of £10.3 million for its first six months, though industry analysts pointed out that the loss was to be expected since the airline traditionally made all its profits in the summer period when passenger volumes and yields were high. More encouragingly, first half revenues rose 43 per cent, while passenger numbers increased 31 per cent to 3.2 million, with 86 per cent of bookings made on the Internet.

Meanwhile, the major carriers were recording falling passenger numbers. The US economy was entering recession, and as transatlantic travel fell away the large carriers saw their margins being eroded. Airlines had grown accustomed to taking the easy way out, and many were fat and complacent after pampered decades of government control. Fragmented and financially fragile, the European aviation industry was reeling from rising fuel prices, an excess of seats and hefty costs, particularly for labour. Earlier in 2001, Germany's

Lufthansa had capitulated after a strike of just three days and awarded its pilots a 12 per cent pay raise. Airlines were acutely vulnerable to industrial action; even the threat of a strike encouraged passengers to switch allegiances to rival carriers. As Daniel Solon of leading London aviation consultants Avmark International pointed out, 'The cabin unions realise they have a grip on the windpipe of the industry.'

British Airways bade farewell to CEO Bob Ayling. In Ayling's place, the flag carrier welcomed Rod Eddington as its new chief executive; speculation arose that Eddington was brought in because his greater popularity with employees might make it easier for him to push through as many as 20,000 job cuts. Credited with revitalising the fortunes of domestic carrier Ansett Airlines, the second largest airline in his native Australia, Eddington had grown up in the country-side in Western Australia and was incredibly down to earth. A Rhodes scholar, he had married an air hostess at Cathay Pacific, where he was formerly managing director, and had two children. After running Ansett, in which Rupert Murdoch had a 50 per cent stake before selling to Air New Zealand, Eddington became a non-executive director on the board of Murdoch's News Corporation. He was expected to leave the airline industry and run Murdoch's Australian media opera-tions but an offer to take the £500,000-a-year job at BA proved too hard to resist.

During his first twelve months as CEO at BA, Eddington got rid of BA's much-mocked ethnic tail fins, held and then broke off merger talks with KLM and suffered the aftermath of the Concorde crash in July 2000. Eddington had walked into a tough job. At the start of September 2001, the new CEO predicted an annual pre-tax loss of £65 million for the year ending March 2002, his first full year in charge, compared with a previously forecast full-year profit of £150 million.

Labour costs at the British flag carrier were rising as pilots demanded more money. It looked increasingly likely that BA would cut more jobs in 2001, having already shed 3,000 in

2000. It had already announced its intention to reduce its passenger-carrying capacity by 25 per cent by March 2003. Airline traffic volumes for BA's crucial long-haul business were nose-diving as Western economies deteriorated faster than expected and competition intensified. Profits from the long-haul business were simply no longer robust enough to cover the spiralling costs of its short-haul flights, which were losing customers in droves to the no-frills airlines such as easyJet.

'We are getting to a crossover point where the likes of BA will say "enough is enough",' Webster predicted. 'They will recognise we have deep pockets and they will concentrate on long-haul business and leave short-haul to us. I believe in the near future there will be two ways to travel over any distance in Europe: either high-speed train or low-cost airline.'

BA's new CEO worked hard at consolidating and rationalising the company's short-haul UK and European businesses, which had been losing BA £300 million a year. He cut BA's long-haul flights from Gatwick, transferring some to Heathrow, and reduced the number of companies using the BA brand. He also promised to fight back in the domestic and European short-haul market against easyJet and Ryanair, who by now were both larger than BA in terms of market capitalisation. Given that BA's cost base was three to four times higher than those of its no-frills rivals such as Ryanair, it seemed a quixotic quest.

Ryanair liked to compare itself with Walmart in the US: 'pile it high and sell it cheap', a philosophy that was making the company Europe's fastest-growing airline. Having carried 7.4 million passengers in the year to 31 March 2001, a rise of 35 per cent on the year before, Ryanair raised annual pre-tax profits by 44 per cent to £104.5 million on revenues up 32 per cent to £487 million. Ryanair's strong growth was accompanied by a stellar share performance. The airline was a darling of the City, with brokers showering it in 'buy' notes.

Almost synonymous with Ryanair was the airline's irreverent Irish boss, Michael O'Leary, who was only too happy to offer cheap seats to keep people flying, with promotions such as 1 million flights for £9.99 one-way.

O'Leary, one of six children whose father was an entrepreneurial type with a background in farming, rabbit-breeding and property, had trained as a tax consultant with KPMG in Dublin, where he met Tony Ryan, Ryanair's founder, and became his adviser. By 1990, when Ryanair was on the brink of going under, he agreed to become chief executive in return for a 25 per cent stake. Habitually dressed in old Levi's, a rugby shirt and a baseball cap, O'Leary transformed Ryanair from a money-losing carrier serving Ireland and Britain into the leader, alongside easyJet, of Europe's low-fare airlines. By emulating the same low cost, no-frills model pioneered by the US's Southwest Airlines, Ryanair offered fares as low as one-tenth of the price of the national carriers on intra-European routes.

Unlike easyJet, Ryanair didn't compete head-on with the national carriers or fly into major airports such as Amsterdam. Instead, the airline flew to secondary airports outside main cities, targeting the discount market, which the majors had long shunned in favour of the business-class traveller. A hop to Paris with Ryanair, for example, really meant a flight to Beauvais, 43 miles north of the city in Picardy, where the terminal looked like a bus depot stuck in the middle of farmland.

While easyJet had to pay standard airport fees at major airports, out-of-the-way terminals were so hungry for business that Ryanair could negotiate airport fees of as little as €1.50 per passenger and get marketing and training support for as long as twenty years. That was a fraction of the €15 to €20 per passenger charged by Europe's major hubs. Because there was so little congestion at these locations, Ryanair's planes were back in the air no more than twenty-five minutes after landing.

Far from fearing the recession, Ryanair and easyJet

embraced it as the best business opportunity for years, largely at the expense of BA and the other large carriers. Like Ryanair, easyJet maintained it was well positioned to withstand any economic slowdown, arguing that it would benefit from passengers trading down to cheaper carriers. 'We have been praying for a downturn for years,' said Webster. 'There is a cascade effect as people trade down from the traditional carriers to the new low-cost operators.'

The percentage of easyJet customers who had 'business travel characteristics' (they booked last minute and left and returned within the week) had increased to 55 per cent from 36 per cent a year previously. 'There is an increasing acceptance among business travellers of easyJet and if there is a recession then there could well be a further migration of these passengers,' Webster reported enthusiastically.

British Airways' no-frills arm, Go, was also enjoying success. Go ran services to twenty destinations from Stansted and in May 2001 opened a new hub at Bristol, offering flights to eight destinations with plans to fly over half a million passengers from the new base in the first year. Go also had smaller-scale operations in Glasgow and Edinburgh, and was aiming to grow total passenger numbers from 2.8 million in 2000 to 'closer to 4 million' for 2001. The company had already expanded its fleet from thirteen to fifteen aircraft in 2001 and hoped to increase this to seventeen by 2002.

Aviation analysts at Merrill Lynch expected Europe's burgeoning low-cost airline market to grow between 25 per cent and 35 per cent over the following five years, and easyJet was in a prime position in that market. 'EasyJet looks to be positioned to grow at least in line with its sub-sector peers, and we believe it could be a beneficiary of any consolidation opportunities within the sector going forward,' Merrill Lynch analysts said.

And then, in just one day, the world changed irrevocably. Millions of people saw the devastating pictures of planes crashing into the World Trade Centre on 11 September 2001. The world was plunged into grief and fear.

Several European carriers had already been wobbling before 11 September, and now many airlines were left struggling to survive. Many people decided it was too dangerous to fly and rapidly cancelled their holiday plans. Businesses axed travel budgets. Big national carriers – Belgium's Sabena, Ireland's Aer Lingus, Spain's Iberia, Italy's Alitalia and Switzerland's Swissair – came under enormous financial pressure, some even teetering on the brink of insolvency as passengers were scared away from flying.

To counteract falling passenger volume, Europe's major airlines cut flights, grounded aircraft, raised fares, and sacked workers in their tens of thousands. Alitalia called the situation 'the worst crisis commercial airlines have faced since the end of World War II'. To meet it, Italy's national carrier announced cost-saving measures including the cutting of 2,500 jobs, or 12 per cent of the workforce. Aer Lingus dismissed almost a quarter of its 7,000 employees. Lufthansa cut catering from European flights and asked staff to accept a four-day working week, pay cuts and early retirement. The crisis may have had a silver lining for some; as Seamus Conlon, at the time managing director of Airtours Holidays, commented, 'Everything that the airlines had wanted to do for years suddenly became possible.'

Many airlines cut fares in a bid to encourage passengers back on to their planes. From mid-October British Airways offered 5 million tickets to twenty-one European destinations at bargain prices, with 500,000 tickets to cities such as Amsterdam, Paris, Berlin, Brussels, Barcelona and Madrid at £69, and an additional 'children go free' deal. Despite the promotion BA announced a 73 per cent fall in profits in the six months to September 30 and stepped up its ongoing jobs cull, announcing 7,200 job losses and a 9 per cent cut in capacity, while executives accepted pay cuts. The carrier reported an 11.6 per cent drop in passenger numbers for September, including a 32.1 per cent reduction on routes to the US. BA's passenger numbers fell by 24.7 per cent in October, and by November the flag carrier was losing £2 million a day.

The terrorist attacks precipitated a massive shake-out in the industry as airlines battled for survival. Ansett Airlines of Australia went bust within a few hours of the disaster in New York. Swissair, already on the brink before the attacks, owing to an ill-judged spending spree buying stakes in some of Europe's worst-performing airlines such as Belgium's Sabena and Air Lib of France, grounded its fleet on 2 October 2001 and filed for protection from creditors. Swissair's collapse helped bring down the ailing Belgian national carrier Sabena.

Europe's major aviation industry was experiencing a financial crisis that bore 'no relation to anything we have ever seen', declared Karl-Heinz Neumeister, head of the European Aviation Association in Brussels. The AEA predicted full-year losses of $8.9 billion, far more than the industry's previous largest annual loss of $2.4 billion after the Gulf War. Between 11 September and 4 November, North Atlantic air traffic fell by 35 per cent and European traffic by 10 per cent for major European airlines.

Industry experts predicted that many of the continent's money-losing flag carriers were headed towards bankruptcy, mergers or take-overs. BA's Eddington believed that Europe's fourteen national airlines would be replaced by just three main airlines grouped around Europe's largest carriers – British Airways, Air France and Lufthansa.

But as other European airlines cut thousands of jobs and dramatically scaled back services amid escalating losses, one sector of the airline industry continued to boom. Not only did 11 September fail to have any adverse effect on low-cost airlines, paradoxically it actually helped their business. People were queuing to travel on low-cost carriers such as easyJet, Ryanair and Buzz, which were recording unprecedented heavy bookings. Low-cost airlines traditionally did better during slow-downs; ten years previously, US discount airline Southwest

Airlines had seen its business increase four-fold immediately after the Gulf War.

While major European flagships such as Air France and Lufthansa saw double-digit declines in their business after the terrorist attacks, easyJet's bookings recovered to their pre-11 September levels within a few days, after falling by 26 per cent on the morning after the terrorist attacks. The carrier flew 680,383 passengers in September, 150,000 more than in the previous year. In October and November, when most European airlines were watching their traffic disappear, easyJet's traffic rose 32.5 per cent and 39 per cent respectively year-on-year.

The number of tickets easyJet sold over the Internet also increased. During November, 90.1 per cent of sales were made online, up on November 2000's figure of 79.4 per cent. The update came just days after British Airways reported a 17.8 per cent slump in passenger traffic during November, which it attributed to 'challenging' trading conditions.

One of easyJet's key strengths was that it didn't fly to the US. 'Our competitors suffered more because they fly the Atlantic,' said Stelios. 'I am almost embarrassed to admit we have benefited from the events of September 11.' Another advantage was that its costs were half those of leading European carriers, allowing it to offer rock-bottom fares. In the weeks after the attacks, easyJet slashed 150,000 seat prices by up to 60 per cent, with flights from London to Glasgow and Belfast for £12.50.

It seemed that people were willing to accept the additional risks of flying, provided it was with a budget airline such as easyJet or Ryanair. Part of the explanation was the assessment that terrorists were less likely to attack an airline with a name such as easyJet than a flag-waving carrier such as American Airlines or British Airways. People also reasoned that it was unlikely that a terrorist would blow up a plane that flew from Stansted Airport to Malaga or Tenerife.

There also seemed to be a widespread willingness to accept

a higher risk of death in return for lower prices. Money is regularly traded for risk when people decide not to buy a smoke alarm, a bicycle helmet or the safest car available. 'After the terrible tragedy we cut our prices even lower and seats on our planes sold like hot cakes,' Webster said. 'If the price is right people will accept your offer.' Michael O'Leary, chief executive of Ryanair, which was offering flights for just £1, echoed Webster's views in an interview with the *Sunday Telegraph* newspaper: 'Drop your prices and you'll be amazed how demand comes back!'

Stelios declared that easyJet was proof of public confidence in the economy. He praised shoppers for taking to the high street to help arrest an economic downturn after the attacks: 'The worst move to make at the moment is to give up. If you sit around waiting for a recession, it will find you. I'm taking a more positive approach. Business may not be as easy as it was but there's still a profit to be made.'

Indeed, easyJet's maiden set of results as a plc proved that the tragedy had done little to dent the airline's fortunes. In October 2001, easyJet announced that full-year pre-tax profits were up by 81 per cent to £40 million, well above even the highest forecasts of £37 million, on revenues of £356.9 million. The airline carried 7.1 million passengers in the twelve months to September 30, up 27 per cent on the previous year. The full-year load factor, or proportion of seats filled, increased by 2.2 per cent to 83 per cent. By now, easyJet was operating thirty-five routes out of seventeen airports. 'September 11 proved something that we have always been very confident of, namely that in a recession the low-cost model is a lot more resilient than traditional airlines,' said Webster.

By the end of October 2001, easyJet's share price had doubled in a single year relative to the average share price of the European aviation sector. EasyJet said that while traditional airlines had suffered from the slump in demand and disruption caused by the hijackings, it saw a chance to expand faster than it had expected. Stelios commented, 'I believe that easyJet is well placed to take advantage of the changing market conditions and the continued strong sentiment towards low-cost airlines. I am cautiously optimistic and believe that out of every crisis there is opportunity.'

The carrier predicted that as rivals merged or reduced services, then landing slots, aircraft and even cheaper pilots would become available. The company started to draw up growth plans with the aim of taking over vacant slots and services being abandoned by national airlines such as British Airways.

Webster flew to Brussels in October to demand the right to take over spare capacity at Gatwick Airport and make the airport its main base. EasyJet managers thought that a move to Gatwick would allow easyJet to tap into a bigger and wealthier market. Webster aimed to make easyJet's Gatwick operation two to three times bigger than that at Luton by around 2005, and said easyJet was also in talks with Paris Orly, Brussels and Zurich airports to gain control of take-off and landing slots vacated by airlines that were cutting capacity.

Webster's demands put easyJet on a collision course with BA, who wanted the Commission to relax its 'use-it-or-lose-it' rule, which forced airlines to give up any slot not used for 80 per cent of the time. BA felt it should be waived until passenger numbers rose back to normal levels, while easyJet argued that while transatlantic routes should be safeguarded, such a move within Europe would amount to an unfair state subsidy. Webster believed BA was trying to hold on to the slots to stop low-cost airlines taking them over. 'They know they have no future in continuing to develop European operations,' he said. 'Any airline that chooses not to fly a route should return its slots and they should be reallocated.'

At the end of October, with £244 million in the bank, easyJet announced it was planning to expand. It had ordered twenty-five new planes from Boeing, and wanted more. Webster said easyJet would put down a deposit on thirty Boeing 737s. At cost, the aircraft would set easyJet back as much as £20 million. But Stelios insisted that the new planes were necessary to boost easyJet's fleet and let it expand into airports such as Gatwick. Webster also said that the airline was looking to hire additional staff to cope with the company's growth plans. The aircraft announcement came just weeks after BA chairman Lord Marshall admitted that he was seeking to wriggle out of aircraft contracts with Boeing in a bid to reduce costs.

EasyJet moved to bolster its financial position. A year after its flotation, it announced plans to raise more than £90 million to exploit the turmoil afflicting rival airlines. The extra money would help fund expansion of the easyJet fleet, create new routes in the short-haul market and take over routes abandoned by other airlines.

Stelios also revealed that he wanted to sell some of his holding to raise as much as £67 million to support his other ventures. He needed the proceeds from his share sale to recapitalise the struggling easyEverything Internet cafés venture and launch more businesses under the 'easy' brand. After Internet cafés, rental cars and a credit card, he was 'looking at cinemas'. He said that the share sale would allow him to retain a significant stake, while freeing cash to invest in other ventures. 'After six years building this company up, I now wish to monetise some of my investment to invest in my new ventures,' he announced, 'although I will still retain a very significant investment in easyJet and have no present intention to sell any more shares.'

Stelios was in an unusual position: he was both benefiting and suffering from Europe's economic downturn. His London-based easyInternetcafé chain, which he hoped to make the McDonald's of web access, had burned through $58 million in two years. Faced with price-sensitive customers and spiralling expenses, the founder had to dig into his own pockets for $22 million to keep twenty outlets open in twelve European cities and New York. He sacked the company's CEO and closed stores in Rotterdam and Antwerp to preserve cash.

The planned share sale was the first time Stelios had taken cash out of easyJet. He denied that his proposed sale betrayed a lack of confidence. 'Of course not,' he said. 'It is only 7 per cent of the family's holding and I have no other income from the business except for capital gains. Every shareholder would prefer me to do it this way alongside the results than surprise them.' He added, 'Remember I come from a rich family. I do not need to sell easyJet shares to fund my lifestyle.'

In November, easyJet issued 26 million new shares and Stelios and his family sold 13 million. The combined share deals left Stelios with a holding in easyJet of 27–29 per cent and his family with 30.9 per cent. UBS Warburg and Credit Suisse First Boston sold the placing and open offer of 26 million shares on a three-for-forty basis at a price of 375p a share. Webster announced that the rights issue was 4.5 times over-subscribed; it raised £93.3 million for easy Jet.

'I am delighted at the success of this fund raising which will enable us to accelerate the expansion of our services to Europe's flying public,' Stelios said. 'To have succeeded in raising new money of this level is very encouraging in today's market.'

EasyJet also announced that it had resolved its long-running dispute with Luton Airport's owner TBI over landing charges, with a twenty-year agreement keeping easyJet charges at existing levels (£5.50 per passenger and 50p for baggage, an amount easyJet had previously said was excessive), which could be reduced if passenger numbers grew, compared with the airport's standard tariff of £8 per passenger. At the time, 2.1 million of the airline's passengers used the airport.

EasyJet now had an incentive to grow at Luton rather than moving its extra business to Gatwick, as threatened. Webster added: 'This announcement gives us certainty over our operations from London Luton Airport.'

Normality in aviation seemed barely possible in late 2001. Two months and a day after 11 September, just as the wounds were starting to heal, the world learned that American Airlines flight 587 had crashed on take-off from New York's Kennedy airport. The crash killed 260 on-board the Airbus A300 and five people on the ground. Even though terrorism was rapidly ruled out, the accident piled on the agony for Europe's major airlines, and many introduced fuel or insurance surcharges to compensate for rising oil prices and higher industry costs.

EasyJet continued to bypass the industry's turbulence; between 24 September and 12 December, easyJet's shares soared by 49 per cent. Stelios encouraged people back to flying, pronouncing, 'You can't save souls in empty churches.' He was blunt about why easyJet had prospered since 11 September: 'It affected Americans flying to Europe, so our competitors, especially BA, suffered a lot more than we did. The Europeans are more familiar with terrorism, and went back to flying much faster. So we could accelerate our growth while BA had to start retrenching.'

The terrorist attacks made it unpleasantly obvious that in security terms the airline industry had become a soft target, and airlines throughout the world increased their vigilance, with tighter security and better policing at airports and on planes. British pilots agreed to reinforced steel cockpit doors, extra searches on crews and passengers, and restrictions on sharp implements. Pilots were told that not even their spouses could join them in the cockpit. Plans to deploy undercover armed guards on British planes sparked fierce debate. The Israeli airline El Al had carried armed marshals on all its flights for more than thirty years, and Lufthansa also used guards on some flights. EasyJet made no attempt to follow their example; Stelios argued that guns on planes could fall into the hands of would-be hijackers and put the lives of passengers at risk.

People continued to be scared away from flying. In an attempt to relax nervous passengers, easyJet hired drag queen May McFetridge, alias comic John Linehan, to provide in-flight entertainment on its flights from Belfast to Glasgow and Edinburgh. Dressed in an orange and green kilt, green Dr

Marten boots, a sporran with poodle hair, waistcoat and blouse and a Scottish 'Jimmy' hat, the comedian handed out sweets and told bad jokes (one example was: 'If you are going to be sick throw up in the bag in front of you, whether you know her or not'). The tactic proved popular with most passengers, but not all; one Scottish businessman complained that he couldn't concentrate on his preparation for an important meeting.

In general, people continued to perceive the budget carriers as unlikely targets for any terrorist attack. Until that is, twenty-nine-year-old Kerim Chatty was caught trying to board a Ryanair flight from Vasteras in Sweden to Stansted with a pistol in his hand luggage. Half Tunisian and half Swedish, Chatty was an experienced pilot who – like nine of the 11 September hijackers – had undergone training in the US. The CIA believed that Chatty had planned to hijack a Ryanair Boeing 737 and fly it into a US embassy in Europe – probably that in London.

Chatty, who had previous assault and weapons convictions, told investigators he found the gun in a borrowed car a few weeks before his arrest. He said he put it in his bag and forgot about it when he left for the airport to fly to an Islamic conference in Birmingham. The district court in Vasteras said Chatty's explanation could not be dismissed, and prosecutor Thomas Haeggstroem dropped hijacking charges because of lack of evidence. Instead, Chatty was jailed for four months for weapons violation.

Then a reporter from Scotland's *Daily Record* newspaper used a fake identity card in the name of Hani Hanjour, who crashed an airliner into the Pentagon on 11 September, to travel on flights with both easyJet and Ryanair. No one at either of the airlines challenged him over his false identity.

EasyJet was resolute about adopting a zero-tolerance approach when it came to security measures; short shrift was given to even the most obvious of jokes. In October, Malcolm and Betty Ashworth, both in their late sixties, were checking in at Liverpool John Lennon airport when they were asked if they had any dangerous items. Mr Ashworth turned to his wife and jokingly inquired: 'Have you got your pistol, dear?' The couple were escorted away for a thorough baggage search; although no offending items were found, they were not allowed to board their easyJet flight to Belfast.

EasyJet's policy even extended to children. An easyJet pilot turned away a group of thirty ten- and eleven-year-old schoolgirls on their way from Belfast to a netball tournament in Liverpool because they were a 'security risk'. The pilot refused to allow them to board the plane because he claimed that the four teachers accompanying them weren't enough to look after the children, leaving the girls in tears. The pupils from Rockport School in Craigavad, Co Down, had to take a ferry and an eight-hour coach journey instead, though easyJet later apologised and refunded the cost of their outward flight.

The carrier was determined to enforce its security policy that passengers, even on domestic flights, had to carry a valid form of photographic ID, namely a passport or national identity card, with visas when applicable. Age made no difference; lack of the correct ID meant that Scottish fourteen-year-old Jamie McGovern was not allowed to fly to Liverpool for trials with Everton football club, while ninety-four-year-old Elsie Brigg from Liverpool missed the family reunion her daughter had planned for months after easyJet staff refused to accept her bus pass as identification. Her daughter Jacqueline Gee complained that easyJet staff had made her 'feel like a gun-wielding maniac'.

One person tried to take advantage of the heightened sense of security. Alan Burton, who lived in the flight path of Liverpool's airport, became so frustrated with the noise of planes flying overhead that he called the airport in the early hours of the morning twice in three days, telling staff there were bombs on two easyJet flights to Belfast. Each time Special Branch officers became involved. Burton was jailed for twelve months at Liverpool crown court after pleading guilty to two charges of making hoax bomb calls.

Meanwhile, easyJet was busy planning its expansion into the French market. The airline applied to Cohor, the body which distributed take-off and landing slots at Paris Orly Airport, for 20,000 of the 35,000 slots that had become available following the collapse of AOM and Air Liberté, France's second largest airline.

Air Liberté, which together with its sister, long-haul and charter carrier AOM, employed 5,200 staff, had been struggling to overcome losses for years. Until May 2000 it was owned by British Airways, but after failing to turn it round, BA booked a big loss and sold it for £50 million to Swissair, which held 49 per cent, and its 51 per cent sleeping partner Taitbout Antibes, controlled by Paris-quoted Marine Wendel. Losses mounted to £500,000 a day and had helped plunge Swissair into loss too, causing Air Liberté executive chairman Marc Rochet to file his company's insolvency in June 2001.

EasyJet saw great potential for its low-cost model in the French market, which had no domestic equivalent. 'Paris and London have a similar passenger base, but the difference is four low-cost carriers serve London,' said easyJet spokesman Toby Nicol. 'How many serve Paris?'

EasyJet aimed to become the first low-cost carrier operating out of France, and to use Paris Orly as its second major European operating base after Luton. The airline wanted to base ten Boeing 737-700 and 737-300 short-haul aircraft at Orly, reroute some of its existing cheap flights from Luton and Liverpool and provide cheap, high-frequency flights to European cities such as Nice, Barcelona, Madrid and Geneva. It projected building up a 2.5 million per year passenger base from Orly 'very quickly'.

In response to easyJet's French ambitions, O'Leary was planning to expand Ryanair's presence at Beauvais Airport, outside Paris, to compete head-to-head with its no-frills rival in the French market. There were no slot restrictions at Beauvais, so Ryanair's presence there was limited only by its willingness to invest. Like easyJet, Ryanair was increasing the size of its fleet and had plans to open other bases in continental Europe. The Irish airline began flights from Brussels Charleroi airport, its first base outside the UK and Ireland, in March 2001.

Ryanair had also thrown down the gauntlet to Lufthansa, mainland Europe's biggest flag carrier, announcing its plans to make Frankfurt-Hahn a hub airport. Ryanair already flew a handful of flights from Hahn and planned to ramp up its operations at the German airport to offer more than thirty flights a day from February 2002. O'Leary claimed he could undercut Lufthansa's fares by as much as 75 per cent. Ryanair was already engaged in a bruising price war with Go on routes between Ireland and Scotland, with both airlines offering tickets for as little as £9.99 for a return flight between Dublin and Edinburgh.

However, easyJet's French aspirations were met with resistance from the outset. The French authorities refused to provide take-off and landing slots on the grounds that the airport was full. Webster hoped the prospect of 300 new jobs at Orly, at a time when Air Liberté was poised to shed 1,400, might tip the balance, and he flew over to Paris to lobby the French Transport Ministry officials. In the meantime, easyJet offered employment to potentially displaced employees at AOM/Air Liberté, in the event that the regional carrier failed to secure the appropriate financial backing it needed to survive. AOM/Air Liberté were continuing to operate in what amounted to the equivalent of US Chapter 11 bankruptcy, while its employees participated in sporadic strikes. But the beleaguered carrier's employees refused easyJet's offer and pressed for a solution to protect all jobs.

Management at the carrier clearly liked the concept of introducing low-cost flights into France. In the event Jean-Charles Corbet, the former pilots' union leader, backed by

Canadian bank CIBC, bought Air Liberté and AOM for a token sum and attempted to turn them into a low-cost carrier named Air Lib. Corbet planned France's first low-cost internal flights from Paris to Nice, Toulouse, Toulon, Perpignan and Lourdes, adding Marseilles, Nimes, Bordeaux and Montpellier later, with one-way fares as low as £20. Unfortunately, the high fuel burn of its aircraft and stubborn union resistance to more flexible working and low-cost business practices left the new chief executive officer with low fares but high costs.

Air Lib was watched closely by easyJet, Ryanair, Go and Virgin Express, all of whom had expressed interest in expanding their development in France, especially Paris. Only Buzz flew at low prices from anywhere in Britain to Paris, with Ryanair using Beauvais Airport north-west of Paris for flights from Dublin. Air Lib wasn't about to help easyJet fulfil its ambitions, however. The new carrier had agreed to hand back 35,000 of the 75,000 slots it controlled at Orly Airport, following the French authorities' request for it to abandon 40,000 of the slots. But then Air Lib changed its mind about the number of slots it was willing to relinquish, giving back only 12,000 instead.

EasyJet, which was still hoping to gain 20,000 of the slots given up by Air Lib, was outraged. 'It is scandalous that Air Lib has not fulfilled the terms of its restructuring,' said Webster. 'It is a piece of blatant anti-competitive protectionism. This company should at least have the decency to abandon those slots it knows it cannot use.' In the end, Cohor awarded the bulk of the available slots to Air Algeria, Iberia and Air Malta. EasyJet's Swiss arm, easyJet Switzerland, was given a few slots from Paris to Zurich and Geneva, but easyJet was no nearer to fulfilling its French ambitions.

But the company was still able to expand elsewhere. Webster felt that the airline's strong post-11 September performance strengthened its position at airports. 'Four to five years ago, airports treated the low-cost sector as a very risky experiment. I think we have now created enough good experience in airports around Europe that the word is that the low-cost business is a good business. It's viable. Every major airport nowadays contacts us and says, "Can we talk?"'

The carrier continued to develop its presence at London Gatwick by announcing four new routes (to Edinburgh, Malaga, Majorca and Zurich) in December 2001, making easyJet the second largest scheduled airline at the airport after British Airways. By the end of the year, easyJet was flying thirty-five routes between seventeen airports.

Webster was already looking ahead. 'I've always stressed as intrinsic to the airline that the trick is not making it profitable today, it's making it profitable when it is very large. If you want to get from roughly thirty aircraft now to three hundred aircraft, you've got to make sure the things you do are repeatable. You can't get there by just taking opportunistic moves when one comes up. Opportunities, whether it be cheap airports or cheap planes, are not predictable enough in their availability. If you want to grow 25 per cent a year for as far as you can see into the future, you have to make sure you have a business that can continue to retain the same business model . . . By picking major airports and brand-new planes we build what we call a cookie cutter. Having every passenger buying exactly the same seat on exactly the same plane is an example of how we apply the concept of simplicity. You move complexity, you move costs.'

Meanwhile, O'Leary estimated that Ryanair's business would double to 15 million passengers by 2003, and double again by 2008, making Ryanair Europe's number one international airline. In November, Ryanair reported a 39 per cent surge in interim profits to £55 million. The tragic events of 2001 may have left many European airlines in a tailspin but Ryanair and easyJet were soaring even higher.

6. Going, going, gone

EASYJET'S ARCH-RIVAL GO was also growing in leaps and bounds. Just as Go had been beginning to perform successfully in November 2000, Ayling's successor, Rod Eddington, surprised Cassani by deciding to offload it. Eddington didn't want to wait to find out whether Go's promised profits would arrive the following year, after estimated losses of about £25 million in the previous two. Eddington thought Go was cannibalising British Airway's customer base, nipping away at its parent's undercarriage with fares of £39 return to Munich and £49 to Rome. 'It's not a business segment we're in,' said Eddington; though the joke ran in aviation circles that Eddington should have sold the rest of British Airways and kept Go.

EasyJet already had its eyes set on its rival, and for a while, there was talk that the orange airline would take over Go, thus eradicating a powerful competitor and increasing its size and strength. But it wasn't easyJet's turn yet. In June 2001, after months of negotiations, BA let Go go for £110 million to a management buyout team. The management team then sold it on to their financial backers, the private equity group 3i, retaining a 22 per cent stake. Go was now a rival to BA. But a BA spokeswoman maintained that the airline had made the right move: 'We believe we got the timing right and that we got an excellent return of some 400 per cent on an initial investment of £25 million.'

Chief executive Barbara Cassani hurried home to play Monopoly with her two children after completing the deal. 'I wasn't able to spend a lot of time with them while we were putting the deal together,' she admitted. Cassani relished running the airline and was clearly proud of it. Moreover, she was determined to quash speculation that Go had only survived until then because of BA's financial support. She planned to open one new base a year for the following three years, buy new aircraft and set up operations on the continent on her own terms. 'Now we can grow,' she exulted. We want to double in size every couple of years. That was never possible under BA.'

Charismatic, a stylish dresser and a witty conversationalist, Cassani was a public relations dream. She combined an informal approach with a steely determination and a hard-nosed American business style. Go employees loved her easy-going, approachable manner. She became known for hosting dinners at a pizza restaurant near Stansted, where she gave cabin crew and back-office staff lessons in share ownership. She told one interviewer: 'All of a sudden you see a light come on in their eyes – and the first thing they say is, "Is there a catch?" And I say, "Yes there is a catch. The catch is they aren't going to be worth this unless we do something."' Diners were always restricted to two courses only; their boss liked to remind them they were working for a low-cost airline. Like Stelios, Cassani wasn't afraid to muck in with the troops – she was once an air hostess for the day, making coffee and cleaning seats with the rest of the cabin crew. In 2002, she was named Veuve Clicquot's businesswoman of the year.

Expansion was rapid. In March 2002, Go increased its passenger numbers to 428,999 from 358,626 passengers in February and 319,000 in January. It was now the UK's third-largest airline. Go flew on thirty-eight routes within the UK and mainland Europe, with a fleet of twenty-four 737-300s and another three aircraft due to be delivered by June 2002. Go's load factor was an impressive 76.5 per cent, and some 83 per cent of its ticket sales were sold via the Internet. It announced a four-fold increase in pre-tax profits to £17 million for the year ending 31 March 2002. Full-year sales rose 46 per cent to £233.7 million and passenger numbers increased 55 per cent to 4.3 million. Cassani was understandably proud of her achievements and planned to float the airline in the next two years; she was confident that Go could repeat easyJet's success and raise close to £1 billion on the stockmarket.

And then the bombshell was dropped: easyJet was in talks to take over Go. Cassani was outraged, but easyJet had had the takeover in mind for years. Unlike Ryanair, Go followed near-identical business models to easyJet and targeted the same passengers. Taking over Go would annihilate easyJet's fiercest opponent and at a stroke make easyJet Europe's largest low-cost airline.

Unsurprisingly, Cassani was fiercely opposed to easyJet taking over what she called her 'third baby'. She told staff she was 'extremely disappointed' that Go might no longer be an independent company. Her ambitions to float Go now lay in tatters. Cassani claimed that her management was '100 per cent' behind her opposition to the transaction. But easyJet was confident not only of 3i's support but of that of Go's management – which would be essential as easyJet integrated the two companies. Go's senior management accounted for the bulk of the 18.5 per cent staff equity holding in the company; the twenty-seven top managers at Go would become millionaires when easyJet bought the airline, sharing about £60 million. Cassani, who owned 4 per cent of the company, would gain about £16 million from the deal. Ironically, easyJet also had to pay £42 million to Barclays Private Equity in return for its 11.2 per cent of Go, only two years after Stelios had cut up his Barclaycard as part of easyJet's dispute with the Barclay Group about its hike in landing fees at Luton Airport.

Cassani also became embroiled in a personal row with Stelios, who claimed to have offered her the role of Webster's deputy at the enlarged airline with a promise of taking over when Webster retired. 'There can only be one chief executive in a business,' Stelios said. Cassani insisted she had never been offered a role in a merged airline. In an extraordinary move, she issued a formal statement saying that she had 'never been offered a role', did not want one and would quit if the deal went ahead. Stelios countered by saying that he had offered her the number two job over dinner in a private room at Mark's club in London's Mayfair the previous year.

Stelios branded her version of events as libellous. 'She is calling me a liar and she is calling my chief executive a liar,' he said, rubbing salt in the wound by insisting that Cassani was allowing 'emotion and ego' to cloud her judgement. He added that Cassani would not be allowed to stand in the way of a deal, pointing out, 'No company is ever a one-man or one-woman show.' Ryanair's O'Leary suggested that Cassani should 'shut up, take the money, be very happy that she's one of the very few people who have made a lot of money out of aviation'.

Cassani's anger wasn't just directed at Stelios. She was also furious with Go's majority shareholder 3i for agreeing to sell to easyJet and cash in so quickly. The venture capitalist had been down a similar flight path before, when it sold British Caledonian to BA in the mid-1980s. The company made a living by buying low and selling high. In an emotive message to her 900-strong workforce, Cassani said, 'When we bought Go from BA they indicated to me that they would wait for a flotation to get their money out, but they felt that the potential offer was just too good.'

Cassani's wrath wasn't sufficient to hold back the deal.

EasyJet got the green light from its shareholders and from competition regulators for the merger to go ahead. The first flights by the enlarged easyJet were due to take off the following March. Cassani called the deal 'a tremendous compliment to all of us at Go' and added that she was 'particularly pleased that everyone at Go will share in the rewards from our success'.

In August 2002, easyJet and Go completed the merger deal to create Europe's number one low-cost airline. Stelios called the takeover 'one of the most exciting developments' in the airline's history, and Webster added that the group wanted to create an airline that could 'capitalise on any opportunity in Europe'.

Cassani continued her fighting talk even after the conclusion of the takeover, claiming that Go was a better company than easyJet. Webster conceded that Go often provided a better service. 'There are certain things that Go does better,' he admitted. 'It is better at looking after customers both on board and in its after sales service. We want to bring these things forward into the easyJet model.' Douglas Johnson, a policy adviser at the Air Transport Users' Council, concurred. 'We got a lot of feedback suggesting that Go was the best of the low-cost carriers. We hope that some of the things that made it successful will be carried over into the merged airline.'

Cassani urged her staff to take the 'Go spirit' with them to carry out a reverse culture takeover. The deal had split the Go management team. Four leading executives, including chief financial officer Andrew Cowen, left the airline. EasyJet persuaded three other senior directors to stay on with the use of 'golden handcuffs', namely chief operating officer Ed Winter, sales and marketing director David Magliano, and director of customer services Dominic Paul. The takeover made Winter, a former British Airways manager who had been Cassani's right-hand man at Go, an instant multimillionaire. He became the new chief operating officer of the enlarged easyJet, provididing day-to-day leadership of the airline while Webster focused on easyJet's longer-term strategic development.

The two companies continued to operate in parallel while easyJet worked out the best way of proceeding with the practicalities of the merger. Go launched a promotion after the takeover was announced, offering flights between its base at Stansted and Belfast for £5. Go moved to reassure its passengers who were calling its booking line that their tickets would not be affected by easyJet's deal. No routes were to be dropped in the short term – not even those to Nice, Barcelona and Malaga, where both airlines flew.

The widely admired Go brand was set to disappear by early 2003, and the name would start to be erased from 1 December, when the sales staff would start selling all tickets under the easyJet banner. All cabin crew were to wear easyJet's uniform, and all the old Go aircraft were repainted in easyJet's trademark orange. Webster said that easyJet's most urgent task was to decide on the location of the combined company headquarters, as easyJet considered moving from Luton to Go's base at Stansted Airport in Essex, 30 miles away. In the end, easyJet decided to stay in Luton. It hoped Go staff based at Stansted would want to relocate to Luton.

EasyJet financed the £374 million acquisition partly by raising £276.7 million through a rights issue. Credit Suisse First Boston acted as the sponsor and financial advisor to easyJet and was the sole book runner in placing the rights, underwriting the issue alongside UBS Warburg and Schroder Salomon Smith Barney. EasyJet financed the rest of the deal out of its own capacious pocket. The company was financially stable: it reported pre-tax profits of £1 million in the half-year ending 31 March 2002 compared with a loss of £103 million a year earlier. Revenues rose 36 per cent to £194 million pounds during the six-month period. EasyJet shareholders had to pay £9.5 million in advisory fees relating to the acquisition and £5.5 million relating to the rights issue, and existing shareholders were offered four new shares for every eleven held at a price of 265p.

The takeover enabled easyJet immediately to reach a size it

might otherwise have taken several years to achieve, not to mention giving it another London base at Stansted. 'Buying Go will produce a 100 per cent step-change in growth by bringing expansion more quickly and smoothly,' said Webster. The purchase put blue sky between the combined airline and European rivals such as Buzz and Virgin Express, and made it even larger than Ryanair. The purchase increased easyJet's fleet to fifty-four aircraft from thirty, compared with Ryanair's forty-four planes, and almost doubled its routes to eighty-one from forty-five, compared with Ryanair's seventy-six routes. EasyJet and Go together flew more than 12 million passengers during the twelve months ending in March 2002, compared to 11 million passengers on Ryanair. The enlarged company had a turnover of almost £490 million – £210 million more than its Irish rival.

But O'Leary maintained that he wasn't concerned by the takeover, adding that it would probably be good for Ryanair if the three main low-fares airlines were reduced to two. Ryanair said it had no interest in muscling in on the talks. '[Go's] fares are about 50 per cent higher than ours and their costs are about 60 per cent higher,' said O'Leary. 'We spend our time trying to drive down costs, forget it.'

Stelios said that the planned acquisition would 'contribute significantly to our objective of becoming Europe's leading low-cost airline by strengthening our position in important target markets and providing a larger, stronger platform from which to exploit growth opportunities profitably'. The real point of easyJet's deal seemed to be to outfox the competition. Increasingly, that didn't mean Ryanair, which was growing by offering super-cheap fares to ever more out-of-the-way destinations. EasyJet and Go, by contrast, took the more expensive option of flying to major airports in places where people already wanted to go. Taking over Go meant taking out one of the players.

The Consumers' Association worried that easyJet's purchase of Go might lead to a fare increase for passengers. 'The downside is that we will see less competition on the routes where the two carriers currently overlap,' the association said. EasyJet and Go had competed fiercely on busy domestic routes, from London to Edinburgh, Glasgow and Belfast and on routes to holiday destinations such as Malaga. But Webster told BBC radio that the combination with Go would not mean an increase in fares. 'This is an opportunity to keep prices low,' he said. 'That is the beauty of our model. We need low fares to stimulate the market that we are developing.' Stelios likewise dismissed warnings of raised fares, arguing that because of its increased size the easyJet/Go combination would be able to make savings on purchases of fuel, insurance and aircraft.

Go was not easyJet's only takeover target. At the same time as its acquisition of the former BA subsidiary, easyJet announced that it had acquired an option to buy Deutsche BA, the German subsidiary of British Airways. Deutsche BA operated 130 flights per day on seven German internal routes with a fleet of sixteen 737-300s. In the last financial year it had had a turnover of £212.5 million and carried 3.5 million passengers. Deutsche BA had embarked on a no-frills strategy earlier in 2002, cutting fares to €39 on its domestic network. Other low-cost measures included launching a €48 million cost-cutting drive through September 2003, charging for on-board services and promoting Internet ticket sales. But it hadn't worked; the carrier hadn't made a profit since it was set up in 1992, though it didn't reveal the extent of its losses.

The agreement with DBA gave easyJet the option to acquire 100 per cent of the chronically unprofitable German airline at any time up to 3 July 2003. In the interim, BA would retain full control of Germany's second-largest airline but easyJet would place three managers with Deutsche BA, contribute £3 million towards capital expenditure and pay BA £366,000 per month. BA estimated the deal to be worth between £18.3 million and £28 million.

Observers were concerned that the bigger easyJet became, the more it would change to become like a conventional airline and thus lose its point. Size meant complexity, and one of the reasons easyJet had been such a success was that it had kept its operations simple and cheap. London aviation consultants Avmark International noted that easyJet was straying from the low-cost business model it originally embraced, that of Southwest Airlines in the US, which championed organic growth, and pointed out that Go and Deutsche BA had both been started by British Airways and had different business cultures.

Analysts were even more concerned about easyJet's proposed takeover of Deutsche BA than its purchase of Go, and several investment houses downgraded easyJet's stock to 'underperform'. Lehman Brothers commented: 'We believe the market is over-estimating the profitability of future growth and that the management has under-estimated the structural differences in the German market and the task at Deutsche BA.'

Jürgen Weber, chairman of Lufthansa, said he could not see how easyJet would manage to turn around unprofitable Deutsche BA and claimed he was unfazed by the prospect of easyJet's entry into his home market. Weber emphasised that budget airlines catered to a different customer base from Lufthansa, Germany's flagship airline. 'The tasks ahead for easyJet are enormous: the integration of three companies – Go, Deutsche BA and easyJet – into one firm has to be established first. According to our estimates, the acquisition of Deutsche BA by easyJet does not create a more competitive environment.' BA itself said that selling Deutsche BA was a step towards improving the performance of its European short-haul business.

Webster characterised the deal as a quick way for easyJet to establish itself in Germany. EasyJet would follow in the footsteps of Ryanair, which had established a base at Frankfurt/Hahn – its second in continental Europe – in February 2002.

A combined easyJet/Deutsche BA would immediately be propelled into pole position in the German market, with significant opportunities for growth, declared Webster. Time would tell.

7. Stelios quits

EASYJET WAS PROSPERING. Its sales were buoyant, its share price was at an all-time high and it was taking over its greatest rival. Which, as far as Stelios was concerned, meant that it was time for him to leave. In April 2002, in a statement to the London Stock Exchange, he announced that he was going to give up the chairmanship of easyJet. The statement startled investors and fans of the airline alike. EasyJet without Stelios? Surely that was like jam without bread? Virgin without Branson?

EasyJet's impromptu press conference held later that day was, true to form, a no-frills affair. Reporters who made the trek to the airline's bright-orange headquarters at Luton Airport to hear about Stelios's resignation first-hand had to pay 80 pence each for their plastic cup of coffee.

Stelios told a gathering of surprised reporters that he was to be replaced by Sir Colin Chandler, the chairman of Rolls-Royce subsidiary Vickers Defence Systems and deputy chairman of engineering group Smiths. Chandler, a City veteran and part of the blue-chip establishment, turned up at the press conference in a tie that was swiftly dispensed with before the photo shoot. EasyJet banned ties except on the flight deck, a rule that applied equally to senior management.

Stelios told the media that he had a low boredom threshold and had lost interest in what he called 'the tedious business of chairing a major plc'. He maintained that he wasn't cut out to be a corporation man. 'I like taking risks,' the easyJet founder explained. 'And taking uncalculated risks is the privilege of the entrepreneur, not a chairman. You have to recognise your strengths and weaknesses early in life. It is all about finding what you are good at. In my case it is starting a company, coming up with ideas and turning dreams into reality.'

To outsiders, Stelios's decision to give up control of the business might have seemed strange, but it was typical of the thirty-five-year-old millionaire, who didn't believe in standing still. 'For me, this is like growing up – easyJet is not a baby any more,' said Stelios. 'I like having a dream and making it a reality, but I prefer other people to run the companies once they are set up. When people ask me what my favourite business is, I say the next one.'

By leaving, Stelios was also bowing to pressure from City investors, who did not like him being a major shareholder as well as chairman. Institutional investors feared that Stelios had been running the airline as his personal fiefdom and worried that other investors' interests were not being properly represented. 'The City likes to have its cake and eat it,' Stelios complained. 'They need you there to drive the business when it is growing but once it gets successful they turn around and say they want someone else to chair the company.'

London-based Pensions Investment Research Consultants, the shareholder voting advisor and corporate governance consultants, had issued a circular in March 2002, just prior to Stelios's announcement, recommending that clients block Stelios's re-election to the board, as well as that of his appointed non-executives. Boardroom best practice, enshrined in the Cadbury and Greenbury codes, dictated that all non-executives were to be independent of the company. Stelios had also infuriated institutional investors by attempting to change the articles of association to give the controlling shareholder (namely himself) the right to appoint the chairman and two non-executive directors in perpetuity.

Representatives from the Co-operative Insurance Company (CIS), which owned 17,205 shares out of easyJet's total of 292 million, turned up at easyJet's annual general meeting to rage about the board structure and the total absence of an environmental impact policy.

Christopher Hirst, CIS's chief investment manager, said that while a company such as easyJet might have delivered good shareholder value, the concern was about sustaining that performance. 'Proper corporate governance is needed to ensure that the right structure is in place in case things go wrong,' Hirst said. 'CIS has major concerns about the way easyJet is run. The corporate governance failings are so severe, we felt we had no option [but to vote against accepting the report in the accounts].'

EasyJet's other leading institutional investors included Standard Life, Britannic Asset Management, Fidelity of the US and Wellington Management. Shareholders were also keen to have a more experienced company chairman at the helm as easyJet expanded rapidly and headed for a possible place in the FTSE100. Stelios admitted that his colourful personal style might not be what the company needed most as it reached adulthood. 'It is a sign of maturity in a young company to have a chairman who is independent from the controlling shareholders,' he agreed.

Stelios denied being driven out of his chairman's role but said that he agreed with investors' complaints that he had too much control over the business. 'I have taken their views on board and I have decided this is best for us. I am doing it voluntarily. Nobody has forced me to do this. It is part of natural evolution. Starting a company requires different skills to those needed to chair a plc and I consider my strengths are in the former. I am a serial entrepreneur. The history of the City is littered with entrepreneurs who held on to their creations for too long, failing to recognise the changing needs of the company, its business and its shareholders.'

Asked if he might follow Stelios's example and take a back seat at the airline, Ryanair boss O'Leary glowered, 'There are very few examples of where I would follow Stelios in anything. He's Greek and I'm Irish. The Greeks will never outdo the Irish in anything. We'll even outdo them in drinking.' At least O'Leary had something nice to say about Stelios. 'He's the son of a billionaire,' proffered O'Leary. 'He could have been a rich tosser but at least he did something and set up an airline.'

Understandably, some outsiders were apprehensive about Stelios's move. Stelios had turned a £5 million cheque from his father into a business worth £1.5 billion with his drive and vision. A well-known personality, he was generally popular, depending on whether you had just enjoyed a cheap flight to Amsterdam or had suffered a delay at Luton Airport. He still got complaints addressed to him personally, even if the days when he had time to answer them personally had long gone.

But Stelios was aware of the danger of just one man being behind a company. 'The problem with very personal businesses is they are not saleable,' he said. 'If you build a whole business around your own personality, it can't grow. At some stage you must step back and say, "This business has to deal with its customers through its departments rather than through its founder."'

Stelios's decision to leave easyJet also meant that he could spend more time in the easyGroup headquarters in The Rotunda, a converted piano factory in Chalk Farm, London. He intended to carry on as chairman of the other companies within the easy empire and declared that his intention was to rebalance his portfolio between 'cash, listed equities, unlisted companies and risky start-ups'.

Stelio's car rental business, easyRentacar, was on track for a stockmarket flotation at the end of 2004. It had been a bumpy ride. The sales pitch for easyRentacar was impressive. With prices from £19 a day for a Mercedes A-class car in cities such as London or Glasgow, it sounded like a steal. But the final bill with all the extras was often a shock. There was a £15 'preparation and cleaning fee' for the first day's rental, mandatory insurance charges that varied depending on the customer's driving record, and a penalty of £100 for returning the car late. Moreover, the daily mileage limit was a mere 75 miles, then 20 pence for each extra mile.

Ever one to change the rules, Stelios had also decided at the launch of easyRentacar to recover the cost of damage in a different way from usual. Passengers returned rented vehicles in what they insisted was immaculate condition and later discovered that their accounts had been debited because of alleged damage, such as a scratched hubcap, even though the damage had been noted by the rental office before they collected the car. Stelios ended up with what he himself admitted was a huge customer backlash and a sizeable embarrassment, including at least two appearances on the BBC's *Watchdog* and damage to the easy brand.

Meanwhile, Stelios was working on a new bright-orange business called easyCinema. Stelios planned to offer prices as low as 20 pence for those who bought a ticket a month or two in advance, with higher prices for last-minute or peak-time bookings. EasyGroup held talks with estate agents to find a suitable location. The site turned out to be at what Stelios dubbed the 'centre of the entertainment world', otherwise known as Milton Keynes. Cinema buffs could forget Hollywood for true glamour and catch a bus up the M1 to the bright-orange box with ten screens. They might have to wait to see the latest hits: the big studios would not let him show their new movies.

Another one of Stelios's brainwaves was easyDorm, a chain of hostels providing cheap accommodation. Rooms were nine times bigger than a phone box and made from fibreglass. The little box's soft furnishings were in the company's familiar lurid orange, which no doubt didn't aid a restful night's sleep. Guests had to clean up after themselves or else pay a fee. But at least the rooms cost as little as £5 a night, if booked in advance.

Stelios was on a mission to prove wrong the sceptics who taunted that he was just 'lucky first time' with easyJet. 'Film distributors say, for instance, that I cannot change the cinema industry,' he said. 'Everyone thinks their industry is different, more difficult than the others are. But I will come along and tear up the rule book.'

He planned to use easyJet as the bank account for all the nascent easy businesses. Stelios did not receive a salary from any of his companies, nor any dividends, so he relied on occasional share sales to raise fresh funds. 'I have made clear on several occasions in the past,' he explained, 'I have no other source of income from easyJet other than disposal of shares and as I engage in new ventures, I may need to liquidate some of my stock from time to time. As I have said before, I need to sell my past to finance my future.'

Stelios said he intended to remain a 'significant' shareholder in the airline for a very long time. 'I have no present intention to sell any easyJet shares in the near future,' he said. His stake was diluted from 27.4 per cent after easyJet's rights issue to finance the Go deal. His brother and sister owned a further 24.4 per cent.

When Stelios announced his resignation as easyJet chairman in April 2002, he said that he would be standing down in early 2003. But after the speedy takeover of Go, he brought the date forward and said that he would quit the post in November 2002, when easyJet released its full-year results.

Not everything was going smoothly at the airline. After completing the takeover of Go on 1 August 2002, easyJet expanded by 60 per cent, ballooning overnight to a network of eighty-one European routes. While easyJet enjoyed the fame associated with its new ranking as Europe's largest low-cost airline, employees were left struggling to cope with the increased workload and the inevitable collision of cultures that followed a merger. EasyJet admitted that it was 'stretched to the limit' in the two weeks following the acquisition of its former rival.

EasyJet's pilots were among those who had to work the hardest following the merger and they consequently complained the loudest. Growing numbers of pilots at the company called for industrial action, claiming that easyJet was paying them less than their peers were receiving at Go. An easyJet spokesman said that while its pay scales were lower than starting salaries at Go, the overall package was almost identical when pension contributions, food and other elements were considered. On average, easyJet paid captains base salaries of £60,000 and first officers £38,000. Pilots also benefited from a bonus scheme and a share option programme. Pay at Ryanair was higher; the Irish airline had just agreed a five-year pay deal with its pilots which would see their annual salaries rise to more than £82,600.

A number of easyJet pilots in the British Airline Pilots' Association called for a strike vote if the company failed to improve its offered pay increase of 2.3 per cent for captains and 1.3 per cent for first officers, at a time when the management had enjoyed a collective £10 million bonus following the Go acquisition. The pay offer was rejected overwhelmingly by postal ballot and Balpa demanded an urgent meeting with Webster to discuss pay and pressures on the airline's staff.

EasyJet had recently employed more pilots after going on a recruitment drive in 2001 and offering pilots 'golden hellos' worth up to £30,000, believed to be the first scheme of its kind in the industry. The company needed to recruit over 250 pilots to fly the new planes it had on order for its fleet, due to reach forty-four aircraft by mid-2004. The new enlarged airline employed about 750 pilots and 1,000 cabin crew. But that still wasn't enough to cope with the surge in passenger numbers.

Almost as soon as the Go acquisition took place, nineteen flights had to be cancelled because easyJet did not have enough staff or extra aircraft when two planes developed technical problems. Thousands of passengers suffered delays and many abandoned their journeys.

EasyJet's troubles reflected wider problems in the budget airline industry. Many customers of no-frills companies such as easyJet, Ryanair and Buzz had come to expect delays, wayward baggage and bad service as part and parcel of a bargain flight. Ryanair's customer service department – consisting of five staff – said only one in 1,000 passengers complained. But with 1 million passengers a month, that was still 12,000 complaints a year. Despite the best efforts of those involved, delays at the two main no-frills airports – Luton and Stansted – were also the worst of all UK airports, exacerbated by shortages in air-traffic controllers and by increased security checks.

EasyJet admitted that it was struggling and warned that it needed to cut flights to regain control over its schedule and ease the severe pressure on its pilots and cabin crew. As part of its restructuring, it planned to end all Go flights from Belfast to Glasgow and Edinburgh and contacted the 9,882 affected passengers to offer them alternative easyJet flights where available. The cancellation of the Belfast flights raised questions over easyJet's ability to cope with other services it had taken over from Go.

A bungled new rota system added to easyJet's problems and pushed many of its pilots to the point of resignation. The rostering system, introduced in June, forced easyJet to cancel twenty-eight flights in July. The airline said it tried to cancel flights that hadn't been heavily booked. EasyJet said that air-traffic control delays, building projects at Luton Airport and bad thunderstorms worsened the situation. Almost 10,000 people had their flights cancelled in August and many more suffered delays. The new rostering system was splitting up crews, meaning that a re-fuelled plane and a pilot could be waiting at Luton Airport while the cabin crew was stuck in Barcelona or at another easyJet destination.

'EasyJet pilots complain a lot about the roster pattern,' explained one pilot who moved over to easyJet from Go after the takeover. 'The Go pattern used to be very stable. Since the merger, pilots operate a system of three early shifts and three late shifts, meaning that they will get up three times at 5 a.m. and then work late three times until, say, midnight. Obviously adjusting your body clock like that makes you very tired.' An easyJet spokesman said: 'We thought that the new rostering system would be more efficient and better. It proved to be anything but that. Hands up, we got it wrong.'

Morale sank among easyJet pilots. One pilot, who moved over to easyJet after the merger with Go and didn't want to be named, complained of a poorer working atmosphere following the takeover: 'Go had a lot more company pride than easyJet. It may be a result of easyJet being a larger company now following the merger. There was a lot of ill feeling and loss of morale after the merger as Go employees felt patriotic towards Go.'

Employees also missed the team spirit they had enjoyed at Go. 'Cassani was very popular and had all the staff on-board working as a team and pulling together,' the pilot continued. 'With easyJet management you just do as you're told. Webster keeps himself in the background and is not so close to the day-to-day running of the company. He is more interested in keeping the shareholders happy.' Former Go pilots also griped about the ending of Go's travel scheme, whereby staff could fly to any destination for £25 return including taxes. 'EasyJet, meanwhile, doesn't really believe in staff travel,' the pilot complained. 'It does have a scheme but its fares are often higher than the standard ones advertised for passengers!'

On a day-to-day basis, the pilots' workload didn't change when they moved over to easyJet, the pilot said. 'Both airlines are pretty similar in the way that they try to get the most productivity out of their employees. As far as I can see, airlines are low cost by getting the highest staff productivity for the least money. I subsidise the passengers' air fares by accepting lower pay.'

It wasn't just the pilots who were feeling the strain brought on by easyJet's rapid expansion. EasyJet cabin crew were also toiling hard. Michael, one cabin crew member, commented: 'EasyJet is expanding so much. It's getting bigger and bigger every day. But it's getting too much and is expecting too much from its staff in terms of long working hours and the amount of work you have to do in those hours. Some days are short. I have to report to work at 6 a.m. and can fly for example to Rome and be back home by 1 p.m. On the other hand, if there's a flight delay or an emergency then I may not get back until 7 p.m. Or some days I might do a double shift, for example from East Midlands to Venice and back and then to Prague and back, which is a very long day.'

Some pilots feared that the pressure placed on flight crew might lead to mistakes or even prompt an accident. One pilot said: 'I have repeatedly told managers the situation has become dangerous but their only concern is profits. They have pushed staff to the limits and now we are seeing the consequences. It would be terrible if it took a crash to force them to rein back on this breakneck expansion.'

An easyJet spokesman said: 'I'm alarmed if one of our pilots is saying those things. We have worked our pilots incredibly hard and made great demands on them in the past two months. We are negotiating with them over pay and they have rejected our first offer.' EasyJet decided to try to improve working conditions and dispel pilot unrest, and planned to return to its old rostering system. Eventually the airline won an alleviation from Civil Aviation Authority rules to change the rostering pattern to five early working shifts for pilots followed by five late shifts, which meant that pilots needed to readjust their body clocks less between shifts.

Fears over pilot safety at easyJet and at its fellow no-frills carriers escalated again when an air-traffic controller who feared a crash in the skies above London raised his concerns in a safety report to the Confidential Human Factors Incident Reporting Programme, which was then published in *The Times*. He claimed that pilots in the no-frills sector, which thrived on keeping its planes in the air longer than traditional carriers, were so desperate to avoid delays that they were putting passengers at risk.

The air-traffic controller said that pilots ignored instructions from ground control to allow them to meet tight deadlines. He alleged that pilots sometimes approached landings too fast and had to abandon the manoeuvre because they were too close to the aircraft in front. Pilots also ignored longer flight paths to cut down on noise disturbance and instead took shorter routes over nearby houses, he claimed; they frequently challenged the order in which jets took off and landed, and gave 'overly aggressive responses' to air-traffic control. '[This] is occurring with increasing frequency and, in my judgement, is due in part to the aggressively commercial ethos that exists within some airline companies,' the air-traffic controller stated in the report.

A spokesman for easyJet said it was a common misconception that shortcuts were taken by budget airlines. 'Low-cost airlines become more effective by squeezing the time on the ground. It's got nothing to do with air-traffic controllers; it's [about] effective baggage handlers and getting people on and off the aircraft.'

No-frills aircraft typically travelled four return journeys to Europe in a day, double the number of a typical British Airways jet. Planes and people worked much harder than on traditional airlines. In particular, the turnaround time – from the moment the pilot of the inbound aircraft applied the parking brake at the gate to the start of the push-back at departure – was typically scheduled to take only twenty-five minutes at easyJet and at other budget airlines. If the arrival was delayed, there was no slack to help make up time.

Budget airlines quashed speculation that their pilots cut

corners to keep to tight schedules. A spokesman for easyJet said: 'We would refute any allegations that our pilots are disobeying air-traffic controllers' orders. Safety is absolutely paramount and all our pilots conform to very high standards of training and supervision.'

But a letter by Stelios to the *Financial Times* in June 2002 served only to re-stoke the fire. Stelios argued in the letter that those low-cost airlines who used old aircraft were unwise to do so because their reputations would not survive in the event of a crash. 'Combine a low-cost airline with old aircraft and the odds of your reputation surviving an accident are against you,' he argued. 'Old aircraft flatter profits in the short term and, in my opinion, have more to do with management's attitude to the risk of damage to reputation as a result of an accident involving an old aircraft than to the long-term business model.'

Stelios mentioned Ryanair in his letter. The Irish-registered airline operated some of the oldest aircraft in Britain at the time, with twenty Boeing 737-200s dating back to the early 1980s. EasyJet, meanwhile, swore by a young fleet – the average age of its planes was 4.6 years. But if Stelios hoped to make the City think twice about Ryanair, his rambling letter raised more doubts about himself. One analyst declared: 'Stelios has lost the plot. It doesn't matter how old aircraft are – it's whether they are maintained properly. Stelios has broken the golden rule in airlines – you never hit out at rivals over safety because you never know when it might happen to you. The letter smacks of desperation.'

Nor did Ryanair take the blows lying down, stating that it adhered to the 'highest standards of international safety'. 'What surprised me was that he would put his name to such nonsense,' cried O'Leary. 'It would seem that those of us who offer the lowest air fares just get on with it, and those who do not, write whinging letters to newspapers.' Ryanair marketing director Tim Jeans added: 'We don't cut corners while the aircraft is airborne. Turnaround times are tighter but safety and security are an absolute priority and there is nothing we would do to compromise that.'

Even as it struggled to assimilate Go's flights to its network, easyJet kept up the rapid pace of its own expansion, announcing in August that it would introduce new routes from Liverpool to cities including Prague, Milan and Rome. More than 2 million passengers a year were using Liverpool's newly rebranded John Lennon Airport and the airport had just upgraded terminal facilities that would lift annual capacity to more than 3 million passengers. Two-thirds of passengers using the airport flew with easyJet. 'EasyJet has had a massive impact on the airport; it has been phenomenal,' said Robin Tudor, the airport's corporate affairs manager. 'EasyJet has been a godsend to Liverpool John Lennon Airport,' agreed Mike Doran, a spokesman for Liverpool City Council. 'The airport has risen from the ashes on the back of easyJet.'

EasyJet's new flights met with huge popularity in the north-west. Indeed, easyJet had to rip up posters advertising £17.50 fares for its new services from Liverpool to Paris as it ran out of tickets following a landslide of applications. Other regions also benefited from easyJet's expansion drive. The airline recruited thirty-three new cabin crew and based two aircraft permanently at Belfast International Airport, marking its most significant expansion in Belfast. EasyJet said it planned to introduce seven daily flights to Liverpool and six to London Luton for the summer, bringing its total daily flights to and from Belfast to forty-two. This was a seven-fold increase on its flights from Belfast in just three-and-a-half years, making easyJet's Northern Ireland's largest airline.

Citing research carried out by Ulster Marketing Surveys, easyJet claimed that seven out of ten of Northern Ireland's frequent flyers flew with easyJet on business, as cost-conscious companies recommended that employees use low-cost airlines whenever possible. An increasing number of company heads, directors and senior managers said that easyJet above any other airline was their main business carrier to Great Britain.

EasyJet announced that it planned to set up a base in Newcastle in October, the airline's fourth regional base in the UK, creating more than 100 jobs. Go had run a regular service to Newcastle from London Stansted and easyJet promised to unveil a network of routes from Newcastle in December 2002, including flights to Barcelona, Alicante, Paris and Nice. EasyJet planned to base two aircraft on Tyneside, rising to four in 2004. The airline aimed to carry about 750,000 passengers to and from Newcastle in the first twelve months from the start of the base operation.

Nor had the no-frills carrier forgotten Scotland. It also planned to offer up to three flights a day from Glasgow and Edinburgh to Malaga, Barcelona, Nice, Geneva and Paris as part of an expansion of its Scottish services from Glasgow and Edinburgh. One question remained, however: would easyJet have enough aircraft to fly all of its potential new passengers?

8. Airbus soars off the runway

IN OCTOBER 2002 Stelios unveiled plans to enter the big league by massively expanding his fleet. EasyJet already had sixty-four planes in its fleet following the merger with Go and a further twenty-three new Boeing aircraft on order. Stelios decided that it wasn't enough. He announced that he wanted to buy eighty-five new aircraft and then revised his target to an even more ambitious order of 120. To fulfil his ambitions, Stelios opened negotiations with Boeing Co. and Airbus Industrie.

In the middle of what was thought to be the biggest recession in airline history, easyJet was planning to buck the trend with a multi-million-pound deal. People initially scratched their heads, wondering why Stelios should want to buy new planes when a number of airlines such as Lufthansa were trying to cut capacity and sell off their planes secondhand. But Webster defended the move: 'Given the current state of parts of the global aviation industry, this is potentially a very good time to be addressing our long-term aircraft needs.' The new planes were needed to support easyJet's targeted growth rates, he continued. 'We have already committed to grow aircraft capacity by approximately 25 per cent a year until 2004 and need to secure delivery positions beyond that date.'

EasyJet wasn't interested in acquiring secondhand aircraft. 'We like new planes,' said Webster. 'They require less maintenance overnight and are crucial to reliability and therefore short turnaround times and high aircraft utilisation.'

With transatlantic air travel crippled since 11 September 2001 and orders being cancelled worldwide, Seattle-based Boeing and Toulouse-based Airbus were both desperate to win the easyJet contract. EasyJet was aware that a shopping list for aircraft with a total in triple figures might prompt the salespeople to reveal unheard-of discounts. Competition between the world's two largest plane makers was fierce. France's Airbus was starting to win market share from Boeing and threaten the US company's position as the world's largest aircraft manufacturer. Earlier in 2002, Airbus had won the hard-fought competition to supply new jets to Air New Zealand, previously an all-Boeing customer. Boeing alleged that Airbus had sliced prices on its planes so viciously to win market share that Boeing had lost some key sales rather than match its rival's hefty and unreasonable discounts.

The low-fare market had become one of the airline industry's only bright spots. The European carriers, seeking to expand service, were taking advantage of the situation to get unusually steep discounts for new planes. Ryanair had already made the most of the industry slump, announcing in January that it would buy 100 Boeing 737-800 aircraft in the following eight years and taking options on fifty more planes.

EasyJet had also operated an all-Boeing fleet. Its preferred aircraft type had always been the Boeing 737 series, which it kept on adding to its fleet to accommodate its burgeoning network. In July 1998, easyJet had ordered fifteen brand-new 737-700s, followed in March 2000 by an order for seventeen more. Now Stelios was thinking of a change. The Airbus A319 had originally had 145 seats, compared to the 149 offered by the Boeing 737-700 aircraft, which had made the Boeing marginally more profitable for easyJet. But now the A319 would have 150 seats, with the possibility of increasing to 156, which, Webster announced, made it a viable competitive alternative.

The announcement sent shockwaves throughout the industry. The low-cost model was built on a handful of simple principles. One of them was that no-frills carriers only operated one type of aircraft: it saved on crew costs and training, not to mention spares. The doyen of the industry, Southwest Airlines, swore by its all-Boeing fleet. Two types of aircraft required two types of parts and two types of engineers. Only two years previously, in 2000, Stelios had announced, 'part of the process of keeping costs down is keeping the business very simple. You should only have one kind of aircraft, which in our case happens to be the same as Southwest's – the Boeing 737 – and that aircraft sets the limits of your range.'

Stelios had clearly changed his tune. Of course, price paid an essential role in his new thinking. Stelios knew that the dearth of airline orders might make Airbus sink its prices to unknown levels to secure the deal, which would cancel out the additional costs of operating a mixed fleet. And competition for Boeing surely couldn't hurt?

Boeing almost won the contract outright. In November 2001, easyJet received an unsolicited offer from Boeing which Alain Mulally, Boeing Commercial Airlines President, termed the 'deal of the century'. But Airbus heard of the offer and was quick to respond. Chris Buckley, Airbus's senior vice president Europe and the key point of contact for the aircraft negotiations with easyJet, emailed Webster at the end of November, stating that he could almost guarantee that easyJet would benefit from running a real competition with Airbus and Boeing to improve Boeing's offer.

One Friday evening in December, Buckley was relaxing at home when he received an unexpected telephone call from Stelios, who was in the middle of a meeting with the members of the easyJet board. Stelios put Buckley on speakerphone and on the spot, asking him to explain why easyJet should run a competition with Airbus. Buckley told them, 'Let's see what Airbus can come up with,' and encouraged easyJet not to sign a deal with Boeing immediately.

His persuasion worked. In January 2002, easyJet started a detailed evaluation process of both Boeing's 737-700 and Airbus's A319 – painfully detailed from Buckley's point of view, as the easyJet management pored over every aspect of Airbus's performance. And then, on a Friday evening in October 2002, several months after easyJet's initial call, Webster called Buckley and told him, 'I want you over tomorrow.' Buckley immediately cancelled his plans for the weekend, hopeful that victory was in sight.

The next morning a small team of easyJet executives, including Stelios, met Airbus executives at a hotel on Marylebone Road in central London and worked throughout the weekend to try and thrash out a deal. They reached a compromise on Sunday night. After months of playing off the world's biggest aircraft makers against each other, easyJet had finally made its decision. The airline held a press conference on the following morning, Monday 14 October, to announce its new aircraft order to the world. Stelios told journalists that easyJet was going for a deal with Airbus, thereby breaking Boeing's stranglehold on the European low-cost airline market. The industry was stunned.

Stelios became emotional during the press conference as he talked about Boeing and how it had repeatedly offered a lower price than its original one. Stelios had met Boeing's Mulally before Christmas. 'He said this is the deal of the century, so take it. It wasn't. He undercut himself again and again. Why should I believe him again?'

EasyJet placed an order with Airbus for 120 A319 aircraft,

plus ten-year price-protected options for 120 more A319 planes as well as the possibility of larger-sized Airbus A320s and A321s. The contract would see the no-frills airline take delivery of two A319 planes every month for five years as of August 2003. The A319 planes would be introduced at easyJet's Geneva hub, operating under the airline's Swiss air operator licence, but would eventually interchange with existing Boeings on all routes.

The order would almost treble easyJet's size from 9,500 seats to nearly 25,000 seats by 2007, but easyJet insisted that it could maintain the growth. 'By 2007, we will overtake Alitalia, Iberia and SAS and we will remain fractionally bigger than Ryanair,' the company explained. 'We're planning on compound growth of 25 per cent per year for seven years.'

Nobody was vulgar enough to talk about the price of easyJet's aircraft order, but given the state of the industry at the time, with the Arizona desert full of the white tails of parked aircraft that airlines no longer needed, easyJet was guaranteed a good deal. The A319 had a notional sticker price of $50 million, but, by buying in bulk, Stelios was thought to have picked up 120 for $20 million apiece – $5 million less than Boeing was asking for its 737 aircraft. 'The Airbus deal will give us a cost per seat which is 10 per cent lower than the last Boeing deal,' said Stelios. 'Now how often do you get 10 per cent off your cost base by doing just one transaction?'

The immediate costs of around £70 million to secure the order and down payments for the first aircraft were to be borne by easyJet's £400 million cash pile, which was swollen by two cash calls from the stockmarket over the previous year. The airline had to stump up 1 per cent or at least £20 million to secure the deal, then 30 per cent of the value of the ten or so aircraft it expected to have delivered within the following two years – at least another £50 million, with the balance payable on delivery. Longer-term deliveries could be bought outright (depending on the company's cashflow), mortgaged, or sold and leased back with third-party leasing companies.

The Airbus deal remained subject to shareholder approval, but since Stelios and his family owned 48 per cent of the business, shareholder consent seemed a foregone conclusion. Stelios said that he would personally spend a lot of time over the ensuing weeks talking to shareholders to explain the 'benefits of the deal'.

In New York, Boeing's shares fell more than 3 per cent to $31 on receipt of the news. Boeing said that it had 'fought aggressively' but added that it would not 'sell our aircraft at a price that is considerably less than the value of the product', hinting that Airbus had done exactly that. Noel Forgeard, Airbus chief executive, hit back, saying: 'This is a cash-positive transaction for us. At no point will this be cash out of our pocket in spite of the costs initially to help easyJet.'

The fact that Forgeard felt obliged to defend himself against the charge was possibly indicative of the state of the aircraft industry in 2002. Airbus and Boeing knew that there would be far fewer orders in 2002 because of the industry downturn, which made the easyJet competition all the more crucial for the two aircraft makers. The order subsequently gave Airbus an entrée into the profitable low-frills market and helped the manufacturer secure as many as nine consecutive wins against Boeing's 737 with low-cost carriers around the world; it also safeguarded as many as 10,000 jobs at Airbus plants in Broughton, Flintshire, where wings for the planes were made, and in Filton, South Gloucestershire, where key components were manufactured.

But the share price didn't react so positively to the news. Shares in European Aeronautic Defence and Space Company NV, the owner of 80 per cent of Airbus, fell by 4.4 per cent in Paris to €9.70 amid investor concern that Airbus might have agreed to too big a price reduction to secure the biggest order of the year. Investors were worried that Airbus was also taking a risk by underwriting the training costs when the new planes arrived.

Airbus was to provide 'extensive support' to ensure that

crew training and new maintenance regimes did not add to easyJet's costs. As part of the deal, easyJet had made Airbus guarantee that the introduction of the planes would not be more expensive than Boeing's 737-700 planes in the first two years. One industry executive, who did not want to be named, speculated that the easyJet deal might come back to haunt Airbus. 'One consequence of this deal is that Airbus is helping easyJet in further reducing its costs to compete with Airbus's best customers in Europe: British Airways, Air France and Lufthansa. And they are all having a tough time fighting the low-cost carriers in domestic Europe. Clearly these three carriers paid too much for their A319s when they ordered them years ago. We may see a round of negotiations between Airbus and these network carriers to bring their already negotiated prices more in line with the deeply discounted prices at easyJet.'

EasyJet's shares also fell after the Airbus announcement, dropping by nearly 5 per cent to 251¼p. Share prices had nearly halved since March amid fears that easyJet was growing too rapidly and that the airline would find it difficult to integrate Go. Investors were worried by the fact that easyJet would become the first large low-cost carrier in Europe to fly a mixed fleet, and concerned about the rate of easyJet's planned expansion. Dominic Edridge, an airline analyst at Commerzbank, said: 'Taking two aeroplanes a month is a challenge for any airline – the concern is where they can be deployed profitably.'

Stelios and easyJet had broken the mould before, so it was unwise to bet against them now, but there was no disguising the risk that Stelios was taking. After all, easyJet had only just begun to consume Go and it was already eyeing up its next course, Deutsche BA. It had less than a year to digest them before it began the task of integrating a brand-new aircraft into the fleet. Webster was highly rated and for good reason but observers worried that this would stretch even his managerial capacity.

Stelios admitted the decision might unsettle the City: 'I was faced with the dilemma of either following the conventional wisdom in the market place in order to keep shareholders happy in the short term or doing what's right for shareholders in the long run,' he explained. 'We decided to do what's right. We refused to overpay in order to improve the stock price in the short term. It should be an offence to misuse that level of corporate resources. At the end of the day, "low-cost" companies remain "low-cost" by not wasting money. Sticking to old-fashioned fads like "low-cost airlines only fly Boeing" does not reduce costs. The last thing we want is to be held hostage by one supplier.'

The airline argued that it would achieve 'substantial savings' by ordering the Airbus planes. 'About four years ago, as a small airline we bought fifteen B737-700s with no competition,' said Stelios. 'Today, buying 120 aircraft in a competitive market, we can now purchase aircraft at approximately 30 per cent below the prices, adjusted for inflation, we achieved then.' Stelios also cited 'the great success JetBlue has experienced with the Airbus product in the US'; the US low-cost airline JetBlue was able to achieve faster turnaround times because of the aircraft's wider aisles.

EasyJet and Airbus now had forty-five days of exclusive talks to finalise the deal, one of the most significant seen at Airbus. It was tough work. Buckley admitted that there were times when he shouted at Webster and other members of the easyJet team, as their thoroughness frustrated him. 'I'm not a most detailed person and I would shout out of sheer exasperation. Ray and the team were very focused on the deal and interested in all kinds of details.' But by the end of the year, everything was sorted out and all easyJet had to do was to wait for the planes to arrive.

Meanwhile, Stelios had successfully delegated himself out of a job on 26 November 2002, the day of the airline's annual results. Fellow entrepreneur Sir Richard Branson gave him a surprise farewell, presenting him with a model plane and paying tribute to his friend's achievements as the pioneer of budget airlines, adding that easyJet was 'by far the best' in the short-haul market out of the UK: 'Millions of people who could not afford to travel before are now travelling and he has done it with great style and panache.' Asked about Stelios's departure, Branson said: 'Easy come. Easy go. I cannot believe he is ever going to let go.'

Stelios revealed that he had the right to return as chairman at any time, as long as his stake in the company stayed above 10 per cent. But he added: 'I have no intention to meddle in the management and I do not expect to be chairman again. I will have my hands full with other easyGroup activities, but will continue to watch from afar with a close and fond interest.' Stelios's replacement, Colin Chandler, clarified that Stelios would return as chairman only 'if something goes badly wrong'.

The airline announced that for the year to 30 September, pre-tax profits had rocketed 78 per cent to £71.6 million, beating the analyst forecasts for £57 million to £66 million. Revenues for the period surged 55 per cent to £552 million, and the number of passengers increased 59.5 per cent on a year earlier to 11.4 million, helped by eleven new aircraft and a two-month contribution from the twenty-seven planes in the Go fleet. EasyJet also said it had overcome problems integrating Go, which was generating enough cash to pay for its major aircraft order with Airbus without easyJet having to seek fresh funds from the equity market. Stripping out Go from easyJet's annual figures, revenues had still risen 36 per cent to £486 million, with passenger numbers up 43 per cent at £10.2 million and operating profits 49 per cent stronger at £57 million. 'This is the last set of results that I will announce as the company's chairman and I couldn't have hoped for a better send-off,' Stelios said.

There was some negative news, however. The airline said the average fare paid by the customer had fallen 4 per cent from £48 to £46, while costs per available seat kilometre declined 1.3 per cent to 4.46 pence. EasyJet did not provide numbers for the second half of the year but Gert Zonneveld, analyst at West LB Panmure, estimated that easyJet's fares fell 7.5 per cent in the period. Other analysts said that the drop was closer to 9 per cent. Zonneveld commented, 'The shares have had a very good run, rising from 240 pence since early October. This is by no means a profit warning but these companies are not cheap. If anything goes wrong, you will immediately see people taking profits.'

The news of the results pushed easyJet shares, which had made a partial recovery in the last couple of months, down 14 per cent to 337p as a result of City concern that increased competition could put pressure on the group. One analyst, who declined to be named, said: 'The worry is that if current growth targets look too optimistic, it will savage the share price further. While easyJet has said that it doesn't need to return to the stockmarket in the next year, it has said that it may have to alter that. A steep share price fall jeopardises the confidence the City has in the group.'

Webster insisted that the airline remained well placed to prosper although it faced uncertainties, including the threat of war in the Middle East and fears of a consumer spending slow-down. 'Notwithstanding the uncertainties, market demand continues to be strong, but at lower average fares.'

EasyJet's employees would no doubt miss Stelios's presence at work. Staff had always felt a buzz from working for the jolly Greek giant. Stelios was dynamic, full of energy and liked to have a laugh in the office. One of the cabin crew said: 'He's totally down to earth and friendly. We all call him Stel Boy or Steli Babes. None of the girls would dare make a pass at him, even though we all want to. With that much money I'm sure that most of the guys would too!'

Stelios didn't take himself too seriously and that was part of the 'no-frills' ethic he had built into the company. He occupied the same space as everyone else in the open-plan office. No one had a private office and there weren't any secretaries. Instead, people were encouraged to book their own travel on the Internet, take care of their own administration and run a paperless office. Document control scanned everything in, and documents were filed and forwarded to staff via email. Everyone organised their own email, correspondence and filing on the network.

One of Stelios's achievements at easyJet was instilling an 'orange culture' of being 'up for it', 'passionate' and 'sharp'. The 'orange culture' remained in place after his departure. Every Friday, the staff continued to socialise with each other at easyJet's weekly barbecue, even if 'Stel Boy' was no longer taking his turn at flipping hamburgers.

Stelios also succeeded in cultivating an attitude of friendliness among staff, which continued after he left. EasyJet attracted eager young cabin crew, some of whom seemed more akin to Butlins' Redcoats entertainers or local radio DJs in the way that they joked and jested with passengers. On a flight from Zurich to London, passengers were treated to the following announcement: 'We hope you have enjoyed your flight with us. If you have, thank you for choosing easyJet. If not, then thank you for choosing Ryanair.'

EasyJet prided itself in not employing 'trolley dollies'. Take for example, Pauline Mors, who didn't start work as an air hostess until she was forty-five, an age at which most airlines were retiring their flight attendants. The company believed that the life skills of mature workers far outweighed the youthful good looks favoured by their competitors, and used Pauline in a high-profile campaign against ageism. The carrier valued those with team working skills above those that knew how to apply make-up correctly. Crew needed an exceptional sense of humour and a 'get stuck in' attitude towards work and customers.

Pilots also needed to work hard yet remain jolly. 'You are reminded that smoking is not allowed on the plane,' quipped one pilot on an easyJet flight from Liverpool to Palma. 'Anyone found doing so will be asked to leave the aircraft.'

And you just knew that it had to be easyJet when you heard that pilots from an airline had posed for a nude charity calendar. The Christmas calendar featured photographs of nine naked male pilots from Nottingham East Midlands Airport on the flight deck and on the runway. They planned to donate the money from the calendar to Britain's National Society for Epilepsy.

9. Continental drift

AIR LIB, FRANCE'S second-largest airline, stopped flying in February 2003, stranding thousands of passengers. Air Lib was weighed down by €100 million of debt, most of which was owed to the French government. A Dutch company, ICMA, offered to re-float the airline but withdrew its offer after the French government declined to persuade Airbus to provide thirty new A319 aircraft, on credit, at bargain prices.

Many of Air Lib's 3,200 employees blocked access to roads to Orly Airport, near Paris, accusing the government of throwing them out of work. There were angry scenes at airports in Corsica, the French West Indies and several French regional cities as passengers found Air Lib check-in desks deserted, meaning they couldn't exchange or cash in their tickets. Jean-Charles Corbet, the airline's president, called on French President Jacques Chirac to intervene. But government officials made it clear that they believed hopes of saving Air

Lib and the fifteen-year-old dream of creating a second French airline to rival Air France were over.

EasyJet and its rival cut-price airlines waited patiently for the Air Lib saga to end, hungrily eyeing the extinct airline's take-off and landing slots at Paris Orly and Charles de Gaulle. EasyJet hoped to gain 20,000 slots a year at Orly, which would allow it to fly to London, French provincial cities and other capitals. The airline already operated services from Charles de Gaulle to Liverpool, London Luton and Nice, as well as flights from Orly to Nice.

Webster, who had bought easyJet's flock of white planes from Airbus around the same time as Air Lib was going under, had a blunt message for the French government: 'We bought your bloody aircraft, now give us somewhere to land them.' But his comments were in vain. The French government preferred to avoid further competition for state-owned Air France, and handed over most of the slots to Air France.

The French officials' decision frustrated easyJet but it decided to make the most of the meagre slots it had secured, announcing in April 2003 the launch of services from Paris Orly to Barcelona, Marseilles, Milan Linate, Nice and Toulouse. People were attracted by the airline's low fares, said Elodie Gythiel, in charge of marketing for easyJet in France: 'The French people like small players and have been pissed off by Air France before, either because of high fares or delays or other bad experiences. We have established a strong position as a consumer champion.'

Anne Dusoleil was one of the many French passengers who regularly used easyJet, largely to travel for her job in marketing at materials maker Saint Gobain. Dusoleil was growing accustomed to the easyJet way of doing things on her frequent business trips with the airline. 'I normally fly with easyJet on business but a lot of families travel with the airline too. Having all those children running around and shouting in the plane is not very relaxing so you can't really work on-board. Then again, the fares are cheap and travelling with easyJet helps my company cut travel costs so you can't really complain,' she commented. 'The downside of travelling with easyJet is the absolute chaos before passengers board the plane. The hostesses call out the numbers on our boarding passes for people to get on to the bus but nobody takes any notice at all. We French people can be so disorganised. And then the resulting chaos and people who try to jump the queue annoy those passengers who are trying to queue properly.'

Flights from the UK to Paris were among the most popular in easyJet's network. Passengers in Britain enjoyed being able to hop on a plane and spend a romantic weekend in the French city for a reasonable price. As with all airlines, however, not every flight ran smoothly and sometimes customers' expectations were thwarted.

Howard Elliot-Jones from North Wales was particularly unimpressed following his easyJet flight from Liverpool to Paris Charles de Gaulle. The commercial property developer wanted to whisk his wife away for a romantic, relaxing few days to celebrate her thirtieth birthday. The result was anything but. Arriving at Charles de Gaulle, the couple waited for their suitcase to appear, eager for their holiday to commence. But an hour later it had still failed to turn up. EasyJet staff quickly reassured the two passengers, telling them that they would be compensated if the suitcase were lost and handing them a form to fill in.

Over the next few days, the couple continuously phoned the airport to try and find out if their suitcase had been located. 'I can't speak French so it was all difficult, really,' remembered Elliot-Jones. 'I never seemed to speak to the same person on the phone and was constantly re-routed around an automatic voicemail system. Each time we finally got through to someone we were told that my luggage hadn't turned up. It was really frustrating. The holiday was awful. EasyJet basically ruined what was a very special occasion. I didn't have anything to change into so I had to wander around Paris in the same clothes I had travelled in. What is more, I didn't have my glasses as they had been in my suitcase. As I can't wear my contact lenses for long, I couldn't see the sights, never mind the restaurant menu in front of me. What was even more worrying was that my tablets were in my bag. I have to take Tenormin, high-blood-pressure tablets, and it was worrying to be without them, particularly as the situation was making me more and more stressed.'

As soon as they returned to Liverpool, the couple informed easyJet what had happened. Elliot-Jones waited for an apology and compensation. Instead, all he received was a standard letter headed 'Without Prejudice', meaning that the airline's comments couldn't be admissible as evidence in a court of law. 'The letter wound me up as soon as I saw it,' said Elliot-Jones. 'It was very matter-of-fact and unapologetic. EasyJet told us bluntly that it could give us £25 in compensation and asked us to sign yet another form. I was outraged by the paltry amount offered. I had about £750 worth of possessions in the suitcase, including glasses worth £300, new clothes that I had bought specially for the trip, as well as my best shirt and pair of trousers.' Elliot-Jones became even more outraged after he had spoken to an easyJet employee. 'What was worse was the attitude of the woman when I rang her up. She basically didn't give a damn and was completely unbending in her attitude. She just muttered standard responses.'

Three days later Elliot-Jones received a call from Liverpool Airport telling him that they had identified a piece of luggage as his. He was outraged to learn that the only reason it had been traced was because of the discovery of some letters addressed to him inside. 'There was absolutely no correlation between my complaint and anything being done to find the suitcase,' he fumed. 'In my opinion, what easyJet clearly offers is a cheap flight with nothing on top. What annoyed me about the whole thing, apart from messing up our holiday, was that there was no apology and absolutely no consideration shown at all. I fly nowadays with British Airways. They treat you a lot better.'

In response, easyJet referred to the terms and conditions listed on its Internet site, which stated: 'You are strongly advised to take out your own insurance to cover the value of your baggage and its contents, particularly if you are carrying important or valuable items. Claims are dealt with up to the airline's limit of liability based on the weight of the items concerned.'

Now that it had established a foothold in the French market, easyJet turned its attentions towards Germany. The country was the largest domestic air market in Europe but traditionally had been poorly served by low-cost airlines. EasyJet wasn't the only company that was eager to bring cheap airline seats to Germany. The number of planes operating on the 'pile 'em high, sell 'em cheap' principle in Germany was expected to reach eighty-six by the end of 2003, compared with just seven at the end of 2001. German charter airlines, including TUI AG (whose budget arm was Hapag-Lloyd Express) and Air Berlin (which ran the no-frills City Shuttle), were making moves into the budget sector to offset weakness in their core business. In TUI's opinion, there was only room for three budget players in the German market, indicating that there was disappointment ahead for some.

Lufthansa, the national carrier, had slashed fares to compete with domestic low-cost carriers such as Germania Express, offering round-trip fares including taxes as low as €88 as of early 2003. Lufthansa had also chased Ryanair through the courts after the Irish airline set up in Germany, offering flights to London Stansted, Glasgow, Dublin, Shannon, Charleroi, Girona-Barcelona, Milan, Pisa and Oslo. Lufthansa challenged Ryanair over its description of its German base, 120 kilometres (70 miles) from Frankfurt, as 'Frankfurt-Hahn'. In July 2003, a German court blocked Ryanair from using 'Dusseldorf' for an airport near the German–Dutch border, 70 kilometres (42 miles) from the city.

Meanwhile, Ryanair was considering whether to shut down

its operations at Belgium's Charleroi Airport after discovering that the European Commision was set to rule against it in a key competition probe over illegal state aid. Much of Ryanair's business model was based on negotiating payments from under-used airports and regional public bodies in recognition of the economic boost the airline generated. Some of Ryanair's competitors complained that these payments, when made by public entities, amounted to state aid that distorted competition. The EU challenge over Charleroi was not the first such problem for the airline. In September 2002, Ryanair was forced to suspend services to Strasbourg in eastern France after a French court barred local authorities from subsidising its advertising. Ryanair moved services to Baden-Baden, about an hour away over the border in Germany.

Despite its legal setbacks, Ryanair was booming. In November 2003, it unveiled record interim profits of €175.5 million and vowed to keep cutting fares to drive passenger numbers higher. The airline claimed it would be Europe's largest airline within eight years. Indeed, Ryanair had once again pipped easyJet to the position of Europe's largest low-cost carrier after buying unprofitable Dutch carrier Buzz from KLM Royal Dutch Airlines for €23.9 million in February 2003.

Even amid strengthening competition from the likes of Ryanair, easyJet was determined to establish itself as the biggest low-cost carrier in Germany. Taking over Deutsche BA as planned would provide easyJet with seven of the eleven crucial internal routes and hundreds of German crew and pilots in one swoop. The airline continued to pay €600,000 per month to hold its exclusive option to buy the British Airways subsidiary, as well contributing €5 million towards the cost of converting it into a low-cost operation. An integration group, comprising executives from both airlines, met once or twice a week to discuss strategy and progress.

EasyJet was aware that the acquisition would require a substantial restructuring of the German airline. While Go had complementary business models, culture and routes to easyJet, the Deutsche BA deal required its buyers to transform an airline which was over-manned, operated in a complex and hostile labour market and had a high cost base. Unlike easyJet, Deutsche BA concentrated on attracting business travellers, who paid higher fares. It filled around 65 per cent of available seats, compared with easyJet's targeted load factor of 85 per cent.

As a first step in its restructuring, easyJet aimed to put more seats in Deutsche BA's planes. Other key changes that easyJet wanted to implement included increasing the number of hours flown by Deutsche BA aircraft and changing over to easyJet's own distribution and yield management system. Deutsche BA was encouraged to abandon its traditional airline contracts with suppliers and to simplify all of its operations and systems, with the aim of selling 100 per cent of its tickets over the Internet within a year. It was an ambitious target. Deutsche BA only sold between 5 per cent and 10 per cent of its tickets online, as companies in Germany still tended to use travel agents.

That wasn't the only difference that easyJet encountered. EasyJet was eager to learn about the German political and business environment to work out how a British company could become successful in Germany. But it didn't count on how difficult it would be to change working practices for Deutsche BA's 800 staff, including introducing performance-related pay for 200 pilots. Every minor change required consultation with unions and workers' councils. The initial reaction from DBA middle management to the takeover had been one of fear – fear of losing their jobs through the merger process and fear of changes within the company. Only three Deutsche BA executives had known about the planned merger before Stelios made his announcemen to Deutsche BA employeest in an aircraft hangar.

Even those employees who welcomed the merger were daunted by the changes needed to make the transition from a traditional German airline into a British low-cost one. Webster and some of the key easyJet players took part in road shows, showing German employees how easyJet's so-called 'orange culture' worked and encouraging staff to exchange ideas. But easyJet's open culture simply didn't translate. Many German workers were simply left feeling uncomfortable by practices that were commonplace in the UK. German employees gasped in horror when they saw how little space easyJet employees were allocated in the easyLand head-quarters. Accustomed to large, individual offices, they were appalled at the prospect of having to work in close vicinity with each other in the same room. There were laws against it, they told easyJet. Deutsche BA pilots put up even greater resistance to easyJet's plans. In February 2003, easyJet was forced to halt negotiations with the German pilots' union after failing to persuade pilots to adopt easyJet's salary structure.

The deal now stood on shaky ground. It was unlikely that easyJet would exercise its option unless the pilots agreed to the terms on offer. They did not. Eventually easyJet threw in the towel, announcing in March 2003 that it would not take up its option to buy the German carrier.

EasyJet's decision threw Deutsche BA's future into doubt. The German airline had been losing up to £25 million a year for the past ten years. British Airways insiders admitted that it had 'burnt a pretty big hole in our pockets', and it was now losing even more than it was before the easyJet purchase was signed. But with over 800 employees, the airline was too expensive for British Airways to shut down. British Airways said it would continue to develop DBA as a no-frills carrier. However, it admitted that it would be open to offers.

EasyJet's withdrawal shocked Deutsche BA managers, who had been convinced up until the last minute that easyJet would exercise its option. After all, the integration team had worked diligently to implement easyJet's proposed changes. Webster himself had spent weeks in Germany, working hard on the project. But easyJet, just like British Airways, simply failed to understand how Germany worked, said sources close to the negotiations. 'Everybody told us it was going to be difficult in Germany but there is nothing like getting first-hand experience,' Webster admitted. 'It is disappointing that we have had to make this decision. However, we always made it clear that we would not compromise the easyJet business model.'

EasyJet blamed its decision on Germany's unbending labour laws. Webster declared that the airline had been forced to recognise that German bureaucratic processes were incompatible with the needs of businesses today and a changing aviation market. 'Despite months of exceptionally hard work . . . there have been two insurmountable hurdles,' Webster explained. 'Firstly, the rigidity of German labour laws has made it impossible to get acceptance of easyJet conditions of employment from key staff groups, despite numerous attempts and different approaches.' Secondly, Webster said, the situation was exacerbated by 'a substantial deterioration in the financial performance of all airlines in the German market', including Deutsche BA. 'This is in large part due to the specific characteristics of the German market and in particular the highly aggressive pricing policies of Lufthansa.' Lufthansa declined to comment about the allegations of anti-competitive behaviour.

Sources close to the negotiations said that the real reason behind easyJet's decision was that it had simply taken on too much. The airline was already working hard to integrate Go into its business. By March the combined airlines were flying entirely under the easyJet brand. All cabin crew now wore easyJet's orange uniform and the on-board easyJet kiosk had been rolled out across the whole network. On top of that, easyJet's first Airbus 319 was set to go into service in Geneva in October 2003. Webster said that the decision to abandon its deal with Deutsche BA would not affect easyJet's deal with Airbus. 'We reaffirm that the order for 120 Airbus A319 aircraft has always excluded any aircraft needed in relation to the DBA option and we remain committed to organic growth of 25 per cent per annum,' he said.

Dropping the Deutsche BA deal meant that, on one hand, easyJet had removed a major investor uncertainty. On the other hand, easyJet's German presence remained limited to a Munich–London route. EasyJet was to develop flights out of Germany to connect the dots of its existing network. In November 2003, the airline announced plans to establish a new base in Berlin. EasyJet was to base six planes and operate flights to eleven destinations from Schönefeld Airport, about 20 kilometres (12 miles) from central Berlin. The first of the flights, to Luton, was due to start on 1 May 2004, with the rest – including flights to Paris, Copenhagen, Athens and Barcelona – to follow by the end of June. The introduction of the new services was expected to create about 300 to 400 jobs in Berlin.

EasyJet succeeded in attracting pilots by offering higher pay than many of its competitors, according to Michael Hahn, an easyJet pilot based at Berlin Schönefeld. Other budget operators already flying out of Berlin included Ryanair, Air Berlin, Germania, Lufthansa-affiliate Germanwings and travel giant TUI's Hapag-Lloyd Express. Only half of the pilots working at the Berlin airport were German, said Hahn. 'No German would leave Lufthansa to join easyJet as Lufthansa pays good money and it is still in the German's head that you either fly with Lufthansa or take the train.'

Bart Schöpflin, who worked for a bank in Frankfurt, summarised the German attitude. 'Sorry, I'm a convinced Lufthansa man. There is no way that I would choose easyJet for corporate trips. You can't buy flexible tickets with easyJet and I need that in case a meeting finishes later than planned. I also need to be able to fly at peak times and I'm not aware that easyJet offers those flights. Basically I don't care how much it costs when I go on corporate trips so I take the most convenient flight and that is usually with one of the larger airlines. Also I can then earn Air Miles, which I can't with easyJet.'

By moving into Schönefeld, easyJet had secured access to Germany. German passengers gradually learned to value the cheap tickets offered by the likes of easyJet, even if that meant not flying with Lufthansa. But flight attendants' lack of language skills sometimes caused problems with passengers; far from all of the cabin crew could speak German. One German passenger hit a member of the easyJet cabin crew during a flight to Cologne, as she failed to understand that she couldn't use her large holdall as a footrest but needed to stow it away in the overhead locker.

'I explained to her that for safety reasons, I would have to take her bag and put it away,' said one flight attendant, also called Michael. 'She replied to me in German, which I can't understand. I wondered if she couldn't understand what I was saying either so I used hand movements to explain the situation. But she was very adamant and refused to give me her bag. We play a German demo-tape before take-off which explains that you have to stow away large bags. It didn't make any difference. The woman's voice started to get very high and I could tell that she wasn't happy. By this time, all of the 148 passengers on-board were looking at me and I just wished that I could be beamed up. I was so embarrassed.

'I tried to get her bag off her again but she hit me on the arm and continued shouting. The woman was clearly being very abusive, even though I couldn't understand what she was saying. I told her that she would have to leave the aircraft as part of an emergency procedure as she was being so abusive. Eventually she moved her bag and the man who was sitting behind her apologised to me on behalf of the German people for the woman's behaviour.'

Problems with low-cost airlines weren't always what one might expect. Sometimes it was the older passengers who were the most demanding, Michael explained. 'The winter period is particularly difficult as the passengers tend to be more mature people with higher expectations. Some people who fly think that they're flying with British Airways. When I tell them that we don't have the extras such as blankets and pillows that they want, they go absolutely barmy and shout at me. People take it out at me and I'm often told things such as, "You don't get this with BA." But you can't win them all. It is a tough challenge trying to educate people that you can get cheap deals on easyJet and you can do different things, such as bring your own food on-board, but at the end of the day, it is not BA.'

Of course, there were good sides to the job, added Michael. He particularly enjoyed working on flights during the summer months, when lots of young couples escaped on romantic breaks, and introducing new passengers to the joys of flying. 'I've had lots of passengers on-board who have never flown before. There was a woman yesterday who was flying for the first time and she was very nervous. I try to be down to earth and to talk people like that out of their nerves. I told her to try and spot her house when we were taking off. It is a good tactic to calm down passengers as they can concentrate on something else. Some get scared if the plane is a bit wobbly during take-off or during turbulence. I try to be a bit cheeky to make them feel better, telling them that wouldn't their car be a bit wobbly if it had 150 people in it.

'My Mum is not a good flier. She is probably typical of people her age who think that easyJet planes are going to be fifty years old and that the tickets are too cheap and therefore wonders what is wrong with the airline. I went out to Spain with her on easyJet. She was dreading landing back in the UK but ended up pronouncing her landing the best one she has ever had and that was during a snowstorm! Nowadays my Mum flies with easyJet all the time. She travels up to Edinburgh for £25 return to go shopping for the day with her friends. After all, it is only a thirty-five-minute flight from East Midlands.'

Michael said he enjoyed seeing the many celebrities who travelled with easyJet, including Barbara Windsor, Delia Smith and various football players. Some of his passengers were distinctly less well heeled, however. 'Yesterday was funny. I had two women on-board who were in their late forties but dressed as if they were twenty-five years old, wearing cropped tops, which unfortunately showed off their caesarean scars. They were carrying their shopping bags from the shop New Look and trying to act as if they were young and posh but it just wasn't working. They asked for a glass of Chardonnay at 6.30 a.m. Well, we only carry one brand of white wine and one brand of red wine on-board and certainly don't stock Chardonnay. It was obvious that they just wanted to go away for a few days and pretend they had a really glamorous life and simply feel a bit special. They managed to get a cheap ticket with easyJet and could carry out their fantasy. They probably couldn't have afforded that otherwise.'

10. Honeymoon over?

STELIOS'S DEPARTURE MARKED the end of a winning streak for easyJet. In early 2003, the US and UK were preparing to go to war in Iraq. The conflict could hardly have come at a worse time for the industry, as airlines struggled to cope with terrorism fears and the weak economy. The International Air Transport Association expected international passenger travel to drop by 15 to 20 per cent during the war. As well as fuelling passengers' fears of flying and denting consumer confidence, war in the Middle East would also push up fuel costs as the price of crude oil soared; with the added factor of a strike in Venezuela that had choked off the country's oil exports, oil prices had soared above $30 a barrel in January 2003.

In January 2003, easyJet announced that it would slip back into the red for the first half of its financial year, September to March, and that annual growth would fall back from 40 to 25 per cent. EasyJet insisted that the announcement was not a profit warning but illustrated that the company was 'trading as normal'. The airline traditionally posted a loss in the first half, which did not include the key summer months. In the previous year the company had managed a £1 million profit, but easyJet insisted that the previous year's result had been 'exceptional'. 'EasyJet was helped last year by very mild weather and the fact that Easter fell in the first half,' said a spokeswoman. 'Also, post September 11, we dropped prices last year to excite the market and many people were flying short-haul. Furthermore we have had a high level of disruption this year such as bad weather and air traffic control problems, which mean we have had to suspend flights and compensate passengers.'

Concerns about easyJet's welfare escalated in February when the airline warned that average ticket prices in the first half would be lower than previously expected. In a circular to shareholders, the company declared that its average fares in the four months to January were 6 per cent lower than the same period last year, as it cut prices to boost passenger numbers while also having a much greater seat capacity to fill. In a thinly veiled profits alert, the no-frills airline said that it was not at all certain about the outcome for its full financial year: 'Although current forward bookings are robust, the overall profile of the last quarter's revenue, and hence the full-year outcome, will not become apparent for at least several months.' The warning sent easyJet shares tumbling down 34 pence to 208p, a dramatic fall from the airline's high that year of 504p.

EasyJet's interim results were as bad as predicted. In May, the company reported a pre-tax loss of £48 million for the six-month period ending 31 March 2003 – its greatest-ever interim loss. The loss included £18 million of charges for integrating Go and the company also spent £9.2 million on its aborted attempt to buy Deutsche BA. Stripping out one-time costs and goodwill charges of £8.9 million, largely from the Go acquisition, easyJet's underlying losses were £24.4 million.

However, first-half revenues increased 92 per cent to £373 million – a 25 per cent increase on the combined revenue of easyJet and Go the previous year.

To compound the bad results, Webster announced that fifty middle management jobs would be shed at the firm's head office in Luton, as part of easyJet's restructuring following the acquisition of Go. The job cuts came on top of 116 job losses resulting from the closure of the Go call centre at Stansted, announced in March. EasyJet insisted that the integration of Go was making better progress than expected. Although the airline ran up integration costs of £5.6 million in the first half, Webster said that the combined company had been able to make significant cost savings. But investors couldn't yet breathe a sign of relief. The outlook remained 'challenging', added the CEO, warning that profits for the year to September were dependent on the summer months.

Analysts stated that easyJet was suffering from the old problem of trying to expand too fast. EasyJet's purchase of Go brought it lots of extra seats to fill, while Iraq war fears and the economic downturn hit demand. The airline was quickly learning that greater scale meant greater complexity and resulted in declining margins and falling return on capital. This was particularly the case when an acquisition with different systems and methods of operation needed to be integrated, but it was even more so for easyJet as it moved from one centre of operations to multiple hubs in different countries with different types of planes. Managing growth is always difficult – managing growth with added complexity, growing competition and a worldwide slump in demand was even tougher.

While passenger numbers were up by 40 per cent to 9.3 million, the average fare paid by passengers was 10.7 per cent lower than in the same period a year earlier at £37.45. EasyJet dismissed claims that this was the result of competition from Ryanair, which had itself reported an 8 per cent year-on-year fall in fare revenue to the end of December. Webster argued that O'Leary's incessant attacks on easyJet were designed to distract attention from his own carrier's underlying problems. 'I think a lot of the profit growth at Ryanair is coming from Ireland while the new routes he is launching, particularly since taking over Buzz, are unprofitable,' said Webster.

Ryanair had launched a new phase in the air fares war in April 2003, attacking easyJet for being more like a flag carrier than a low-cost airline. The Dublin-based carrier ran a series of adverts poking fun at easyJet and disputing its claim to offer the lowest fares available on the routes it operated. One advert depicted Saddam Hussein's former Information Minister, Mohammed Saeed al-Sahaf, who had been dubbed 'Comical Ali', as easyJet's new head of information. Other advertisements described easyJet's claim as 'a load of bullocks' and one of the 'four greatest lies told by man'.

Ryanair's decision to attack easyJet, rather than British Airways or Lufthansa, marked a distinct shift in strategy, particularly as easyJet only competed with Ryanair on six of its 125 destinations. O'Leary said that criticising high-fare airlines such as BA had become a 'bit like kicking a dead sheep', and that Ryanair's objective was now to 'reposition' easyJet in the minds of air travellers. 'We want to eliminate the idea that easyJet is somehow a low-cost airline,' O'Leary declared. 'It isn't. Its average fares are 70 per cent higher than ours. There is only one low-fares airline in Europe and that is Ryanair.'

It was clear that Europe's no-frills market was dis-aggregating. At one end of the spectrum, there was a genuinely low-cost, low-fares operator in the shape of Ryanair, and at the other end a host of wannabes such as bmibaby. EasyJet, with its higher cost structure because of its mixed fleet and preference for principal airports, fitted somewhere in the middle, appealing to those who wanted a cheaper fare than BA rather than the lowest one going.

EasyJet responded that it had always been careful not to claim that it offered the lowest fares available and added that flying with Ryanair was like a geography lesson: 'They go to places you can't spell and have never heard of, and certainly don't bear any resemblance to the destination advertised,' said an easyJet spokesman. 'And by the time you have paid for a taxi to take you into the city centre it would probably have been cheaper to fly with British Airways, let alone easyJet!'

Webster stressed that easyJet operated a different business model from Ryanair's. 'Comparing ourselves to Ryanair is irrelevant,' he argued. 'We are trying to be the cheap operator between airports that people really want to use. If you are flying to Beauvais [where Ryanair lands], it is not Paris. My wife is Parisian and if you mention Beauvais she says it is the country.' Ryanair's voluble boss retorted that the majority of easyJet's traffic involved Luton, Liverpool, Belfast and the East Midlands, which were hardly sought-after locations. 'EasyJet is not low cost and it is not low fare. It is much more like BA because it charges high fares and it loses money. Case closed.'

It was somewhat disingenuous of easyJet to talk about inappropriate ads. The orange airline was known for its colourful adverts, including one inviting passengers to 'discover weapons of mass distraction' above a picture of a woman's breasts in a bikini top and the promise 'lowest fares to the sun'. A total of 186 people contacted the Advertising Standards Authority in summer 2003 to label the newspaper advert 'offensive and demeaning to women' and 'trivialising the war in Iraq'. The ASA rejected the complaints. EasyJet said the advert was the latest in a series designed to be 'topical, humorous and irreverent' and dismissed accusations it was either sexist or demeaning to women.

The ASA also rejected a complaint by Charles Ingram, who was convicted in April 2003 of using deception – via the coded coughs of an accomplice in the audience – to win the top prize on quiz show *Who Wants to Be A Millionaire?* EasyJet ran a newspaper ad soon after the verdict with the headline 'Need a cheap getaway?' above a photograph of Charles Ingram with his wife Diana and the words 'No Major fraud required'.

EasyJet's shares received another hammering in August, when Stelios sold a further £19 million of shares in easyJet to fund four new ventures: pizza delivery, minibus services, and budget hotels and cruises. The sale of 8 million easyJet shares, equivalent to just over 2 per cent of the stock, reduced Stelios's holding to 18.8 per cent. EasyJet shares fell 7 per cent to 241p on the news.

Stelios seemed keen to apply the principle of yield management to absolutely anything, whether it was the shiny new Airbuses soaring ahead or cheese and tomato pizzas in cardboard boxes. James Rothnie, spokesman for easyGroup, decribed easyPizza as a 'classic easyGroup concept', allowing people to buy a pizza for as little as £1 at traditionally quiet times like afternoons. Next was easyBus, which would transport passengers not to glamorous destinations such as Paris or Nice but between Hendon in north-west London and Milton Keynes for as little as £1. Another of Stelios's brainwaves was easyCruise: Mediterranean cruise ships on which passengers would have to clean their own cabins and supply their own bedding and toiletries in return for a fare of as little as £29 per night. Forget lavish banquets and white-jacketed stewards; the bright orange-painted cabins wouldn't even have windows. Rooms in easyHotel were only nine times the size of a phone box and guests had to bring their own sheets and toiletries. EasyMobile, meanwhile, planned to offer the lowest tariffs for voice calls and text messaging in the UK.

Stelios conceded that extending the easy brand into other markets was anything but easy. 'I think the mistake I made is I thought it would be easier. In the early days with easyJet, I worked very hard in the unglamorous surroundings of Luton. I now realise that you have to do the same with every business.'

The outspoken entrepreneur blamed the 'catastrophic failure' of managers for £120 million of losses incurred over the previous four years at his easyGroup companies, which excluded publicly owned easyJet. 'The explanation does not lie in the branding strategy,' Stelios maintained. 'It lies in a catastrophic failure of cost control by the managers I chose to run these companies.' And possibly a lack of enthusiasm among consumers for being shuttled up to Milton Keynes in an easyBus to watch a little-known film in the weathered, squat home of easyCinema? At least Stelios appeared to be becoming more cautious, rejecting proposals for an easy-branded undertaker service (with orange coffins?) and a cosmetic surgery service he dubbed easyBoob.

Under an agreement, none of the easy companies were permitted to compete directly with one another. Nor could easyJet set up non-core subsidiaries that generated more than 25 per cent of its total revenue. None of which had stopped easyJet from forming a partnership with Europcar – an easyCar rival.

Stelios argued it was 'slightly simplistic' to focus on easyGroup's accumulated losses. 'It is a bit meaningless. I am a venture capitalist. I invest money in the hope to get it back and more in a few years. I think in decades not years.' He warned that there would be more share sales to come, insisting, 'As I have been consistently saying for a while, from time to time, I will be selling a bit of my past to finance my future'; though in the previous autumn, standing down as chairman of easyJet, he had proclaimed that he had no present intention to sell any easyJet shares in the near future.

The departure of a company's founder, even when he had already put in place a highly competent successor such as Webster, was normally a sign for a company's shares to fall – and once the dust had settled easyJet was no exception. Analysts said that whatever the merits of eliminating a competitor, the Go purchase had also provided a convenient cover for Stelios to sell a significant slice of his shares at a price he would have been hard pushed to get if the institutions had not been excited by the deal. By persistently selling off his past to finance his future, as he put it, Stelios was doing his original and most successful creation no favours at all. Stelios was entirely open in stating that he intended progressively to flog off his shares in easyJet in order to fund his various other easyGroup ventures. Nonetheless, each time it happened, it came as a surprise and knocked the share price, which was still languishing close to its Iraq-war lows.

The umbilical cord with easyJet's founder hadn't been completely cut. Stelios's presence was everywhere to be seen in easyJet's Portakabin-style headquarters, from a framed photo of him to the 'thank you Stelios' poster in reception. But Webster maintained that Stelios didn't intervene in the day-to-day management of the airline. The chief executive briefed the airline's founder after every set of results and Webster and Stelios caught up twice a year at a meeting of the easy companies. That was it. Stelios concurred: 'If they decide tomorrow to fly business class, I'd give them my negative thoughts. But if you ask me to name the routes easyJet flies, I couldn't.'

Webster had no intention of fundamentally straying from Stelios's original strategy but some things had changed since the founder's departure. For one, competition was getting tougher. Low interest rates, a glut of secondhand aircraft and the example of the successful market leaders had lured hopeful start-ups into the market. By mid-2003, there were at least thirty-four no-frills carriers in Europe and seven 'coming soon'. It was hard to keep up with the no-frills scene. Aside from everyday names such as easyJet, Ryanair, bmibaby, Virgin Express, Germanwings and Hapag-Lloyd Express, you could find Basiq Air (Amsterdam), Snalskjutsen (Sweden), SkyEurope (Bratislava, Slovakia), Volareweb (Milan/Venice), Evolavia (Ancona), Jetmagic (Cork) and Air Catalunya (Barcelona).

The reach of European no-frills airline networks had mushroomed. It was easier to count the countries European low-cost airlines didn't serve than those they did. The Baltic states weren't yet served by any carrier that could be realistically defined as no-frills and neither were the more remote Eastern European countries like Belarus, Ukraine, Moldova or

Bulgaria. But outside this handful of nations, there were few exceptions. In central Europe, Poland and Hungary and Slovakia had their own low-cost airlines. Prague was a perennially popular destination for budget carriers from Germany, Scandinavia and the UK. And at least three no-frills airlines were now flying to cities on the Dalmatian coast of Croatia, as well as to Serbia, Bosnia and Herzegovina and FYR Macedonia.

In Western Europe, Luxembourg was unique in being the only EU country yet to play host to a no-frills service – though the private regional airline VLM usually provided a better deal on low-fare flights to London than any competitor. Independent travellers could increasingly find low-cost flights to elsewhere on the continent in every country, from Iceland in the far north-west to Georgia in the south-east, including the most unlikely regions – Denmark to Kosovo, anyone? A growing trend pioneered by Air Berlin and Snowflake was to provide cheap connections from Europe to destinations in North Africa, such as Egypt and Morocco, as well as to eastern Mediterranean countries like Turkey and Lebanon.

Meanwhile, the low-cost boom continued in the UK, which played host to more no-frills carriers than any other country in Western Europe. Coventry Airport greeted Thomson Fly, a new low-cost airline run by TUI, the same German parent company that operated Hapag-Lloyd Express. Full-service airlines had added to the competition by creating their own no-frills clones – Britain's British Midland had set up bmibaby and Scandinavia's SAS had established Snowflake Airlines. Other full-service airlines added to the competition by matching many no-frills fares, especially for late booking, with one-way prices and no Sunday-stay requirement.

While British Airways and the other large established airlines could partially ignore easyJet when it flew from Luton to a handful of destinations, they were inclined to compete more vigorously as easyJet got larger. Martin George, marketing and commercial director of British Airways, said that BA had no intention of relinquishing short-haul routes to no-frills carriers: 'Some may retreat but we're fighting to make money on short-haul.' As the cost of jet fuel soared, some network carriers tried to compensate by raising ticket prices, only to give up within days. Budget airlines controlled pricing in the market and the larger airlines were being forced to respond. Passengers were being offered more choice and better prices.

Competition wasn't the only thing easyJet had to worry about. The airline also needed to find new routes and landing slots. It had to fill sixteen additional aircraft in its fleet in 2004 and twenty-three more planes in the following year. Ryanair, meanwhile, had about 100 Boeings on order whose seats it needed to fill. Keith McMullan of Aviation Economics calculated that each of these aircraft would have to carry 250,000 passengers a year to earn their keep. It was a tough target to meet. In 2003, easyJet carried 21.1 million passengers, while in the year ending March 2004, Ryanair carried 23.1 million passengers. In order to fill up all the new planes, already arriving in the airlines' fleets at the rate of one every fortnight until the end of 2008, easyJet and Ryanair needed between them to attract 52 million new passengers – more than double their current numbers.

Webster revealed that he had short-listed half a dozen airports for talks about expanding the airline's network of 105 routes between thirty-eight airports. He wanted to pick one or two of the short-listed airports to launch new services the following summer. The problem was that most of the bases operated by easyJet and Ryanair were in Ireland or Britain. The London airports were dominated by low-cost traffic, with the sector's share at almost 40 per cent, against only 12 per cent in Paris and less than 20 per cent in Frankfurt's airports. EasyJet and Ryanair held a measly 7 per cent of intra-European flights at Paris Charles de Gaulle, Orly and Beauvais combined. EasyJet complained about discrimination at Charles de Gaulle, where it paid the same landing fees as Air France but was relegated to Terminal Three, a bus ride away from the main airport. Unless the two airlines could gain greater access to airports in France or Germany and so tap new markets, both would struggle to maintain their growth and would have to continue their bitter price war. They were making some progress, but it was an uphill struggle.

Industry analyst Chris Tarry of research consultancy CTAIRA commented: 'Ryanair and easyJet are very much of a UK phenomenon and here the full-service carriers BA and bmi British Midland have fought back hard. It is also a market dominated by the M25 factor, where passengers are prepared to pay a little extra for a full-service flight or one that doesn't go from Stansted. Add the collapse in corporate spending and fall in consumer confidence and discretionary spending, and you see the problem. You could say the honeymoon is over.'

In February 2004, Stelios decided to go on a 'little shopping spree'. He came home with more than just a few groceries. Over the course of a few days, Stelios made commitments to buy a cruise ship capable of carrying 250 people for easyCruise, a twenty-five-room hotel in London for easyHotel, and a fleet of Mercedes buses for easyBus. As ever, easyJet provided the cash for Stelios's shopping excursions. He sold 4 million shares, or 1 per cent in the airline, to fund his purchases, bringing his stake in easyJet down to 16.57 per cent, or 66,076 million shares. But the Greek multimillionaire also underlined his ongoing commitment to the easyJet business. 'I have not sold out of easyJet, nor do I intend to sell out. I remain a great believer in the scalability and sustainability of the business model I developed.'

Some observers wondered if Stelios's foray into such a bewildering and unprofitable assortment of businesses was having a damaging effect even on easyJet itself. John Williamson, a director of brand consultancy Wolff Olins, commented, 'Stelios does not live the brand in the way that Branson or Michael O'Leary at Ryanair does. The "easy" brand is worth less now than four years ago.'

Overall, these were trying time for Stelios. Two years previously, in 2002, easyJet had been worth more than £2 billion, Stelios had a host of expanding businesses and more ideas than he had time to implement, and the future had seemed lurid orange. Since then, Stelios had been obliged to restructure his easyCar auto rentals business, which had lost £20 million, in order to save it from oblivion. Stelios also had been forced to rescue easyInternetcafé, which had lost about £90 million, with a multi-million-pound handout and he was still fighting a cartel of film studios that were refusing to let him screen new releases at his low-cost easyCinema.

EasyJet was also suffering. It wasn't that long since no-frills airlines had been cruising above the clouds of a brutal industry shakeout, boasting soaring sales and profits. The low-cost pioneers had been able to flourish simply by feeding off the soft underbelly of the established full-service airlines. It had been pitifully easy to undercut them. Times had changed, and budget carriers were increasingly being forced to compete against each other to sustain the breakneck pace of growth.

Low-cost carriers that had already gone under included Duo, which flew from Birmingham and Edinburgh, Irish airline Jet Greet, Cork-based JetMagic and Luton-based Now, which collapsed before its first flight, backing up the aviation industry's historic statistic that 97 per cent of all start-ups eventually failed. Airline expert Chris Tarry said it was 'inevitable' that more European airlines would go under as carriers fought to the death for bookings. EasyJet's German network of twenty-five routes was suffering from particularly strong competition. EasyJet had opened bases in Berlin and Dortmund to increase its routes and planned to raise capacity by 50 per cent in the winter, adding three aircraft, new routes and more frequent flights to existing destinations. With the UK market relatively mature, executives knew that future low-cost expansion would take place on the continent. That was why hanging on in Europe's most populous and central state was so important. 'Germany is the real battleground,' said

Chris Avery, an airline analyst at JP Morgan. 'The UK and Ireland broadly have the same penetration of low-cost carriers as in the US. So the rest of Europe is where the easy growth is. France is pretty much closed, so everyone has gone to Germany.'

EasyJet's arrival was causing consternation among the German start-ups, including Air Berlin, Germania Express, Hapag-Lloyd Express and Lufthansa-affiliate Germanwings, all of which were soundly based and operated routes to the UK. 'It is an emotional issue for us,' said Andreas Bierwirth, the deputy managing director of Germanwings. 'We will protect our market and we will protect our routes, especially London Gatwick to Cologne, to the last drop of blood in our bodies.'

Major carriers such as British Airways and Air France were an added concern for the budget carriers. Chris Tarry said easyJet was being hit by an aggressive response from so-called 'full-service' airlines like British Airways, after these slashed their fares in Europe. If you fancied a Riviera vacation, easyJet could fly you from Paris to Nice for as little as €84 but then Air France, which at first pooh-poohed easyJet's arrival at Paris Orly airport, had cut its Paris–Nice fare to just over €100. A BA round trip from London to Paris cost as little as €119 – more than the €62 easyJet charged for mid-week travel during off-peak hours but roughly comparable to easyJet fares at other times.

Many Europeans still preferred to fly old-line carriers even if it cost a little bit more, said Tarry: 'It turns out that Europeans are not so price-sensitive that a few euros on a ticket will make a difference.' Moreover, the old-timers were also continuing to adopt some of the discounters' innovations, such as easier online booking and the elimination of some stay-over restrictions. And passengers flying with the likes of British Airways could luxuriate in 'frills' such as frequent flier miles and a free meal on-board. The discounters continued to choose price as their chosen weapon and retaliated with even lower fares than the established airlines. After Aer Lingus started selling one-way Dublin to London tickets for €14.50, Ryanair dropped its fare to €13 as part of an average 11 per cent fare cut.

By April 2004, Ryanair chief executive O'Leary was Armageddon-like in his predictions of what was in store as the price war continued. 'I see a ferocious bloodbath among no-frills carriers. There will be tremendous competition, with the mother and father of all fare wars. We expect the coming year to be tough and the winter to be particularly difficult.'

His comments came as the Irish company announced profits were down 14 per cent. The squeeze on margins prompted Ryanair to axe three of its French routes, Reims, Clermont-Ferrand and Brest. There was more bad news. In February 2004, the European Commission had ordered Ryanair to repay €4 million in discounts it had obtained from Brussels Charleroi Airport – a ruling that took direct aim at the Irish airline's strategy of securing cheap landing fees at under-utilised regional airports.

The Dublin-based airline warned investors that it expected its revenue per passenger to plunge by as much as 20 per cent in the three months to September, the second quarter of its financial year, as it fought to increase market share. Ryanair reminded investors that it remained hugely more profitable in terms of operating margin than even the best of the full-service airlines. In an attempt to boost revenues while keeping fares low, the airline said that it intended to introduce in-flight entertainment on all of its flights but customers would have to pay for the privilege at an introductory price of €7 per flight. The company also worked on plans to ban large luggage.

Ferocious pricing from competitors was also hurting easyJet, which in May 2004 announced a loss before tax and goodwill of £18.5 million in the six months ending March, approximately what analysts expected but an improvement on its loss of £24.4 million in the same period a year earlier. Turnover was up by 18 per cent at £439 million as the number of passengers rose 16 per cent to 10.8 million. 'We are currently seeing unprofitable and unrealistic pricing by airlines across the European industry, seeking to grow or maintain their market share,' said Webster. 'The substantial oversupply of seats, especially in the London market, is unsustainable.'

The airline adjusted its outlook for the full year from 'cautiously optimistic' to 'cautious' because of what it termed an 'increasingly competitive marketplace'. There were further premonitions of doom. EasyJet said it expected its average fares to fall in 2004 from £42 to £38. The profit warning – just as the normally lucrative summer season got into full swing – shocked the City. That, plus disappointing trading over Easter and the collapse over the previous weekend of Duo, sent that day's shares in easyJet plunging a stomach-churning 25 per cent, or 73p, to 219p. More than £275 million was wiped off the budget airline's value and Stelios saw £49 million wiped off his shares.

Even worse, in June, easyJet came back to the City with another profit warning, announcing that profits might only just top last year's £52 million. This was well below market expectations. Even with recent profit forecast downgrades after the interim results, analysts had been pencilling in profits as high as £80 million. The airline claimed it was continuing to face pressure from unprofitable and unrealistic pricing in an increasingly competitive market. High fuel prices, thanks to an unstable Middle East, added to the problems. Airline fuel had risen by 10 per cent in the first three months of the year and the cost of oil had hit a high of $42.30 a barrel. The International Air Transport Association estimated that the fuel crisis could cost the global airline industry as much as $1 billion a month in extra costs.

'While demand for low-cost travel remains strong, the forward pricing environment is exceptionally competitive,' said easyJet in the trading update. Webster also served notice that there would be some 'bloody noses' among its rival low-cost operators as the fares war intensified. 'There is going to be a lot of blood on the floor and it is not going to be O'Leary's or mine. We are not going to sit on our hands as other airlines come along and try to take our market but nor are we going to open up the war chest and go out and pick a fight.'

The colourful words were more typical of one of O'Leary's ebullient outbursts than of the quietly spoken, reserved New Zealander. But if Webster thought that his macho comments might win favour with the City, he was wrong. EasyJet shares nosedived by another 37 pence to 163p on Webster's warning. In under a month, easyJet had issued two profit warnings and shares had crashed by a total of almost 50 per cent. The company was now valued at £629 million compared with £2 billion in November 2000, and some observers saw it as vulnerable to takeover.

Webster admitted that the airline had made a mistake in not being specific a month previously in its guidance but denied that it had been punished by the markets as a result. 'I wouldn't call it punishment; I would call it a correction,' he said defiantly, adding, 'Overall I was surprised at the reaction. We felt we had a good first half; we met our expectations so we certainly weren't anticipating the reaction the market gave back to us. One can only assume their expectations were much higher than ours.'

But City investors didn't like getting caught on the hop. 'EasyJet's second warning in a month dents the credibility of the management led by Ray Webster,' the *Financial Times* pronounced. 'The management's operational expertise is highly regarded but the warning suggests a cultural flaw of over-optimism and a lack of understanding of the stock-market.' Analysts and investors were angry. One shareholder said: 'The whole management process comes under suspicion when things like this happen.' Another investor said he felt that Webster would be viewed as 'damaged goods' for a while, adding that the worsening market conditions had been 'signposted' by O'Leary months ago. 'Mr Webster appears to have been caught out on what is really going on in the market,' the shareholder commented tersely.

These were stinging rebukes for somebody who for nine years or so, along with Stelios, had delivered spectacular growth in revenues, profits and passenger numbers. There were calls for executive heads to roll. 'I think the market is punishing poor investor relations,' said Stelios. 'I've spoken to the company and know that it is doing something about it. You measure investor relations by how well or otherwise the market receives bad news, and twice in the last month the stock plummeted by more than 15 to 20 per cent in one day. That cannot be good investor relations, no matter how bad the news is.'

Stelios also told the airline that it must cut costs. EasyJet announced plans to axe unprofitable routes and lose at least six planes, nearly a tenth of its fleet – the first time that the company had ordered such cutbacks. The airline said that it would stick to its new aircraft delivery schedule for its 120 new Airbus planes, despite the growing fears among analysts that there were too many planes in Europe and too few passengers. EasyJet itself also raised questions over what it would do with the eighty-two new planes Airbus was due to deliver over the following three years. The Luton-based airline was still expecting the market to expand by 20 per cent in 2004 but its predictions of a 25 per cent expansion in 2005 were looking over-optimistic. 'Capacity deployment for financial year 2005 is currently under review,' the airline said in a statement.

Webster organised a series of meetings with big investors in the UK, continental Europe and the US to try to calm anger over what was undeniably a serious communications failure from the cockpit. At these meetings, he re-emphasised that despite the current fuel price problems and increasing competitiveness in airline prices, easyJet should be able to report pre-tax profits that would exceed the £52 million it made in the previous year. The airline had already acquired the financial strength, size and breadth of network to see it through the turbulence, and, as Webster pointed out, it had a balance sheet that was flush with cash.

Webster reckoned that only two low-cost carriers, perhaps three at a push, would survive long-term in Europe – one of which would be easyJet and the other Ryanair. He recognised that the two had a mutual self-interest in not going head to head. 'Ryanair and easyJet will find a way of co-existing,' he promised. 'The important thing to recognise is that both of us are disciplined by the capital markets. If we ignore that and start depleting shareholders' funds we will get some pretty clear signals from investors.'

The chief executive's words helped calm angry investors but the damage was already done. The City's love affair with low-cost airlines had cooled. Stelios was watching his and his family's combined 41 per cent stake shrink in value by the day and analysts speculated that he would like nothing better than to take his airline private again and prove how wrong the City was to ease him out in the first place. The one question was whether he could raise the finance, given that Stelios's easyGroup businesses had yet to make substantial profits. With the shares now significantly lower than they had been when floated four years ago, the company would be a steal on its current valuation of £575 million, though any bid was likely to be pitched around at least £650 million. Chris Avery, transport analyst at JP Morgan, referred to recent reports that Stelios had received offers for his original shipping business, Stelmar Shipping, adding: 'If consummated, this might fund both start-ups and give Stelios the cash to take easyJet private again at a sensible price, perhaps returning to the stockmarket in a few years' time when the business model would be more mature.'

Webster dismissed the reports, saying that a buy-out 'is not on my radar screen'. He added that Stelios was a supportive shareholder who took a close interest in the running of the business and had his own representative on the board, making him an insider. A month later Stelios backed up Webster's statement, announcing in a letter to shareholders that taking the airline private 'would be something of an extreme measure' and that he had 'no current plan' to do so, though he admitted that he could change his mind if shares fell further or if he lost confidence in the board. At the same time, it was revealed that OMI, an oil shipping company, had withdrawn its £352 million takeover offer for Stelmar. The news didn't help; easyJet's shares slumped to a record low, falling 6½p to 143½p as investors stripped out any takeover premium from their valuations of the airline.

EasyJet did little to soothe fears in the City when it put out a trading statement in July saying there had been no improvement in the market since the previous month's unexpected profit warning. EasyJet carried 2.24 million passengers in June, putting it within spitting distance of the 2.27 million that Ryanair handled in the same month, with easyJet's aircraft flying at 84 per cent of capacity against Ryanair's 87 per cent. The planes were full but the fares were falling.

11. A grim winter

HARD TIMES LAY ahead for easyJet. In a bid to prepare for tougher times, the airline planned to increase the size of its fleet by just 16 per cent in 2005, instead of the 24 per cent previously planned, and retire about eighteen of its older Boeings 737s to ease over-capacity problems – six more than it had planned. Even so, analysts raised concerns that plans to slow the rapid growth rate of its fleet would not come into effect for another twelve months. Shares in the budget airline plunged even lower in September 2004, as easyJet admitted that there was 'continuing volatility in fuel prices' and that yields – average revenue per passenger – would remain under pressure in 2005. The company's stock slumped to 128p, less than half its flotation price four years previously.

Nine years had passed since easyJet's inaugural flight from Luton to Glasgow, when Stelios had pledged to bring flying to the masses. A lot had changed since that first orange Boeing 737 left the tarmac. Running easyJet was not so easy anymore.

With oil prices a hair's breadth away from $50 a barrel, margins were coming under pressure on all fronts.

The wider picture for the no-frills sector continued to look bleak. There were too many players, many of which were under-capitalised. Pressure on prices, relentless cost-cutting and selective route closures meant more players were going to the wall. The German outfit V-Bird was laid to rest, following the fate of others such as Now and Air Planet. The Danish operator Sterling had put itself up for sale. Virgin Express, meanwhile, had responded to the competitive threat by getting into bed with SN Brussels, which itself emerged out of the remnants of bankrupt Belgian carrier Sabena and its regional affiliate, Delta Air Transport, at the end of 2001. Then there was Hop – backed by Kit Malthouse, the deputy leader of Westminster council, and Tony Camacho, the former Buzz airline chief executive – which flopped before it even got off the ground after the financiers got cold feet.

There was little doubt that Ryanair and easyJet, two of the best-capitalised players in the sector, would survive. But for a while, the pickings would be thinner. The next duel that broke out between the pair concerned hand baggage. Ryanair raised its cabin baggage allowance to 10kg from 7kg. A week later, easyJet responded by abandoning the weight limit altogether. The only constraint was volume: your bag had to fit the 55cm by 40cm by 20cm maximum dimension, which corresponded to 22 litres. If you took a container of those dimensions full to the brim with lead weights, it would amount to 250kg. And if this generous allowance was insufficient for your needs, easyJet also allowed you to bring a laptop on board in addition. EasyJet hoped that the check-in process should be smoother and faster as a result of the eased restrictions although the boarding process could be slower as passengers tried to find places to stash their newly expanded baggage allowance.

Ryanair was testing the spartan spirit of its passengers by dispensing with its planes' window blinds, reclining seats,

Velcro-anchored headrest covers and the seat pockets where customers normally found a safety notice and free magazines. The required safety notice became a mere sticker on the back of each seat. EasyJet, meanwhile, was considering the introduction of a frequent flier programme. Webster, speaking at the International Air Transport Association annual conference in Singapore, said: 'We may have to do a frequent flier programme cheaply. It would be along the lines of a coffee shop stamp on a card.' He denied that such a programme would amount to easyJet adding frills. But in analysts' opinion, the move would inevitably further blur the distinction between low-cost and full-service airlines. In the end, easyJet didn't introduce the scheme, deciding that such frills didn't fit in with its low-cost plan, and perhaps also that it could fall victim to fraud.

Meanwhile, easyJet was experimenting with fully automated check-in kiosks at East Midlands Airport to replace check-in staff and counters. 'In due course, this could revolutionise the airport process in the way that the Internet revolutionised the booking process,' said Webster. The airline announced that if it was successful the system would be rolled out in other airports across its network, which would 'ultimately see kiosk-only check-in'.

EasyJet injected a degree of optimism into the sector when it announced that trading in its last quarter had been better than expected, with load factors remaining in the high 80s during the summer. The airline now expected pre-tax profits for the year to the end of September 2004 to top £60 million, up 16 per cent on 2003, improving on its previous predictions that profits would 'at least' exceed last year's £52 million. In the end, easyJet's full-year profits nudged higher than expectations. Profits rose to £62.2 million, up 21 per cent on a year earlier. The shares rose 2.86 per cent to 188½p on the news. The annual load factor, or how many seats were sold, improved to 84.5 from 84.1 per cent. With planes fuller, easyJet crossed the £1 billion turnover barrier for the first time, with sales up 17 per cent to £1.09 billion. But increased competition led to a fall in passenger yield to £42.28 in 2004 from £43.28 in 2003.

The airline warned the remaining winter months would be 'challenging'. Like other airlines, easyJet was facing pressure on overheads after its annual fuel bill increased by almost 22 per cent on a year earlier to £146.9 million, representing 14 per cent of spending, which had itself risen 20 per cent to £929.3 million.

High oil prices and stiff competition prompted a further drive to focus on costs. EasyJet said it planned to outsource some information-technology operations and achieve savings by using more fuel-efficient Airbus A319s. The airline also aimed to reduce spending by pulling out of poorly performing markets and over-priced airports. Airports and ground handling charges accounted for almost a third of easyJet's operational costs – a higher proportion than for most other airlines.

As part of its costs drive, on 31 October easyJet axed its Luton to Zurich service, which it claimed had become its most expensive route, and switched its Swiss services to Basel Mulhouse EuroAirport. The carrier accused Zurich Airport of ripping it off, describing a 132 per cent hike in landing charges over the previous two years as 'ludicrous', while castigating the airport's 'onerous operating restrictions'. Webster said Zurich 'now realised' that carriers would go to other destinations if airport operators thought they could raise prices as they wished. 'At any one time we are talking to a number of airports about future services – to date we have six new European cities for this winter,' he continued. 'Airports that "get it" and grasp the new reality will be rewarded with growth from Europe's leading low-cost airlines.'

Zurich wasn't the only airport to be shunned by easyJet. The airline reduced the number of flights it operated to Copenhagen Airport, scared away by its high airport tax of 75 kroner per passenger, and also decided to discontinue flights from Amsterdam to Barcelona and Nice as a result of rising landing fees, reducing the number of easyJet flights from Schiphol each day from twenty-seven to twenty-two. EasyJet was the second largest airline user of the airport after the national carrier, KLM. The total number of low-cost passengers at Schiphol in 2004 was around 4 million, almost 10 per cent of all passengers using the airport, and easyJet flew around half of those passengers. Leon Verhallen, manager of the passenger marketing business unit at Schiphol, said the airport was 'working hard to reduce its visit costs in general, but also to offer special facilities to reduce cost reductions'; the airport planned to open a new pier that it hoped would be attractive to low-cost carriers and free space in the central terminal area for airlines with a high level of connecting traffic.

Meanwhile, easyJet was still trying to establish a footing at French airports. The airline had boosted its number of flights out of Orly and Roissy from zero to thirty-five over the past two years. But as easyJet pointed out, it had taken only three months to build a comparable network in Germany. The airline asserted in a statement in *Les Echos* business newspaper that 'the French market is still closed to the development of airlines capable of competing with Air France . . . it is incomprehensible that a country such as France, which sees itself at the forefront of European legislation, does so little to permit the emergence of real competition to the national company'.

EasyJet's next area of conquest was Italy. Both easyJet and Ryanair, lured by Italy's position as the second largest low-cost airline market in Europe, announced plans to extend their reach in the country following the collapse of Italian no-frills airline Volare, which had declared insolvency. EasyJet planned daily services starting in April or May 2005 from Gatwick to Olbia, Luton to Cagliari and Berlin to Olbia and Pisa. The airline said it expected to see its passenger numbers on all Italian flights 'significantly increase' in 2005. Ryanair, meanwhile, said it would start a twice-daily service from Paris Beauvais to Venice Treviso and also announced that it wanted to hold talks with the Italian airports affected by the collapse of Volare about beginning low-fare domestic flights within Italy on routes previously served by the Italian carrier.

Then both airlines started to aim punches below the belt. In September Ryanair announced it would start flying from Britain to provincial Spain, previously seen as the preserve of easyJet. In a matter of days easyJet launched a surprise attack on Ryanair in the latter's home territory, announcing plans to introduce its first routes to the Republic of Ireland in January 2005. Weeks later, Ryanair said it would launch on the same Irish routes out of Gatwick as easyJet. The new easyJet services from Gatwick to Shannon, Knock and Cork were the only routes in Europe on which the two airlines competed directly.

In a side-sweep at its Irish rival, Webster declared: 'These are our first services to the Republic of Ireland, where air fares, in many cases, have remained stubbornly high and have generated consistently strong year-round returns for the incumbent airline.'

Ryanair co-deputy chief executive Howard Millar hit back: 'They are free to fly where they want to and if they want competition they can have competition. We will be happy to take the game to them.'

EasyJet's move into Ireland was ironic news for Ryanair. O'Leary had spent years calling for Irish airports authority, Aer Rianta, to be privatised. Eventually, in mid-2004, the Irish government proposed a bill which would break up the company that ran Ireland's three major airports by April 2005. Aer Rianta was to be split into three separate, competing state-run authorities operating the airports in Dublin, Cork and Shannon respectively. It must have come as a blow for the Irish CEO that the airports immediately chose to strike a deal with his competitor.

Meanwhile the two airlines battled to keep costs as low as possible. Whereas O'Leary famously banned highlighter pens from the office, Webster banned photocopiers, which he considered a more compelling example of cost-cutting. EasyJet employed more than 4,000 people but its headquarters remained in what Stelios had dubbed a 'giant Portakabin in Luton'. Not even the most senior managers had PAs; they all did their own administration.

EasyJet ran paperless offices, with documents scanned into the intranet where they could be picked up on a screen wherever employees might be in the world. An accountant complained in a flyer on the wall at easyJet's headquarters that she found 1,113 sheets of printer paper in the rubbish. 'If you rely on technology to run the business then you don't need pieces of paper,' said Webster. 'The problem with paper is that if you want lots of people to be involved you need lots of bits of paper. The great thing about technology is that 500 people can read the same piece of information simultaneously, three or four seconds after it was sent. It is not about the cost of paper. It is about unleashing the management potential by ensuring people have access to information as quickly as possible.'

The airline's only major administration expenses were IT costs, the lease on the head office and the salaries of management staff. EasyJet kept to its original formula of keeping costs low by selling directly to consumers, cutting out middlemen like travel agents, call operators and sales staff, with nearly all of its reservations made online; it sold a higher proportion of seats online than any other airline. Not paying commissions to travel agents added a healthy 6 per cent to the bottom line, and being a ticketless, web-based operation contributed another 3 per cent. Instead of a ticket, passengers received an email containing their travel details and confirmation number when they booked online. This avoided the cost of issuing, distributing and processing millions of tickets each year.

EasyJet reckoned they could get people on their planes quicker when people didn't have allocated seats. This was because people would be anxious to sit together and so would make sure they were at the gate, ready to board as soon as possible. Lone travellers, who didn't have anyone to sit next to, were a minority. Passengers were normally called to the gate by the number on their boarding pass number so the earlier they checked in the better the seat choice. EasyJet passengers also handed in their boarding card at the gate rather than the door of the plane where possible and used two sets of stairs, front and rear. Again, these were time-saving measures, necessary if easyJet were to achieve its tight turn-around times.

EasyJet worked hard to 'sweat the assets' by making sure that its planes were as full as possible and up in the air as many hours as possible. It wasn't unusual for an easyJet plane to make eight or nine hops around Europe in a day, beginning before dawn and ending around midnight. The planes had to be checked between each flight and the airline had to have a stock of spare engines and parts should any of the fleet need repairs. All planes had to undergo a yearly MOT, which required them to spend a day or more in a hangar being given the once-over.

Many fixed services, such as handling and maintenance, were outsourced to reduce costs. EasyJet held an outsourcing agreement with Danish-owned FLS Aerospace, under which base maintenance was carried out at a fixed price plus the cost of materials and time. Component maintenance was charged by the flight hour, while technical services, which included maintenance planning, was charged on a per aircraft basis. Ground handling covered the cost of check-in staff, baggage handlers and the workers who refuelled the planes. These employees were usually employed by an outside agency, such as Servis-Air or Aviance, who had a deal with the airline. At its large bases, such as Luton and Geneva, easyJet employed its own check-in staff.

In total, easyJet enjoyed a massive profit per employee. According to a study from the European Cockpit Association, easyJet's profit per employee was an impressive 350 per cent greater than that of the traditional airlines. Overall the cost per available seat kilometre, the industry yardstick, worked out at around half that of the full-service carriers and revenue per employee was almost double.

Flight crew working for the likes of easyJet weren't paid peanuts, as was often assumed, but pilot pay was still around 25 per cent lower than at traditional carriers. A captain with easyJet would earn around £80,000 a year, a first officer (the second in command) £50,000. And unlike large airlines, low-cost operators expected their staff to arrive fully qualified. Air France, British Airways and Lufthansa counted between twelve and fourteen pilots per aircraft in their short-haul fleets, while easyJet and Ryanair had between nine and ten, as its pilots and planes were more productive. Cabin crew earned significantly less than pilots, with salaries ranging from £14,000 to £17,000.

Of course, easyJet could employ fewer staff than full-service airlines as it eschewed free food service, which kept costs low. Plastic trays of reheated food were not the low-cost way and feedback indicated that most customers would prefer to pay less for a short-haul flight than be given a big meal, saving a surprisingly high 6 per cent from the bottom line. EasyJet had even managed to turn inflight catering into a money-earner. From the trolley on easyJet flights passengers paid £3 for a can of lager, £1 for a small tub of Pringles and £1.60 for a cup of tea or coffee. The decision to charge for coffee on easyJet flights generated two sources of additional revenue: one from the brew itself and the second from the fact that easyJet could eliminate one lavatory from its planes thanks to lower demand for them, making room for a few extra seats.

EasyJet managed to wring an average of £2.52 from each passenger for food, drinks and duty-free goods, on top of its average £38.06 fare. Perhaps unexpectedly, the airline gave away its in-flight magazine, *easy Come easy Go*. As it said on the cover, the magazine was 'easyJet's only freebie, get it while you can!' But in fact the publication provided another way for the airline to make money, thanks to advertising revenue brought by scores of adverts for second homes and ski resorts close to easyJet destinations.

Clearly the price paid for the aircraft, and each seat, was a key element in easyJet's low-fare business model. EasyJet had managed to secure lower aircraft prices via its mega aircraft order with Airbus. Getting more aircraft helped fleet economies. The newer the jets, the easier they were on fuel and thus the cheaper to run. Packing as many seats as possible into each aircraft played an important role in keeping costs low. The high-density seating configuration in low-cost carriers' aircraft provided an average 16 per cent cost advantage compared with the full-service airlines, which typically would offer business or first-class cabins in addition to 'cattle class'. With almost all of easyJet's costs incurred whether the aircraft was full or empty, it was desperately important to get as many bums on seats as possible. EasyJet managed to get 83 per cent of its seats filled on an average flight but worked as hard as it could to get more. An empty seat at take-off was money lost. Any price it could get for it was worth having, which was what drove it and other budget airlines to offer seats at lunatic prices. EasyJet made full use of its sophisticated yield management system, the brainchild of Webster, to work out the optimal fares. The software-driven pricing system could set an almost infinite number of fares for a given flight.

By using a number of secondary airports such as Stansted, Luton and East Midlands instead of Heathrow and Manchester, easyJet avoided congestion and paid lower airport charges per passenger. BAA Plc, which ran Stansted, charged £4.89 per person and TBI at Luton charged £5.50 per passenger. Heathrow, also a BAA airport, was more expensive, at £6.48 per person.

EasyJet's determination to hack away at costs and overheads wherever they occurred sometimes meant it took an unconventional approach, such as in its decision to supply dual-purpose sick bags on-board. The airline teamed up with

Scottish-based film laboratory Klick Photopoint to combine airsickness and photo development in one handy bag. Passengers who did not empty their stomach contents into the pre-labelled bag could leave their holiday films inside, to be sent off for processing by Klick, from whom easyJet received a commission. The Klick/sick bags were found in the seat backs of all of its aircraft marked with the catchy motto, 'Don't be sick, try out Klick – yes'.

'We thought this was an excellent value for money service,' said Alastair Gilchrist, head of commerce at easyJet, 'but I hope passengers don't post the wrong contents off to be developed.'

12. Go east

ON 1 MAY 2004 a swathe of former Communist countries, from Estonia in the north down to Slovenia on the shores of the Mediterranean, became proud members of the European Union. Budget airlines were swift to recognise the enormous business potential in Eastern Europe. On 24 April easyJet launched services from Gatwick to Prague, followed six days later by bmibaby on the same route. On 29 April, Jet2 began flying between Belfast and Prague, then on 1 May easyJet started services from Stansted to the Slovenian capital Ljubljana, and from Luton to Budapest, from £6.99 one-way.

Airlines wanting to fly into the new EU countries no longer had to wrestle with mountains of bureaucracy to obtain a licence. Out went complex bilateral agreements, which favoured a country's national carrier, kept competition to a minimum and ensured that fares cost hundreds of pounds. All of a sudden, it was a free market and airlines could fly anywhere they wanted. 'Within a couple of years, there will be a large number of airlines travelling to these new countries, within these countries and between them,' said Toby Nicol, the head of corporate affairs at easyJet.

The Iron Curtain was well and truly down, and easyJet and other budget operators benefited from the enormous increase in travellers flying in and out of Eastern Europe. For the first time citizens of the new EU countries could work legally in Britain without permits, and more than 175,000 Eastern Europeans arrived in Britain in the twelve months to 1 May 2005 – about twelve times the UK government's highest estimate.

Prohibitive prices had kept generations of Eastern Europeans on the trains and away from the airports. But the low-cost airlines changed all this. Many of the travellers from new European Union members such as Slovakia, Hungary and Poland were flying for the first time. Tens of thousands of immigrants flew into Britain using budget airlines to seek high wages in the service industries or professional jobs. The Lithuanian Association, for example, predicted that as many as 50,000 Lithuanians arrived in London – propelled from the Baltic State by mass unemployment. Migrant workers were needed to fill vacancies in the UK building industry, restaurants, hotels, food production and farming. They also found jobs as plumbers, labourers and lorry and coach drivers. Stagecoach Group, one of the UK's biggest bus operators, planned to recruit 100 Polish drivers, saying it had struggled to hire British staff.

Ryanair thanked the thousands of Eastern European migrants who flew with the airline for its 21 per cent increase in profits to £44.4 million in the three months to June 2005. Passenger numbers were up by almost a third on 2004 to 8.5 million – and a large proportion of these new passengers were people from former Communist countries. 'Back in the old days, we started off flying migrants from Ireland to England. Now we fly to Lithuania, Poland, Slovakia and the Czech Republic,' commented Howard Millar, Ryanair's deputy chief executive.

Moreover, the quick journeys and cheap tickets offered by easyJet and its competitors meant that the thousands of Eastern European immigrants who worked in cities such as London could now fly home cheaply to visit their relatives. Inevitably, the ease of travel brought problems with it too; according to an official police report quoted in the *Daily Mail*, organised crime bosses were also taking advantage of the cheap tickets, smuggling illegal immigrants from Africa or Asia into Eastern Europe and then using fake documents to board flights to the West. 'The widespread availability of low-cost flights provide a relatively cheap method of transporting illegal immigrants to the UK,' the report stated.

No-frills travel changed the lives of Eastern Europeans who ventured west to earn a living; it also changed the lives of their families back home, as Western tourists in their millions discovered the beautiful landscapes, eye-opening cultural heritage and astonishing low prices of the former Communist bloc. Budget airlines were expected to bring some 340,000 tourists to Hungary in 2004, raising direct revenues from tourism by some €90 million, according to regional development minister Istvan Kolber. At the beginning of 2004, one out of every eight tourists landing at Budapest's Ferihegy airport flew in on a budget airline. By October, that figure had risen to more than 22 per cent of all arrivals. Tourists arriving in Hungary on budget airlines stayed an average of 2.7 days in the country and spent around €100 per day, said Gabor Galla, managing director of the state tourism office.

In October 2004, easyJet increased its range of Eastern European services with new routes to Krakow and Warsaw in Poland and more services to Budapest. The airline now offered five flights to Prague a day, with services from Newcastle, Bristol and London. Meanwhile, Ryanair announced that it would operate flights to Riga from London starting at €50, while easyJet planned a Berlin–Riga route at €21. Other airlines operating in the region included

Wizzair, Germanwings, Snowflake, AirBerlin/Niki and Air Polonia.

At the end of October 2004, easyJet started flying from London Stansted to Tallinn, with one-way fares from as low as £26.99. Ryannis Capodistrias, easyJet's marketing manager for Greece, Italy, Hungary, Slovenia and Estonia, said that the company hoped to serve 185,000 passengers in twelve months on its Tallinn–Berlin and Tallinn–London daily flights. 'We plan to seize a 65 per cent share of the Tallinn–London route, and we predict that passenger traffic on this particular route will increase by 150 per cent after our arrival,' said Capodistrias.

The new easyJet route would raise the number of travellers to Russia as well as to Estonia, courtesy of the eight-hour bus journey linking Tallinn to St Petersburg, said Dimitry Paranyushkin, editor of waytorussia.net. 'About 47,000 British tourists visited Russia in 2003 according to Moscow's information office,' said Paranyushkin. 'At the same time, there are a few million independent travellers in the UK who would like to go to Russia but don't want to pay €400 for a ticket. Once the travellers learn about this offer, I reckon the number of travellers will double.'

Cities like Prague welcomed the huge increase in tourists shipped in by the budget airlines. 'It was all quite flat two years ago because of SARS, the Iraq war etc.,' said Iveta Schoppova, press officer with the Czech tourist board. 'EasyJet flying to Prague has meant that more young people now visit the city. The young generation now come here for a long weekend to profit from low-cost flights. Prague is not just for older people visiting museums and monuments. There has also been a boom in new hotels and lots of new and lively bars.'

Cheap flights had a cost too. By day, Prague's Old Town was a delightful area of cobbled streets and pavement cafés. Tourists of all nationalities mixed without trouble, taking in the culture and history of a city that since its Velvet Revolution had been happy to open its doors to the West. But come nightfall, capitalism in its brashest form came to Wenceslas Square as the stag parties emerged, running from bar to bar and screaming in the streets. Thousands of Britons, dressed in wigs, tutus and rabbit costumes, descended on the Czech capital every weekend on budget flights that could cost just £18. The men were often already drunk when they arrived for their 'last night of freedom', which tended to involve copious quantities of alcohol and the services of local strippers.

Bored with glugging Guinness in Dublin and puffing pot in Amsterdam, the British hordes were seeking pastures new and heading east. The invasion began with Prague and Budapest, where they rapidly wrecked Britain's reputation with central Europeans, whose touching belief in the gentility of the British was replaced by a far darker image. Cheap flights and cheap alcohol then took thousands of holidaymakers and stag parties to Tallinn, a quaint city of cobbled streets, which soon filled up with young British men. Latvia's Riga developed into a hotbed of post-Communist carousing and Slovenia's Ljubljana became a magnet for British stag parties, drawn by the cheap beer and strip joints in a Disney setting.

It didn't take long for businesses in the UK to get in on the scene. Praguepissup was one of the companies which organised stag weekends to the Czech capital. The blurb on its website said it all: 'An all-nighter costs less than five quid ... a night exercising the ferret costs 30 quid! Pub crawls, strippers and milkmaids – it's stag heaven.' The company boasted of its database of hundreds of girls, adding that they were the company that had exclusive rights to Andrea Miss Strip Czech Republic 2002. The weekend's cultural highlight was often a brewery tour.

Praguepissup was set up by thirty-five-year-old Tom Kenyon after he went to the city for his own stag weekend. The Mancunian moved to Prague in 1996, married a Czech girl and began his business with 'a mobile phone and a piece of paper'. By the end of 2004, he and his business partner had twenty staff and his clients could stay at more than 100 local hotels.

Kenyon soon added stag party tours to Budapest and Tallinn. Prague remained by far the most favoured destination, but Tallinn soon became popular too, though the Estonian city was so small that its founder said its capacity was limited to 500 to 600 groups a year.

'Low-cost flights and stag parties in Eastern Europe go hand in hand,' Kenyon explained. 'Low-cost flights are most definitely the number one driver in the whole business. We've been operating to Prague for more than five years now. During the first few years, business was okay but it was more of a hobby as it wasn't that easy to get cheap flights. Then it all really mushroomed when easyJet started adding flights to Prague and other low-cost airlines started operating here. Our business has taken off. It has more than quintupled, growing in direct relation to the number of flights on offer.

'The other direct effect of easyJet and the other low-cost airlines is that they've brought down the prices of the regular airlines too, such as British Airways. It used to cost me about £200 to fly from Prague back home to Manchester and now it is more like £100.'

Kenyon's customers were attracted by cheap flights, cheap accommodation and cheap beer. An average weekend booked through the agency, plus flights, cost around £200. 'Everything is so much cheaper when you get there that it almost pays for itself,' said Kenyon. 'You can pay £200 for a good weekend in Prague, which is the same price as a weekend in London as everything there is much more expensive. It's become such a good proposition because of the cheap flights. Without the likes of easyJet it would be just for the well-heeled stag parties.'

Praguepissup's typical client flew over from London Stansted and was in his mid-thirties. Some 99 per cent of customers arrived on the Friday and stayed until the Sunday. After a spot of sightseeing on the Friday, the men started drinking beer before heading to a strip show. 'We don't employ prostitutes but only professional strippers and steer away from drugs,' Kenyon explained. 'After dinner, the men will head to a strip club or night club and stay out until 3 a.m. or 4 a.m., getting drunk.'

Additional entertainments of a boyish sort, such as machine-gun firing with live rounds, were a pull for macho refugees from safety-mad Britain. Some men, it was rumoured, had even paid locally for the privilege of firing rocket-propelled grenades at live cows. 'They'll get up at midday on Saturday and will then do some adrenalin sports such as shooting, go-karting or paint-balling,' Kenyon continued. 'Then Saturday night, it is the same again – beer and girls. Sunday they'll spend recovering and might do a bit of sight-seeing or something cultural like a museum, before flying home.'

Kenyon emphasised that he steered his parties towards hotels, bars and restaurants that liked his kind of business. 'I wouldn't send them to a small family-owned hotel,' he said firmly. 'We spread them around as much as possible in big hotels. We operate in a hundred hotels in Prague and thirty-five in Tallinn. Plus we have guides with all the groups, who tell the lads what they can or can't do. We take them to places where stag groups are welcome and which don't have any nastier connections.'

The delights on offer appealed to a certain type of customer. 'Couldn't have managed it without you, especially Ulla. We lost one lad who fell in love with a lap dancer and isn't coming home but everyone else got back okay, which is the best I hoped for,' posted one punter called Phil on the company's website, www.praguepissup.com.

It wasn't just the 'lads' who were succumbing to the temptation of a cheap flight away and a riotous weekend in Europe's eastern lands. Women were increasingly flying with the likes of easyJet to Prague for their hen weekends. 'I had a wicked time, all the activities were quality and have already recommended you to my mates for a great piss up weekend, as I want to join them!!!!' posted Tracy on the Praguepissup home page.

The revellers were big spenders. Research for Morgan Stanley Credit Card showed that friends of a bride or groom spent an average of £365 each celebrating a final fling, and that money went much further in Eastern Europe than it did back home. 'Beer 50p, hotel 13 quid, cocaine 10 quid – you wouldn't get more than a bread roll, a cardboard box and a packet of aspirin in London for that,' declared one happy reveller, twenty-three-year-old Gareth from Port Talbot.

Prices were just as low in Tallinn, which was becoming the second most popular stag destination after Prague. Prior to 2004, the relatively few Brits that had visited Estonia had for the most part charmed Tallinn's citizens: the British tourists were considered friendly, laid-back and polite and tipped well. About 2.7 million foreigners visited in 2003, attracted by the high-quality eating and drinking, high culture and fascinating history. Behind the fastidiously well-preserved façades of the medieval buildings were chic bars and expensive boutiques. You could have been in a fashionable part of Stockholm or Helsinki.

But things changed after easyJet and its rivals added Tallinn to its network. An increasing number of Internet-based tourism companies started to market the city as the new destination for binge-drinking Brits. Targeting stag parties in particular, they promised cheap deals, cheap beer and cheap women. It wasn't long before the locals started to notice that a new breed of Brit was coming to town.

EasyJet marketing manager Capodistrias dismissed the importance of stag parties to the airline. 'Stag parties happen at weekends,' he argued. 'We fly every day. You can never make money by flying a route on weekends. You cannot rely on seats you sell on a Friday heading out and a Sunday coming back.' And, as easyJet pointed out, the airline operated a policy of zero tolerance to alcohol on board its aircraft and could hardly be held responsible for the behaviour of their passengers once they had reached their destination.

But although stag parties were a minor part of the airline's business as a whole, they had a disproportionate effect on the cities that suffered invasion. Kenyon said that his company's annual bookings to Tallinn tripled between 2003 and 2004 to 1,500 following easyJet's flights into the cities. 'We chose to add Tallinn as a destination after we heard that easyJet would be offering flights there,' he explained. 'We're going to expand in the future wherever easyJet is going. We plan to set up a new place a year and are currently looking at Sofia, Bucharest and Warsaw. It depends though whether the cheap airlines will be flying there in the future.'

'Stare at the buffage with ample cha-chas,' read the company's website, www.Tallinnpissup.com, which, with a nod to the city's history as a Hanseatic trading city, offered a 'medieval lesbian stripper show and banquet'. Among the other 'bonking good' activities on offer in Tallinn were ten-beer pub crawls and 'tottie tours'. Britain's press was also getting in on the act. 'Tallinn-ho!' shouted the headline of one red-top newspaper. 'It's cheap, full of some of the world's most gorgeous babes and is fast becoming the destination for Brit stag parties.'

But the combination of cheap flights and Tallinn's growing reputation as a stag destination were making some locals worried about the future. The Estonians, a reserved people, were puzzled by British stag parties. 'The Finns have been coming here for year but they just fall asleep,' said one. 'The British are different – they get loud and then they want to take their trousers off. We can't understand it.'

Unsurprisingly, Tallinn's café and bar owners were starting to tire of stag party antics. Aimée, manager of Café Anglais on Tallinn's Town Hall Square, said: 'A lot more people have come to Tallinn since the introduction of easyJet flights. I've seen a lot of trouble caused by young and single English, Irish and Finnish men. They can be very drunk and do stupid things. The men dress up in women's dresses and skirts and scream and shout in the middle of the street. Sometimes there are nice, well behaved people but unfortunately the groups are mainly always drunk and noisy.'

Several hotels had 'taken measures' against stag parties who offended other guests with their drunken behaviour, and the Estonian embassy in London was growing critical of companies offering 'cheap, low entertainment'. Behind the scenes, the Tallinn city authorities had already asked the police to crack down on noisy Brits. Kalle Klandorf was one of Tallinn's most senior police officers and had years of experience dealing with foreign troublemakers. 'The city authorities have asked us to deal with Brits making noise on the streets. Until now we've taken a liberal standpoint.' Klandorf added, 'We'd like people to come here and behave well. British tourism companies might try to attract people here who are wealthier and interested in other things apart from drinking.'

Unsurprisingly, like the residents of Dublin and Amsterdam before them, the inhabitants of Prague, a conservative people with strict rules of behaviour, were also beginning to tire of the stag weekenders. Journalist Johana Grohova talked of her resentment of the drunken men who boarded the bus she took home: 'They bother the women on the bus. They come here thinking this is a poor place and they have money and can do whatever they want. They treat us like we are stupid.'

The tourists who sought out Prague for its culture were equally unimpressed. A columnist in the English-language *Prague Post* proclaimed: 'Those all-time record holders, the Americans, have been dethroned as the No.1 tourist plague of Prague . . . When instant gratification isn't provided, the English can be expected to put on a dazzling display of chair throwing and beer glass smashing.'

Martus Havira from Prague Holiday Company said, 'We welcome the increase in tourists from the flights. But when it is a stag party of twenty young men from England then sometimes it isn't very nice. I heard of one instance when six to seven men checked in to an apartment and totally wrecked it. There was blood in the elevator because of fighting. A neighbour asked them to be quiet and they sent over one of the escort girls as a present. The neighbour was so angry.'

The police on patrol in the city centre were equally unenthusiastic. The citizens of Prague boasted reputedly the world's best beer and the highest consumption rate – an estimated 330 litres, or 580 pints, per person per year – but they noticeably did not roam the streets in packs of twenty, wearing false breasts and singing loudly. 'We are the biggest beer-drinking people in the world, but there is a difference,' said one policeman. 'We can handle it.' The Prague city police increased their numbers and improved their language skills to deal with weekend rowdies. The British embassy conceded that budget flights had brought a new type of tourist to Prague, along with a sharp increase in the consular workload: lads visiting brothels often got their passports stolen. The Czech Ministry of Foreign Affairs also urged the British government to address the problem. 'We are discussing the problem with British authorities to try to find ways to stop British men behaving violently in Prague,' said a senior official.

Czech officials remained reluctant to criticise any visitors publicly because the city wanted the money and they did not wish to admit to a problem that might put off other tourists. This was understandable, for tourism was worth 4 per cent of Czech GDP. But a form of apartheid developed in response to the rising flood of revellers. Several bar and restaurant owners in the city centre rolled up their sleeves and took action. The sign taped to the window at Legends Bar in the city read: 'Please, no groups of drunken British men allowed.'

At Prague's Bombay cocktail bar, a 'no stag groups' sign was put up when the owner finally lost patience after a fight. 'We don't allow stag parties in anymore because they cause too much trouble,' said Deepak Sharma, the manager. 'We've had problems with them in the past and like every bar right now, we don't want them. They are English guys in big numbers of ten to fifteen and think that they own the place. The main problem is fighting. A couple of times they've been really violent, also to our staff, who have been badly injured, as well as to our customers. One Czech man broke his hand after they picked on him because he was out with his girlfriend. He didn't hit them back. They were just looking for some way to create a problem.'

Moskva, a famous café, bar and restaurant looking out over Tallinn's Vabaduse Square, was another establishment that chose to limit its entry. 'If a group of young English guys tries to get in then we reject them,' said manager Timo Tirs. 'We've had tourist groups before asking for catering but if we find out that it is a group of twenty young English guys then we say no.'

Some bars tried to keep a balance between the potential profits the stag parties brought and the possibility of loutish behaviour. 'We've tried to ban the stag parties and groups of English lads altogether but we did retreat from that as we were losing business,' explained Frank Haughton, manager of Caffrey's, who said that in his experience the troublemakers were invariably English; the Scots, Irish and Welsh were well behaved. 'So since then we've tried to be selective. We have a door policy and try to make a judgement on whom to let in. We observe the ones we let in and try to identify the leader so we can make him our ally and then try to calm things down if the situation gets out of hand. Basically, we want the business and are dealing with it.'

In the meantime, Estonia's top brewery, Saku, was opening a 'beer hotel' on Tallinn's waterfront to help large numbers of marauding Brits celebrate their 'last night of freedom'. The conflicting demands of profit and local culture showed no sign of going away, and as easyJet, Ryanair and their rivals opened up more routes to former Communist countries the lives of more Eastern Europeans and their cities would change irrevocably.

13. Home abroad

EASTERN EUROPE IS not the only region to have been changed for ever by the cheap flights phenomenon. At one time, Marbella was synonymous with Britain's movie stars and bank robbers. Recently it has seemed that the Spanish town is becoming more akin to Cheshire-on-Sea. According to Costa del Sol estate agents, some 12,000 properties were built in Marbella in 2002. A study of the real estate figures showed that 70 per cent of all new development purchases in the Spanish town were snapped up by the British and of these buyers around 60 per cent hailed from Cheshire.

Marbella-based Cheshire Estates opened its first UK branch – in Wilmslow – to meet growing demand. 'The demand for Spanish properties among people in Cheshire is phenomenal,' commented manager John Eason. 'Since we opened the UK branch, we have been inundated with enquiries. I think it is a lot to do with the broad wealth of people in Cheshire; anybody who knows the Costa del Sol realises it is not just millionaires and glitzy lifestyle.'

EasyJet and bmibaby flights from Liverpool and Manchester provide the explanation for the migration of the new Cheshire set. Many people are happier to jump on an easyJet flight than to head up the M6 motorway to traditional weekend getaway spots such as the Lake District. 'There are affordable properties and good investments to be made out there, coupled with the low-cost airlines, there has never been a better or easier time to buy,' Eason continued.

The thirty-seven-year-old manager, whose brother-in-law opened the Marbella branch ten years ago, lives most of the year near Macclesfield with his wife and two children. In 2004 they bought a £200,000 house on the fringes of Marbella. 'Our Spanish home is similar to the house over here,' Eason said. 'We also have lots of friends out there. It is like Cheshire in the sun.'

Many of the recent arrivals are men and women in their forties, lured by 360 days of sunshine each year, designer shops, good schools and private hospitals. 'It attracts young, good-looking people who drive around in Ferraris, looking glamorous,' the local Cheshire paper quoted a model called Miki as saying. 'The shops are fantastic too – all the designer names – and there's always a familiar face from Cheshire to chat to.'

Retired people are also attracted by the promise of a better lifestyle in the sun, with cheap links back to the homeland courtesy of the likes of easyJet. 'We don't have any regrets,' said Robert Wilson, who took early retirement and bought a £77,000 home in Spain. 'It is very relaxed and a world away from our old life. The only thing we miss are our children and grandchildren but we tend to see them quite often.' Others enjoyed a more relaxed lifestyle overseas and simply commuted back to the UK for work. John Williams describes himself as 'one of the easyJet generation'. He lives in Spain with his wife and two-year-old daughter, Chloe, and works as a website designer, taking cheap flights to the UK for business meetings every few weeks.

Owning a property abroad has suddenly become an achievable goal for many people. Low interest rates, a relatively weak euro and budget airlines like easyJet and Ryanair mean it has never been cheaper to get to mainland Europe. Before they knew it, would-be buyers could be rubbing shoulders with Claudia Schiffer in Malaga, Elton John in the south of France or Madonna and Cliff Richard in Portugal.

Cheap flights, the promise of sunshine and a slower pace of life prompted more than half a million people to buy a property abroad in 2003, according to a survey by market analysts Mintel. Aviation analysts believed that 15 per cent of all passengers on low-cost flights to southern Europe from the UK were on house-hunting missions. Mintel found that Spain was the most popular country for Britons seeking a holiday home, with 41 per cent of overseas properties bought on the mainland, in the Balearics and Canary Islands. Britons bought 84,000 second homes in Spain between 2001 and 2003, with most properties having a swimming pool and easy access to supermarkets and airports. France was second in popularity, with 32 per cent of overseas properties bought by Britons seeking 'la vie en rose', followed by other European countries, with 10 per cent.

'The time to buy in Europe has probably never been better, with estate agents reporting large numbers of Britons seeking to buy cut-price second homes,' commented the Council for Mortgage Lenders, the trade body representing banks and building societies. Mintel predicted that the value of UK Spanish property market, already worth £12 billion, would reach £21 billion within five years. By then, the company estimated that a further 99,000 new properties would have been sold to disillusioned Britons seeking a better quality of life abroad.

Of those with homes in Spain, 65 per cent said they were attracted by the climate, 45 per cent wanted to spend more time outdoors and 40 per cent were lured by the cheaper cost of living. Tony Holmes and his wife Elisabeth had just bought a villa near Malaga in Spain for £146,000 for themselves and their children, Shaun, eight, and Melissa, five. 'It has always been our dream to buy overseas and we'll eventually retire there – but for now it's a holiday home,' Tony explained. 'Friends recommended a Spanish lawyer who speaks perfect English, and all the documents were translated and verified before we signed. Elisabeth and the kids will spend the school holidays there and I'll join them as much as I can. The kids are even learning Spanish.'

Property-mad Brits were attracted by the fact that houses in Europe were on average cheaper than in Britain. The average price of second homes owned in Europe was £109,000 in 2003, and a run-down property in north-east France could go for as little as £25,000, according to the Council for Mortgage Lenders. On the Costa del Sol, apartments and small two-bedroom properties, usually with a communal garden and swimming pool, were readily available in seaside resorts from about £48,000, and larger, individual properties in the area started at about £100,000. Estate agents advertised bungalows in retirement villages in Malaga for £92,000. Two-thirds of buyers rented out their second home, while the rest used it as a holiday house or a long-term investment, according to the Council for Mortgage Lenders.

Many people remortgaged their own home to provide some or all of the finance for a second home abroad, and British buyers were contributing to a sharp increase in property prices. Data from the Royal Institution of Chartered Surveyors showed that house prices rose by about 15 per cent in 2003 in both France and Spain after similar double-digit rises in the previous year. Portugal and Italy saw a slower pace of price increases, closer to 6 or 7 per cent. Legal experts warned that while property abroad often seemed cheaper than the UK, it would probably take longer to complete the purchase, and that it would often be more expensive in terms of agent fees, local taxes and legal costs. One solicitor said: 'Study the domestic laws of the country you are moving to, you may find out you will be paying the legal costs of the seller as well as your own.'

Property dreams can quickly turn into nightmares. Some people signed the wrong contract and ended up with a different house from the one they thought they had bought, while others discovered that property developers didn't actually own the land in the first place. The dream certainly turned sour for Bob and Jane Alburg, who paid £120,000 for a substantial villa on the Costa Blanca that was supposed to be finished in 2003. A year later, it still wasn't complete and the Alburgs feared the unscrupulous developer who sold them the property would never build it. Their position was made worse because they did not have the completed deeds to the property, having merely signed the preliminary sales contract with the developer.

Still, the overseas property boom continued, and easyJet took plentiful advantage of it. The airline included adverts for estate agents, finance brokers and lawyers specialising in overseas purchases in its in-flight magazine, along with features explaining how best to buy a property in areas served by the airline. Homebuyers quickly learnt to buy close to low-cost airline destinations if they wanted to make money. 'The basic rules that property investors need to apply are how close is the property to an airport and how often there are flights,' said Mike Hayes, editor of *Home Overseas* magazine. 'If you are more than half an hour away from an international airport, then your rental potential drops by 20 per cent.'

'We've seen a steady increase in overseas property over the last couple of years and have seen a lot of more savvy investors,' Hayes continued. 'A third of the market is looking for retirement homes, a third is looking for holiday homes and a further third is looking at property as an investment. The latter third is keeping an eye in particular on low-cost airlines. The Central and Eastern European capitals are full of history and very cheap and are becoming massive weekend break markets. The property investors are certainly looking to follow the low-cost airlines to these destinations.'

A new low-cost flight on the map marked the spot of a future invasion by British homebuyers. Areas of Spain that were neglected before, such as the south-west Atlantic coast of Andalucia, were being opened up to homeowners thanks to the promise of low-cost flights to a new airport, said George Sell, editor of *Viva España* magazine. On the eastern coast in the Valencia area, a new airport was being constructed at Castellon, between Barcelona and Valencia.

'The property market and the tourism market are literally licking their lips and getting ready for a new influx of Brits,' said Sell. 'It is expected to be one of the next hot spots, directly as a result of the new airport and the entry of a low-cost carrier. Low-cost flights are a major, major factor in people buying property overseas and where they buy.'

The French department of Gers was also seeing growing numbers of Brits, thanks to the easyJet service to nearby Toulouse and Ryanair flights to other airports in the region. Jamie Crewe moved his young family from Sussex to Gers after tiring of life as an investment banker. He explained what prompted their life-changing decision: 'Rainy mornings, getting up at 5 a.m. and never seeing my children were enough to make me go – plus the fact that we're still young, so why not give it a blast?' In 2003, Crewe bought a 'great, big, old farmhouse, a ruin' and moved his children into the local school. At first they were the sole British pupils but in 2004 five other English pupils joined them, as purchases and enquiries from British buyers continued to rise following the introduction of easyJet flights.

'We've been getting so many recent requests for this region that we've decided to expand into the area,' said one local agent. But he sounded a note of caution to potential buyers over easyJet's new route: 'It's great when budget airlines expand their routes but this should not be the main factor that buyers base their decisions upon. After all, what if something happens and the airline pulls off the route?'

UK buyers were increasingly seeking second homes on the Costa Blanca, located in south-eastern Spain and including the resorts of Alicante and Benidorm. The Costa Blanca enjoyed 320 days of sunshine annually and an average temperature of 20 degrees Celsius. The World Health Organisation described the region as the healthiest place to live in Europe because of its temperate climate. It had also been changed forever by mass tourism.

The northern part of the region remained largely agricultural, with orange, lemon and olive groves in picturesque valleys, complemented by attractive and historic seaside towns. The southern part of the region, dubbed the Golf Coast, offered more than thirteen championship golf courses between Alicante and La Manga, with ten more planned or under construction. What was more, flying time with easyJet from the UK to Alicante took just two-and-a-half hours.

Ultra Villas Ltd of Cheltenham, an international estate agency offering UK buyers knowledge of the Costa Blanca property market, was currently expanding its operations north to the Costa del Azahar, an area relatively unknown to British property buyers. Huge investment was planned in the wake of the announcement that Valencia would host the Americas Cup in 2007. Low-cost flights with easyJet to Valencia, Alicante and Barcelona was making the area more accessible for Britons wanting to be among the first to invest in properties at prices around two-thirds of those for comparable homes on the Costa del Sol. 'Clients are aware of low-cost carriers and they look for ease of access, to and from the airport, when looking at property,' said Steven Grist, business development director of Ultra Villas Ltd. 'I'm a property owner myself in Alicante and know that I can get from door to door in six hours at less than the cost of a train to London.'

Ultra Villas was also expanding its operations west to the Costa del Almeria in the Andalucia region of southern Spain. The area, which offered spectacular scenery, beautiful beaches and the best weather in Spain, had seen little development so property prices were affordable. Typically a three-bedroom, two-bathroom villa with a private pool twenty minutes from the coast could be bought for as little as £120,000.

But the main reason the estate agency was attracted to the area was the introduction of easyJet's flights to Almeria airport, making it more accessible by air from the UK. The airport had just been opened up to international airlines and the former San Javea military airport was to be replaced by a large, new international airport in 2006. 'Nine out of ten of our clients are happy flying to their second home with low-cost airlines,' said Grist. 'After all it is only a short flight. We subsidise the flights for people who want to view a property and use low-cost airlines as it makes more commercial sense for our business.'

Investors could only hope that beautiful Almeria wouldn't be taken over by an orgy of building as mass tourism turned Andalucia into yet another Costa del Concrete. After forty years of breakneck development, vast stretches of the Spanish coast are built on, including three-fifths of the Andalucian seafront. The Spanish government is even considering buying seaside land itself to stop developers getting their hands on it. Some 70 per cent of the Costa del Sol is already choked in concrete and asphalt. Irish pubs offering Guinness, cafés selling English breakfasts and uninspiring, high-rise apartment blocks litter the view between Torremolinos and Marbella. Greenpeace believe that almost 45,000 houses have been constructed illegally and that 34 per cent of the first kilometre of Spain's Mediterranean coast is built up; around Malaga the figure rises to over 50 per cent. And yet more people keep on buying. In 2003, 1.7 million Spanish homes were owned by foreigners, mostly from the EU. Acute environmental problems have ensued. Development in the wrong locations has destroyed beaches; in Malaga's coastal area alone, 150,000 cubic metres of sand are being added artificially. And unplanned urban growth has caused pollution problems. In July 2004, the European Commission said that almost 200

Spanish municipalities did not respect guidelines on urban sewage for towns of more than 15,000 inhabitants.

Always on the look-out for attractive and unspoilt areas, the estate agency was considering Croatia and Cyprus for possible future properties, as it knew that easyJet was hoping to add the destinations to its network. 'Whether a low-cost airline flies to a destination has a major impact on our decision-making,' continued Grist. 'Low-cost airlines bring a new market to that region. We take stock every time we hear that there is a new route opened up by a low-cost carrier somewhere. There has been a tremendous upsurge in business to Alicante, for example, following the introduction of easyJet flights there. About 25 per cent of passengers on an easyJet flight to Alicante will be either looking at property there or going back to spend time at their property there.'

Meanwhile, the city of Barcelona was emerging as a desirable place for Britons to buy second homes in Spain. A new breed of 'Barça Brits' could be heard converting square metres into feet as they ogled the property brochures and nibbled tapas around the bars in Las Ramblas. The number of Britons buying and looking to buy holiday homes in the Catalan capital rose more than five-fold between the start of 2003 and mid-2004 according to Spanish Property Insight, a company that helped foreigners buy in Spain by introducing them to companies and professionals. Prices were rising by a London-like 20 per cent a year and by up to 50 per cent in the most fashionable districts of the city – to the delight of foreign investors, but less so of Barcelona's inhabitants, many of whom found themselves priced out by the British incomers.

EasyJet flew to the Spanish city from the UK airports of Newcastle, Liverpool, Bristol, Stansted, Luton and Gatwick. The budget airline also offered flights to Barcelona from Paris Orly, Basel-Mulhouse, Geneva, Dortmund and Berlin. Some 1.1 million easyJet passengers were expected to board the low-cost carrier bound for Barcelona by the end of summer 2005. Indeed, Barcelona was easyJet's second most popular summer city break, topped only by Amsterdam, with 2 million passengers due to fly there in summer 2005. 'Britons used to head straight for the Costa del Sol or the "pueblos blancos" of Andalucia without thinking, but they are realising that the real gem of Spain is Barcelona,' commented Mark Stucklin, who ran Spanish Property Insight. 'Barcelona is enjoying a cracking overseas property boom and Britons are big players.'

John Weller was one of the new UK investors in the city. He 'fell in love' with Barcelona and splashed out almost £200,000 on a one-bedroom flat in the newly hip Borne district. The Weller family visited their second home four or five times a year. Among the Wellers' neighbours were Graeme Jones, who had invested a similar sum in a three-bedroomed modern flat in a converted nineteenth-century tenement block, and Robert Collins, who had bought a £220,000 duplex flat. The Wellers, the Jones family and Collins all saw Barcelona as the perfect second-home city, largely because budget airlines made it cheap and easy to get to. 'My son studies, works and plays here, while my wife and I can enjoy terrific culture, good shopping and lazy days on the beach,' Weller explained.

Collins praised Barcelona as a 'proper international city, not a holiday resort'. The city beat the Costas any day, they all agreed. 'We've seen all the unspeakable, football-shirted trash that gathers in the concrete jungles of the Costa del Sol and we don't want any of that,' said Weller. Jones added: 'I'd never invest down south. We've had some great holidays in Marbella, but two weeks of sun, sand and sangria is quite enough.'

Stucklin chucked at the Barça Brits' criticism of the Costa del Sol, where holidaymakers had been flocking to enjoy kids' menus, shopping malls and Robin Hood pubs after Franco opened up Spain to the world in the 1960s. 'Ah, the penny has finally dropped,' he said. 'People may now realise that if you sit around all day in a manicured, culture-free golf resort, reading the *Daily Express* and drinking beer with a bunch of perma-tanned expats, you end up a miserable old alcoholic. Barcelona isn't for everybody but it is perfect for sophisticated people looking for a Mediterranean climate, beautiful architecture and a stimulating cultural environment close to great beaches and mountains.'

EasyJet may have pledged to bring flying to the masses but it wasn't only blue-collared workers boarding the airline. Some flights, such as those to the new stag destinations of Prague and Tallinn, may have attracted the shaven-headed type of punter whose main aim was getting drunk. Other flights, meanwhile, were full of more discerning passengers with fat wallets who were off to visit their overseas property. The rich people who set up home in sunnier climes provided a major boost to easyJet's passenger numbers. The advent of cheap flights might have meant that people could afford an annual trip to Malaga rather than to Blackpool but the real boom in air travel was caused largely by a rich minority taking several foreign holidays a year, according to figures released from the Civil Aviation Authority in November 2004.

Poorer people tended either not to fly at all or to make only one trip abroad a year, according to the CAA figures. Second homeowners took an average of six return flights a year. By contrast, half the population did not fly at all, and a further 25 per cent took only one trip abroad in a year. The CAA's figures, based on 180,000 interviews at airports, revealed that even at Stansted, where low-cost airlines such as easyJet accounted for nearly all the flights, the average income of British passengers was more than £50,000. Even low fares were failing to tempt the poorest section of society to fly; a smaller proportion of them took to the skies in 2003 than in 2002. Those in social groups D and E, which covered low-skilled workers and people on benefits, took only 6 per cent of the total flights in 2004, despite making up 27 per cent of the population. At the opposite end of the scale, the As and Bs, the professionals and senior managers who made up 24 per cent of the population, took 40 per cent of flights.

Of course, the richer passengers flew with the airline more often; and many of the lower-paid passengers who flew with easyJet wouldn't have contemplated travelling abroad before easyJet made flying affordable. And those passengers who previously flew with charter carriers were often choosing to fly with budget carriers instead. The proportion of passengers at UK airports flying on UK scheduled airlines reached 50.1 per cent in 2004, its highest level for the last twenty years, an increase of 8.9 million passengers on 2003, according to the CAA. This contrasted with the proportion of passengers at UK airports flying on UK charter carriers which, at 15.1 per cent in 2004, reached its lowest level in the last twenty years, a decrease of 1.3 million passengers on 2003. Still, the CAA figures undermined the government's argument that airports must be allowed to expand so that less affluent families could continue to enjoy the benefits of air travel. The UK government proposed constructing new runways at Stansted, Heathrow, Birmingham and Edinburgh to accommodate an expected surge in passenger numbers – the total number of flights was expected to grow from 200 million in 2003 to 500 million in 2030. Ministers claimed that the average return air fare would rise by more than £100 unless new runways were built.

John Stewart, chairman of ClearSkies, which campaigned against airport expansion, responded: 'The CAA's figures show that the massive expansion in air travel planned by the Government will almost entirely benefit the rich. The absence of any tax on aviation fuel or VAT on air tickets amounts to a £9 billion subsidy for the better off to enjoy their jet-setting lifestyle.' Stewart also argued that the CAA survey also challenged the Government's claim that expansion was necessary to help British companies to do business overseas; it showed that leisure air travel was growing three times faster than business air travel and in 2003 accounted for 77 per cent of all flights.

EasyJet said that the CAA survey confirmed its own

findings that the rapid growth in budget airlines was being fuelled by people with very high disposable incomes who booked dozens of trips a year. 'We have at least 1,000 people who fly every week from London to their second homes in Nice, Malaga, Palma and Barcelona,' said an easyJet spokesman. 'There is a misconception that budget airlines are used mainly by people on lower incomes. If you are in the airport car park at Luton, you will find it full of BMWs and Mercedes.'

14. Kicking up a fuss

IN MARCH 2004, a group of fifteen friends on their way to Portugal for a golf weekend were banned from easyJet for life for an unusual misdemeanour. 'When the plane landed at Faro we discovered some of them had urinated in their seats and seat back pockets,' said easyJet spokeswoman Samantha Day. 'We are absolutely disgusted and we won't welcome them on easyJet ever again.'

One golfer was told to leave the flight before take-off when his boisterous behaviour towards staff turned 'abusive', Day added. The rest of the group, from Cardiff and Abergavenny, South Wales, carried on with the trip and only became aware of the ban from the airline when they tried to check in for their return flight. They were forced to make their own way back from Faro, costing each of them an additional £170.

Outraged by their treatment, the golfers demanded that easyJet prove its claim that they had urinated on the seats. Bob Bennett, forty-eight, denied easyJet's accusation, saying:

'Nobody would do that on a plane. I got up ten minutes into the flight to tell the stewardess my seat was damp. She brought me a different seat cushion and that was it. I am absolutely appalled at easyJet's claim. Let's have the evidence.' Steve Pandeli, another member of the party, added: 'It is ludicrous what easyJet has been saying. If there had been other people in the crowd doing that we would have been the first to put a stop to it. The main issue isn't compensation; it is about our own reputations. I couldn't care less if I don't fly with easyJet again.'

Whether Bob and his friends relieved themselves in easyJet's seat pockets or made use of the aircraft's sole lavatory remained to be proved. Possibly the most amazing thing about the incident was that such behaviour was perceived as possible on-board an aircraft. Flying was no longer a case of hoping that the passenger next to you didn't snore or jostle for elbowroom on the arm-rest. In-flight entertainment was clearly changing for the worse. Unruly behaviour in the skies was increasing at an astonishing rate in terms of both numbers and severity of incidents.

Air rage wasn't purely a low-cost phenomenon. All airlines suffered from it. Air-rage incident after incident filled the newspaper headlines as abusive passengers turned their aggression against other travellers and often against flight crew. But two factors seemed particularly likely to provoke air rage among low-cost airline passengers. The first was delays. Passengers grew frustrated by the fact that budget carriers often not only failed to inform them why their plane was late but adopted a 'you get what you paid for' attitude towards them. The second factor was the tendency of 'the lads' to use low-fare carriers for their alcohol-fuelled jaunts abroad. In one incident, two men from Ireland allegedly pinned a female flight attendant against the wall of the plane and attempted to sexually assault her during an easyJet flight from Belfast to Liverpool's John Lennon Airport. Both men, in their early thirties, had been drinking.

EasyJet invested heavily in staff training to ensure all employees were able to deal with any situation – no matter how violent. A conflict management course taught staff to calm and even restrain passengers if necessary. 'Obviously restraint is a last resort, but if you are flying at thousands of feet you can't allow a violent passenger to run riot on an aircraft,' explained Samantha Day. 'The course deals primarily with how to calm people.'

Sometimes staff decided that the easiest way to deal with troublesome passengers was simply to stop them from boarding the aircraft, such as the case of one easyJet pilot, who refused to allow 127 drunken Rangers and Celtic fans on an easyJet flight from Glasgow to Belfast after a Scottish Premier League clash at Ibrox. However, angry passengers in Glasgow blamed the trouble on flight delays. 'We were kept waiting at the airport for ages,' complained Gavin Doyle of Dublin. 'There was nothing else for the fans to do but sit in the bars.' The bars were eventually closed in a bid to stop the fans drinking through the night. Airport officials then had to bring in police with dogs after fights broke out. By morning, the passengers were subdued and headed home to Belfast, after being asked to remove scarves and turn all football shirts inside out.

It wasn't just men who were guilty of behaving badly on-board aircraft. Estelle Willoughby was one of the female passengers who were guilty of air rage on an easyJet plane. Willoughby downed three bottles of red wine on the flight before she decided to get to know her fellow travellers by shoving cigarettes in their faces. The drunken woman then stunned easyJet air crew at 35,000 feet during a flight from Copenhagen to Bristol when she put on her rucksack and tried to leave the aircraft, announcing, 'I'm getting off.' She was arrested at Bristol but not before biting stewardess Kelly Brewer on the hand and kicking a police driver. She later told North Somerset magistrates that she had recently lost her job as a mobile phone worker and her relationship had broken up.

But it wasn't just easyJet passengers who were accused of air rage. In well-publicised incidents on other airlines, passengers beat up crew members and even sexually assaulted their own seats. Electrician Lee Thresher was imprisoned for fifteen years for attacking two passengers and punching out part of a window on a British Airways flight from London to Bangkok during which he had been drinking. The pilot had to divert to Delhi.

The question was what caused such atrocious behaviour. One likely trigger was the stress caused by cramming people in an enclosed, claustrophobic space and restricting their movement, industry experts concluded. 'Flying in a plane is a particular set of circumstances and produces a particular set of problems,' explained Dr Helen Muir, a professor of aerospace psychology at Cranfield University. 'That some people cannot cope with those circumstances is not so surprising. If you put mice into a small cage and heat it, they will end up eating one another.'

Leading health expert Professor John Ashton, the UK's North-West Director of Public Health, criticised the cramped conditions economy class travellers faced and called on the industry to plough profits into passenger improvements. 'Evidence is stacking up about the restrictive conditions causing deep vein thrombosis,' he warned. 'When you take that together with recycled air causing respiratory infections and people being cooped up in cramped conditions that can cause fear and panic, it is obvious that things must change. Poor conditions like these turn planes into slave ships without oars and are conducive to air rage, especially when alcohol is available on-board. It is time something was done to improve air travel, especially as the number of flights is expected to increase substantially in the next decade.'

Alcohol makes matters worse as it restricts the amount of oxygen that flows to the brain. A glass of alcohol in the air has the same effect as two on the ground, and the same applies to any recreational drugs. Smoking bans irritate already frayed nerves and have played a part in air-rage increases.

One thing guaranteed to enrage passengers is the chaotic stampede that often results from easyJet's policy of not allocating seats. Mark from Munich dubbed his last flight with easyJet 'a real farce' as he fought to find a place for himself, his wife and his eighteen-month-old daughter. 'We were pleased that we wouldn't have to struggle to get a seat as easyJet tried to board elderly passengers and families with small children first,' he recalled. 'How wrong we were. After our boarding pass was checked, we passed through a door and went down an escalator only to be confronted with a closed door and a bus waiting on the other side to take us to the plane. After a few minutes, all the other passengers were checked through and joined us at the closed doors. It wasn't long before my family and I were squashed against the still closed doors, waiting to get onto the bus. Eventually the doors opened and the free-for-all scramble began as passengers fought to claim a seat on the bus. But that was nothing compared with the fight onboard as we struggled to find seats next to one another. I just don't understand the point of boarding the elderly and young first!'

Laura Wood from London was also enraged by easyJet's policy of not allocating seats. 'I got to the airport four hours before my flight, sat down and watched how all the Germans had already started queuing to make sure they got seats at the front,' she remembered. 'It was ridiculous. Some of them sent their kids to the front of the queue and told them to sit down and make room for them. There was loads of pushing and shoving. When a gate change was announced, I couldn't believe how fast people ran and shoved others out of the way! I felt like I was being pushed along in a herd of cows.'

Sitting around in an airport terminal for hours on end doubtless doesn't calm passengers' nerves. The International Air Transport Association, which represents the industry, suggested that airlines could reduce the potential causes of disruption by trying harder to ensure that flights left on time and explaining why when they didn't. 'The best information should be relayed to people at all times to release tension,' said a spokesman.

Occasionally easyJet employees managed to assuage rising tempers with a sense of humour. One passenger who was waiting at Luton Airport for a delayed flight to Amsterdam was spotted berating an easyJet representative, who responded: 'I'm sorry, sir, but what else do you want me to do?'

'Sing me a carol,' shot back the angry customer. The hapless rep left his desk, rustled up a couple of colleagues, and broke into an apt rendition of *In the Bleak Midwinter*, which seemed to do the trick.

Other passengers, such as the group of easyJet passengers who were delayed twenty-one hours on their way to Belfast, needed more than a burst of song to cheer their spirits. The group's flight from Luton was turned back because of a technical problem. Some then took the option of travelling to Liverpool in the hope of catching an alternative flight but were left stranded because of severe fog and a power failure. One of the passengers, Simon Corless, described the delays they encountered. 'They drove us from Luton, through the night, to Liverpool. From there, we were stuck in a minibus. We never had overnight accommodation or anything. When we got here to get on the plane, to book in, the plane never came. It was delayed due to fog. The service has been terrible.'

EasyJet insisted that it had done 'everything in its power' to take care of them. Indeed, easyJet tended to be praised for its punctuality. The airline published weekly punctuality data on its website. For the week ending 7 August 2005, for example, 74 per cent of all easyJet flights were on time and 94 per cent arrived within an hour.

Simple mishaps caused other delays. Thousands of passengers were left stranded in May 2004 when easyJet cancelled eighteen flights and grounded forty planes after forgetting to put vital insurance documents on-board its fleet. The documents were legally required to be present on the plane for inspection, and more than ten airports in the UK and overseas were plunged into chaos as pilots refused to fly. The cock-up delayed 5,000 holidaymakers by up to eight hours.

Sometimes people resorted to a peaceful protest to express their discontent, such as the group of easyJet passengers who staged a sit-in protest. The problems started when a flight from Nice to Luton was grounded because of technical problems. EasyJet decided to move its passengers onto another aircraft, while a new aircraft was flown in from Britain. But the passengers refused to get off. One passenger told the BBC: 'All of the passengers on our flight protested. There were chants of "no, no, no" and "everyone stay on the plane" and "don't let them do this to us".' The protest resulted in delays of as long as five hours for two other easyJet flights. Their 280 passengers received full compensation but those who staged the sit-in weren't reimbursed.

Other passengers arrived on time at their destination but were then wound up by their experience in the airport terminal. Jesenka Veledar from Bosnia was pleased to see her suitcase appear on the luggage carousel after her flight with easyJet to London. But she wasn't so pleased to discover that her bag had been destroyed. 'It had a huge cut down the side and had clearly been mishandled,' she lamented. 'It was too badly damaged to use again so I bought a new one for the return journey.' She then couldn't believe her eyes when she landed after her return flight and found her new suitcase in tatters. 'The pockets on the outside were torn from top to bottom and one of the wheels was broken. It looked a right mess. So one short flight had cost me two suitcases!

'I would fly with easyJet again as it represents the cheapest deal,' Veledar admitted. 'This time, though, I've bought an indestructible-looking Samsonite suitcase that I've been assured can easily be replaced if need be. I don't want to risk losing another suitcase!'

Travellers also became irritated when they experienced

poor customer service or hostile staff attitudes. Often the problems started at the check-in desk. Norwegian Gunvor Ellingsen described how she was left nearly in tears after 'rude' check-in staff stopped her from boarding her flight with easyJet. Like many fellow passengers, Ellingsen was already stressed when she arrived at the airport after initially forgetting her passport and then battling through London traffic. On getting to the airport, she was relieved to find out that her flight had been delayed by forty-five minutes.

'I ran with my two suitcases to the check-in desk and waited there, only to be told by a sour-faced woman that I was at the wrong desk,' Ellingsen recalled. 'The check-in woman pointed instead to a long queue. Eventually I reached the front of the queue, and feeling very stressed and trying not to cry, I explained my situation to the easyJet employee behind the counter.

'He wasn't at all sympathetic. There was still forty minutes before the flight was due to take off but he insisted that I had to be there forty minutes before the original flight time to get on the flight. I was so upset by the way I was treated.'

EasyJet was particularly slated for its treatment of disabled passengers. In May 2004, easyJet gave compensation of £500 each and free flights to eleven people turfed off a flight minutes before it took off because they were deaf. The friends, from a centre for the deaf in Liverpool, were going to Amsterdam for the weekend in October 2003 when the pilot booted them off. 'EasyJet has apologised profusely for the humiliation and embarrassment they caused,' said the group's spokesman, Geoff Noon. 'But those involved still feel very bitter at their treatment.' Peter Edwards, the solicitor representing those involved, commented: 'One can't imagine the distress they suffered when they were told at the last minute that they would not be able to fly. The fact is that a group of people were denied the right to travel simply because they have a disability.'

EasyJet argued that the disabled people didn't have enough

carers and therefore threatened the safety of the flight, since rules stated that flight crew must be able to evacuate the plane within ninety seconds. The group were later allowed on a different flight after another easyJet pilot overturned the decision, but not before losing precious hours of their holiday. One passenger said: 'The pilot thought that because we were deaf we would not be able to follow emergency instructions. He made us feel like young children.'

EasyJet vowed to retrain its staff to handle disabled people better, but just five days after winning their apology from easyJet, one of the group members was again stopped because of his disability before boarding an easyJet flight. Sign language teacher Steve McKenna was told that he would not be able to understand emergency procedures as he tried to board his return Liverpool-bound plane at Belfast International Airport.

'I felt reassured flying with easyJet because I thought they had learned their lesson,' McKenna recalled wryly. 'The flight to Belfast was fine, and then it happened. A member of the flight crew approached me as I walked through the departure gate. She was trying to speak to me then got into a panic as she realised I am deaf. She was using huge mouth gestures, which made it even more difficult for me to understand. After speaking to the pilot she returned and we could not take off. It was only after they took advice that I was allowed onto the plane. The plane was late taking off and there was great hostility from other passengers. The trip to Belfast was for an international sign language conference – none of the other delegates were treated in this way.'

Just a couple of days later, easyJet caused further embarrassment when it tried to stop thirteen students with learning difficulties flying back from a football tournament, where they represented Wales. The eighteen- to twenty-two-year-olds and five staff had flown with the low-cost airline to Geneva but were initially told they could not board the return flight because they did not have a high enough ratio of carers to students. Student Andy Brown said: 'It's disgusting the way they treated us just because we had a disability.'

The football players – none of whom had severe physical or behavioural problems – were eventually let on the plane after other passengers said they would act as carers. But they were made to wait until everyone else had boarded the jet to Liverpool. 'We have been treated like shit,' complained student David Byrne. Their college, Pengwern in Rhuddlan, North Wales, wrote to easyJet to complain, urging the airline to change its policy on disabled passengers. EasyJet defended its actions by arguing that there should be one carer for two disabled people to evacuate the cabin within ninety seconds in an emergency.

Barry Smith was another disabled passenger who suffered from easyJet's actions. Twenty-five-year-old Smith, who had cerebral palsy, flew from his home in Glasgow for a two-week holiday at a disabled centre in the Midlands. But when he tried to board the return flight, staff at East Midlands Airport told him he could not fly back to Glasgow alone. Instead he had to travel back by train.

Smith's distraught mother, Yvonne, accused easyJet of 'blatant discrimination'. 'They left him stranded,' she fumed. 'They did nothing to help him. He was beside himself with fear and is still very upset.' EasyJet employees admitted they had made a 'huge error' and offered Barry and his mother free return flights on any of their routes, once again promising to put together a new, improved policy for disabled travellers.

EasyJet wasn't the only budget airline to be criticised for its approach towards disabled customers. In January 2004 Ryanair lost a discrimination case brought by a man forced to pay £18 to use a wheelchair – nearly twice the cost of his £10 flight to the South of France. The Central London County Court ruled that Ryanair acted unlawfully by not providing Bob Ross, who had cerebral palsy and arthritis, with a wheelchair free of charge at Stansted Airport. Ross needed the wheelchair for the half-mile journey from check-in desk to departure gate and had to hire one instead. Ryanair immediately described the judgement as 'defective' and imposed a 50p levy on all of its flights to compensate, which it described as a 'wheelchair tax'.

Ryanair's move was condemned as 'obscene' by the Irish Wheelchair Association. 'The levy is low and grotesque, even by Ryanair standards,' said assocation spokesman Olan McGowan. 'Other airlines, including Aer Lingus, absorb the cost of wheelchairs. They hire them for their disabled passengers and pay for them.' Indeed, all other airlines, including budget and charter carriers, met the cost of the service. British Airways offered disability awareness training for all customer service staff and said it was 'delighted' to carry on-board wheelchairs or mobility aids for passengers with additional needs.

It was clear that easyJet and its fellow low-cost airlines still had some lessons to learn about service. Simon Evans, spokesman for the Air Transport Users' Council, the government-funded consumer watchdog, estimated that the council received proportionally more complaints about the main low-cost airlines than it did about other 'full-service' carriers. The council added that a rise in complaints about cancelled flights was probably due to the increased number of low-fare airlines. Figures released by the watchdog showed complaints by passengers about cancelled flights rose to 740 in the twelve months to March in 2004, compared to 558 in 2003 and 354 in 2002.

'The increase in complaints about cancellations is becoming a cause for concern,' commented the council's chairman. 'It appears likely that the rise in no-frills traffic is fuelling the surge. So while we commend the success of no-frills carriers in bringing down fares and hugely expanding the range of destinations on offer, we call on them to convince us that the inconvenience and financial costs suffered by passengers when flights are cancelled are not the flipside to the benefits these airlines bring air passengers.'

The problem for passengers was that they were used to being looked after by an airline when things went wrong. Because low-cost carriers worked to tight margins, they tended not to offer the sort of back-up that passengers had grown used to. Evans said that low-cost carriers as a group were far less generous with compensation and tended to fall back on the strict conditions of carriage, which left passengers with very few clear rights.

For example, if a flight was heavily delayed, or cancelled, passengers were not even entitled to a free cup of tea while they waited – let alone the proper refreshments and overnight accommodation that traditional airlines offered. Evans said he had come across many cases where customers had simply been offered refunds or told that they might have to wait days for the next available flight.

But it seemed that many easyJet passengers were prepared to put up with problems if they felt they were getting a good deal. A survey by the Consumers' Association magazine *Holiday Which?* provided an authoritative account of what passengers thought of low-cost airlines. The survey rated all the budget airlines poorly for their catering, legroom, seat comfort and the cleanliness of the toilets. Yet when rated overall, easyJet was in the top ten places in the survey, above major short-haul airlines such as KLM, Air France, British Airways and all the charter operators. Ryanair came halfway down the table. Passengers' perceptions that they were getting value for money often overrode their discontent.

Some disgruntled passengers preferred to put up a fight rather than accept any mishap. One such passenger was Brian Camp, a solicitor from Merseyside, who won undisclosed damages against easyJet after beginning legal action following a cancelled flight to Paris. He had planned to celebrate his wife Julie's fifty-third birthday, in the company of four friends, with a sumptuous meal in a private dining room aboard a bateau mouche on the River Seine. When the party arrived at Liverpool's John Lennon Airport they were pleased to see that their flight was on time. But, according to Camp, the smiling staff already knew the plane would be going nowhere because there was no flight crew available. He claimed he had learned that easyJet was aware the flight would not operate hours before it was due to take off, and alleged that staff went through a charade of checking in would-be passengers, knowing they would face a fruitless wait.

EasyJet said the problems were caused by delays earlier in the day which were out of their control. 'We did have some disruption during the day which was a combination of air traffic control delays and the effects of a new rostering system,' a spokesman explained. 'This flight was supposed to depart at 19.50 and was delayed to 21.00 but the crew was running out of hours. This meant they would not have been able to operate all the way to Paris. All the other crews were working because we had had delays. We did do everything we could to avoid cancelling this flight. Safety is paramount at easyJet and we accept that, last thing at night, a cancelled flight causes lots of problems. We offered transfers, hotels and refunds.'

The solicitor demanded £10,000 in compensation and encouraged all his fellow disappointed passengers to follow suit. Eventually Camp agreed to accept damages from the airline in a private settlement, with an undertaking that he would not disclose the amount entailed.

New European draft regulations in February 2005 awarded air passengers new rights for compensation for overbooked, delayed or cancelled flights, in cases such as Camp's. The legislation, hailed as a victory by consumer groups and MEPs, meant compensation of as much as £420 for travellers who were bumped off flights due to overbooking. Serious delays also meant compensation for passengers on any EU airline flying to or from Europe, including charter flights and low-cost airlines.

Under the Brussels proposals airlines would be banned from charging elderly or disabled passengers for any special help they needed. They would also be unable to refuse such passengers permission to board their planes. About 7 million European airline passengers need special help each year. Under the new rules, European airports would be responsible for providing free assistance for these passengers, while the airlines would contribute to paying for the expenses. However, according to the Commission the costs should not amount to more than €5.9 million per year.

Jacques Barrot, the European commissioner for transport, argued that the boom in air travel needed to be backed by new consumer rights, and officials in Brussels rejected airline claims that costs would inevitably rise, dragging up ticket prices. According to the European Commission, around 250,000 air passengers were denied boarding at EU airports each year because the flights were overbooked by the airlines. Under the new laws, compensation for passengers not allowed on flights because of overbooking would be £175 for flights of 1,500km or less, with £275 in compensation for those between 1,500 and 3,500km and £420 for longer flights to destinations outside the EU.

Compensation would be the same for cancelled flights unless the carrier could prove they were not responsible or had given passengers at least two weeks' notice. Delays of at least two hours would trigger a range of benefits, from free drinks, meals and phone calls to a free hotel room when the next flight was a day away. Financial compensation was also available after five hours. Previously the maximum compensation offered by airlines had been £205 and budget carriers often offered none. Airlines failing to comply with the new rules could face substantial fines, with the Civil Aviation Authority responsible for complaints affecting UK carriers.

The measures angered the industry, which argued that it would be subject to harsher rules than competitors in other parts of the world. EasyJet said the compensation package for passengers bumped off flights was 'probably the most flawed piece of European legislation in recent years', arguing that it would damage the industry. 'We will look after our passengers and will implement the legislation,' chief executive Ray Webster promised. 'But what started as a good piece of legislation to prevent traditional airlines bumping off passengers through overbooking has become a bad piece of legislation and will cause unnecessary confusion and conflict.'

Still, at least the new rules might calm down the next passenger who was threatening to explode in a fit of air rage.

15. Viking invasion

THE VIKING DESCENDANTS landed in Luton in October 2004. EasyJet became the focus of frenzied takeover speculation after Icelandair snapped up an 8.4 per cent stake in the carrier, splashing out £50 million following a day of hectic trading.

In a statement to the stock exchange, Hannes Smárason, Icelandair's chairman, announced that the deal fitted in with the Icelandic national carrier's strategy of investing in rival companies where it had specialist knowledge. 'The Icelandic Group is financially strong and the company is seeking ways to improve the return on its cash,' Smárason explained. 'We have kept our eyes open for opportunities in airline-related securities.' Icelandair added that it would not be averse to buying more shares in easyJet in the future, since it viewed its easyJet stake as a long-term investment.

Analysts praised Icelandair's investment choice. 'I consider Icelandair to be a sensible investor as it is clearly taking the long-term view about easyJet,' commented Andrew Lobbenberg, airlines analyst at ABN Amro. 'It was a very good deal for Icelandair.'

More than 40 million shares in easyJet changed hands that day and the airline's value rose to £620 million. Shares were driven 16 per cent higher on the news, closing up 21 pence at 152p, as rumours spread through the market about Icelandair's purchase.

Icelandic investors had been among the busiest players in the UK stockmarket in recent months – led by the acquisitive group Baugur, which owned the Goldsmiths, Karen Millen, Oasis, Whistles and Coast chains in the UK and was in talks over a possible offer for Iceland-to-Booker group Big Food. Local analysts had been anticipating investment action from Smárason. The Reykjavik-based airline made little secret of its enthusiasm for overseas expansion. 'We are looking for opportunities to grow in neighbouring countries by mergers and acquisitions,' declared Smárason in an interview with Reuters news agency the week before the investment. 'Our intention is to become very aggressive.'

Educated at America's MIT university, Smárason was a former finance director of DeCode, a controversial bio-technology company that had built a database of the genetic make-up of Iceland's entire 300,000-strong population. One of Iceland's wealthiest entrepreneurs, Smárason was appointed chairman of Icelandair in March 2004 and owned 32 per cent of the airline's shares.

Established in 1937, Icelandair flew to five destinations in America and sixteen in Europe, carrying 1.1 million pas-sengers annually on its twelve Boeing 757 aircraft. Icelandair's Reykjavik hub was popular among travellers seeking a cheap route from Europe to the US. The airline employed 1,000 staff with annual profits of £11 million and a market capitalisation of £174 million. Its biggest investor, with 33 per cent of the holding company, was the Straumur Investment bank.

But the airline was only a fraction of the size of easyJet. After all, Iceland only had a population of 290,000 – fewer than easyJet carried in a week. In contrast, easyJet, at the end of 2005, operated seventy Boeing 737s and twenty-four Airbus A319s to fifty-six destinations in Europe, carrying 20.3 million passengers annually. Its employee count was 3,450 and profits had reached £96 million with a market capitalisation of £608 million.

Despite its small size, Icelandair's management had succeeded in turning the minnow perched on the edge of Europe into a canny investment fund. Icelandair was so confident the market was wrong about easyJet that it went out and sold 420 million new shares to institutional investors at 9.10 ISK per share, raising a total of 3.8 billion ISK (approximately £33.1 million). The airline combined the funds from the share sale with the £60 million in cash it had on its balance sheet to finance its investment in easyJet.

Through buying the shares, Icelandair alerted the market to the possibility that things might not be as bad in the budget airline sector as had been suggested and injected some long-term confidence back into the industry. 'I talk to Icelandair regularly,' commented JP Morgan's airline analyst Chris Avery. 'They are a very well-run small airline. They've got cash to invest and they are airline people. They know about leasing plans and average revenues and all those types of things. They've made the judgement that easyJet is the best investment of all the budget airlines – as I have.'

Another analyst also thought Icelandair had made a wise long-term investment: 'The market at the moment is garbage but in three years' time easyJet will still be here and the world will look different.'

Icelandair increased its stake in easyJet to 10.1 per cent later in October, with the purchase of an extra 6.73 million shares. 'If we want to find ways to grow, we have to look beyond Iceland,' Smárason said. 'There will be consolidation in the low-cost sector and easyJet's fundamentals are strong.' On 1 July 2005, the Icelandic airline purchased a further 2.12 million shares in easyJet, amounting to around 0.5 per cent of the company and thus increasing its stake to 11.5 per cent. Speculation mounted that a takeover bid was in the pipeline.

In common with other low-cost airlines, easyJet had been battered by high oil prices and fierce price competition, making it vulnerable to a bid. Fares had fallen to record lows and, despite the launch of dozens of new routes, the airline had warned that in 2005 it would only marginally beat the previous year's profits of £52 million. But Webster dismissed bid speculation. 'I have no idea,' he replied to questions. 'But we're delighted that at least someone recognises the under-lying value of the airline.'

Morgan Stanley analyst Penny Butcher pointed out that an outright takeover bid by Icelandair would be difficult because the Icelandic company was valued only at £180 million. '[A bid] would deviate significantly from [Icelandair's] stated business strategy which is focused almost entirely on north Atlantic routes,' she said. In addition, Icelandair would also have to get round foreign ownership laws, which put a cap of 40 per cent on overseas holdings in airlines. And any takeover of easyJet would require the consent of Stelios, whose family still owned 41 per cent of the shares.

Stelios informed easyJet that he didn't have any plans to take the airline private or sell out. He vowed always to keep a stake in easyJet, although he would not specify how big, adding that he would not support a takeover of easyJet unless he was assured that the buyer would not do anything that would tarnish the brand. 'I am not about to sell out to any Tom, Dick or Harry,' he declared. Meanwhile, easyJet could continue to act as a source of income for Stelios's burgeoning easy empire. 'I don't think that Stelios wants to sell out,' said ABN Amro's Lobbenberg. 'Stelios likes to use his stake to sell it down to provide cash for his other easyGroup companies.'

Stelios was still busy adding more creations to the easy

empire. *EasyCruiseOne*, easyCruise's first ship, embarked on its maiden voyage in May 2005. The 'floating hotel' with orange ceilings, orange walls, orange bathrooms and orange beds regularly set sail up and down the French and Italian Rivieras between St Tropez and Portofino. Holidaymakers paid as little as £20 a night on the world's first no-frills cruise liner to share a four-berth, fluorescent orange cabin. The cabins were described as 'unique' and 'minimalist' – they didn't even include windows or portholes to escape from the sheer orangeness of it all.

EasyCruise was aimed firmly at the young. Facilities on board the 88-metre, 4,077-ton ship were minimal: there was a sports bar, a coffee shop and a cocktail bar – with a hot tub. Gone were lavish gourmet dinners at the captain's table. People had to pay extra for food and drinks: a burger and chips for £3.90, or a pint of lager for £2.30. Passengers could hop on and off when they fancied but had to stay a minimum of two nights. The venture has met with initial success; more than 83 per cent of its cabins were booked in August 2005.

Meanwhile, easyJet was preparing itself for a winter of discontent as the fare wars intensified. Webster warned that the refocusing of charter carriers such as First Choice and Airtours away from the Caribbean and on to European holiday routes the previous summer was likely to continue: 'These carriers are still desperate and we are assuming that will continue again as early as January on popular ski routes.'

Package tour operators and charter airlines were reeling from the impact of easyJet, Ryanair and other low-cost carriers, which had taken away business by introducing travellers to the concept of booking cheap getaways independently. To meet the challenge, Thomson, a subsidiary of Frankfurt-based TUI, had chosen to restructure itself completely. The company launched a new carrier in December 2003 called Thomsonfly, which began scheduled service in March from

Coventry to cities on the continent for less than £20 each way. Thomas Cook's charter affiliate, Condor, was also trying to compete head-on with low-cost carriers by increasingly focusing on selling just flights rather than traditional holiday packages.

EasyJet's annual sales rose 17 per cent as passenger numbers increased 20 per cent to 24.3 million. But Webster was disappointed that softer yields, the average amount paid per customer, pushed underlying profit before tax down 11 per cent to £85.4 million. The average fare fell by £1 to £42.28, largely due to increased competition from charter airlines and budget challengers such as Ryanair and flybe.

EasyJet's next piece of news stunned the industry. In May 2005, after nearly ten years manning the airline's flight deck, Webster announced his retirement, saying that he intended to resign from the board as soon as a successor was found, although he agreed to continue in a consultancy role until 30 November 2006 before severing his ties entirely.

Webster told investors that he was leaving the airline for personal reasons. The fifty-eight-year-old New Zealander said that his time at easyJet had been the highlight of his career, but that it had come at a heavy personal cost. He continued: 'For the company, it is the right time to step down. For me, it is two years too late. I have lost my mother and father this year and that really accelerated my decision. I had hoped to spend a couple of years with them. I have a nine-year-old grandson and since he was born, I have spent three days with him, which is appalling. I love the outdoors and would love to take him and my two other grandchildren camping while I am still able to. Over the next decade, it is important to protect myself and my family.'

While Webster wasn't pushed, analysts suspected that he was probably encouraged to think about his future at the airline. 'Webster did wonderfully well at building up the airline but then he allowed the company to deteriorate quite sharply in financial terms, while Ryanair was driven far harder under rapid expansion,' said one analyst, who didn't want to be named. 'He didn't always serve as an appropriate figurehead: he wasn't a very high-profile figure internally and didn't have a great profile with investors or the public. I suspect that one of his weaknesses was building a team.'

One employee certainly didn't seem that upset by Webster's departure; a pilot who went by the nickname of 'A Tree' on PPRuNe, the pilot web message board, posted: 'Good old Ray, how we shall miss him. The man who thinks that staff travel is a waste of money and has done as little as possible to allow it to happen at easyJet.'

Webster said that he and his Parisian wife would continue to be based in London, where he hoped to build up a portfolio of non-executive and consultancy jobs. But easyJet would be his last full-time executive role, allowing him to spend more time in his native New Zealand and Australia. He said it was unlikely that he would work for another airline in any capacity.

His successor would be chosen from outside easyJet and would not necessarily be expected to have a background in aviation. 'We are a fast-moving consumer business, which carries 29 million passengers a year,' the company said. 'We will be looking for consumer-driven experience.' Webster said that headhunters had already been appointed and that he hoped a replacement would be in place by the end of 2005. Possible external candidates included American Airlines' chief financial officer James Beer and Gulf Air chief James Hogan. Former Go boss Barbara Cassani might also be interested, although after their history of spats she might find a working relationship with Stelios far from easy.

In some respects, easyJet was as much the creation of Ray Webster, its chief executive, as Stelios, the man with whom it was still identified. Stelios had the original idea, the money and the charisma but it was Webster who had designed the software behind the airline's yield management system that lay at the heart of its low-cost model, and who had steered easyJet to become the first airline to harness properly the selling power of the Internet.

It was therefore with some regret that the airline industry, investors and fans of easyJet alike received the news of Webster's impending departure. Almost as shocking was news that Stelios would be rejoining the board as a non-executive director with immediate effect. The City was in two minds as to whether this amounted to a reasonable trade-off. In his last year at easyJet, Stelios had annoyed investors by trying to change the articles of association to give himself the power to appoint the chairman and two non-executive directors, and he had also sold down his shareholding, which helped finance his other business ventures but didn't do a lot for the easyJet share price.

On the other hand, Stelios knew the business better than anyone, and as a major shareholder he had every incentive to make the company work. 'I hope to make a contribution based on my close understanding of the easyJet business model, and appreciation of its markets and its unique culture,' the Greek entrepreneur announced.

Stelios's return to the board certainly represented something of a U-turn. It was only two years previously that he had quit the board, declaring he had 'taken note of the concerns of institutional investors' about his role at easyJet when he was spending more time building other companies in his easyGroup empire. Now, all of a sudden, Stelios was returning as a non-executive to replace Amir Eilon, his representative on the board and his long-standing corporate finance advisor. Eilon, a former investment banker, joined the board in 1999 before easyJet's flotation and was due to resign at the annual general meeting in February 2006.

Analysts speculated whether Stelios's decision was influenced by the declining fortunes of his other easyGroup companies. 'Not many of his catalogue of easy-branded investments have been successful to date but easyJet was,' one commented. 'Also Stelios had a lot of capital tied up in the airline. No doubt he wanted to take a close look at what was going on given its recent performance.'

EasyGroup's bright orange hadn't always translated into business success. EasyCinema had failed to expand beyond its flagship, a weathered building in Milton Keynes, and continued to face resistance from distributors. EasyCar still hadn't broken even. It had grown to fifty sites since its launch in 2000 but now mainly acted as an online brokerage for 1,100 car-hire firms across the world and was criticised for the large number of disclaimers in its rental contracts. On the introduction of the central London congestion charge, easyCar plastered pictures of London mayor Ken Livingstone on its UK fleet, announcing its customers would not have to pay the £5 charge, but this pledge was quietly dropped by managers.

EasyInternetcafé was suffering from the growing popularity of home Internet access and continued to lose money. EasyBuses were still chugging around but few passengers were keen on journeying between north-west London and Milton Keynes. As for easyPizza, many doubted whether the appeal of ordering a pizza a week in advance would really work.

It was early days for easyMobile, launched in March 2005. While the company carried the easyGroup logo, Stelios had no ownership stake and was being paid only for use of his brand. EasyMobile was 80 per cent owned by Danish phone company TDC, with 20 per cent held by a consortium including Frank Rasmussen, the founder of Telmore, a Danish virtual operator.

Calls to any British network were 7.7p a minute, versus rates often three times higher for full-service operators like Vodafone and Orange. Prices were low because easyMobile was as bare bones as possible. It neither owned nor operated a network, instead leasing spare capacity from Deutsche Telekom's T-Mobile unit, which was happy to get the extra revenue. It also had no retail stores, no marketing, and a tiny customer-support centre. EasyMobile didn't even sell phones.

Instead, customers signed up over the Internet and receive a SIM card in the mail that they slipped into just about any handset, then topped up their accounts online.

Analysts' reactions to Stelios's return were mixed. Morgan Stanley's Penelope Butcher said that the easyJet board changes could lead to a strategic switch, with Merrill Lynch's Anthony Bor saying that Stelios had always been a 'talismanic' focal point for the airline. Ian Jones of the CIS, meanwhile, was quite happy to see Stelios back as a non-executive, adding that easyJet should take the opportunity to increase the number of independent directors on the board.

Stelios said he foresaw no major change to his relationship with the airline he launched. 'By becoming a non-executive director myself, rather than operating through a representative on the board, I expect it to continue to be business as usual,' he said. 'I would like to stress that my role will be in a purely non-executive capacity, given my business commitments with the fourteen other easy-branded businesses.' He told the *Daily Mail* newspaper that he didn't want to be chairman, even though he retained the right to unseat easyJet chairman Sir Colin Chandler as long as he owned 10 per cent of easyJet's shares.

Stelios wasn't returning at a prosperous time for the airline. EasyJet was suffering from rising fuel costs, as oil reached $60 a barrel, as well as increased competition. Losses for the six months to 31 March deepened to £31 million from £27 million in the previous year after fuel costs leapt by 51 per cent. EasyJet said that the high cost of oil would continue to push pre-tax profits below the level of 2004. 'Fuel now represents 18 per cent of our cost base,' Chandler explained, 'and the high prices experienced over the winter months show little sign of abating.' EasyJet shares fell nearly 6 per cent.

In summer 2005 British Airways decided to address its annual fuel bill of some £1.2 billion by introducing a surcharge on ticket prices – £2.50 on all flights, with an additional £12 on long-haul return flights, with the aim of raising £70 million. Virgin Atlantic followed suit, increasing its fuel surcharge from £8 per flight to £24.

EasyJet didn't follow their example. The budget carrier maintained that its financial performance was in line with expectations and the pressure of high fuel prices had masked successes elsewhere, including a 25 per cent increase in the number of passengers on its flights and a 26 per cent hike in group revenues to £553 million. Travellers were spending more money on services such as in-flight food, with ancillary revenues per passenger up by 16 per cent, helping group turnover to continue to grow.

EasyJet had launched forty routes over the previous six months and started flights to fourteen new airports, passing milestones such as the delivery of its hundredth aircraft. The increase in routes meant that a total of 13.5 million passengers travelled on an easyJet flight during the six-month period.

Meanwhile, the airline experienced a further sting in the tail as it discovered that construction of a second runway at Stansted, one of its key bases, might be postponed. The second runway was due to open in 2011–12, but airport operator BAA claimed it would not be ready until 2013 at the earliest due to the UK government's slowness in planning new road and rail links. Moreover, under the existing regulatory regime, enforced by the Civil Aviation Authority, any expansion at Heathrow, Gatwick or Stansted had to be financed by the passengers who used that airport. But funding the £4 billion project entirely from those flying from Stansted would require an increase in charges from £3 to up to £11 per passenger, and would delay completion of the runway 'for several years'.

BAA said, however, that there was an argument for reverting to a 'system' approach to financing the runway on the ground of the wider economic benefits that it would generate in the south-east. If Heathrow and Gatwick passengers paid an extra 50 pence to £1 and Stansted passengers paid airport fees of between £7 and £8, the runway would be able to open in 2013. If the runway were to be self-financing, Stansted charges would have to rise to up to £11.

Ryanair and easyJet, the two biggest operators at Stansted, accused BAA of dropping a 'bombshell' on them by proposing to raise airport charges by almost 300 per cent 'just to finance another BAA Taj Mahal'. Indeed, the two low-cost carriers demanded that BAA return to the drawing board and produce a scheme for Stansted for which its customers were prepared to pay.

Mike Clasper, BAA's chief executive, said that the earlier that an additional runway was built at Stansted, the greater the capacity and the more the competition between airlines, driving down fares and benefiting the economy generally. He rejected claims that BAA was proposing to 'gold-plate' the new runway or build another 'Taj Mahal' at Stansted, and also denied that by airing the possibility of cross-subsidisation BAA was effectively starting the campaign to change the regulator's mind.

Any additional expense was a heavy burden for easyJet, which was battling hard to lower costs and to win customers' affections amid the competitive environment. Webster said the company was basing its longer-term yield forecasts – the amount of money it made per customer – on an outlook of 'continued intense competition'. There were now forty-seven low-cost airlines operating in Europe and all were finding conditions hard. Ryanair reported a 16 per cent drop in third-quarter net profit, blaming high oil prices and intense competition, and British Airways reported a 41 per cent drop in third-quarter earnings.

The low-cost airlines gained some ground by refusing to impose fuel surcharges on customers, thus increasing the price differential with the full-service airlines. EasyJet also saved money by adding more fuel-efficient Airbus A319s to its fleet and withdrawing from poorly performing markets or airports that charged high fees. More full-service carriers were being forced to copy the no-frills carriers' spartan service tactics in a bid to lower their costs and fares in response to their budget rivals. Heathrow-based bmi announced it was to scrap its business-class cabins and make all passengers pay for food and drink in a desperate bid to lift the airline into the black after four consecutive years of losses. New bmi chief executive Nigel Turner launched the shake-up, admitting the former British Midland had lost touch with its customers.

EasyJet, meanwhile, was busily thinking up ways to differentiate its product and raise extra revenue in the cut-throat European market. One innovation was easyJetLounges, which it introduced in June 2005. The lounges offered free drinks, snacks and magazines, as well as the standard flight information and access to phone, Internet and email. Offering a lounge, normally the domain of business-class passengers, seemed a move away from easyJet's no-frills approach, but it was intended to attract the many passengers who flew with the airline on business. And true to easyJet form, passengers had to pay for the privilege of using the lounge. Prices started from £12 per person including VAT.

In a further move, easyJet announced that in the future it would quote fares online that included taxes and charges. From early summer 2005, when the carrier had completed an upgrade of its software systems, easyJet's web bookings would show the complete fare payable, including government tax, airport tax, insurance, security and other charges. Previously, the complete fare was only shown in the last stages of making a booking.

From summer 2005 all-inclusive fares had to be quoted in newspaper, television and outdoor advertising. EasyJet had previously had its knuckles rapped by advertising watchdogs over its fare promotions, including one incident in 2004 when the Advertising Standards Authority upheld a complaint about its cheap flight offers from Newcastle to Barcelona. The ad was headlined 'lots more low fares!' and stated 'Newcastle to . . . Barcelona from £22.49 single'. But an investigation by the ASA revealed that less than 10 per cent of all tickets sold were at that price; by regulation, at least 10 per cent of all tickets sold had to be at the advertised price.

Meanwhile, easyJet was working on another scheme to combat another leading passenger complaint, namely its 'sit anywhere' policy on its flights. The airline had been allowing up to ten passengers on each of its flights from Luton to jump the queue for £10. EasyJet claimed the scheme would benefit passengers wanting more legroom or the choice of a seat in a particular part of the aircraft, but admitted there had been a 'mixed response'.

Slightly more popular was the airline's policy of slowly introducing self-service, automated kiosks for passengers to collect their tickets and boarding cards at its sixty European airports, after successfully testing the scheme at Nottingham East Midlands Airport. The trademark orange kiosks, shaped like slot machines at an amusement arcade, enabled easyJet to handle more passengers for a larger number of flights at the same time.

Ultimately, easyJet and other airlines claimed, the whole airport process would become even easier. One plan was to introduce a system where air tickets were replaced by individual barcodes for each passenger. Baggage tags, meanwhile, could be replaced by new 'smart tags'. The tags each had tiny chips in them that could be tracked by radio, to speed up baggage handling and put an end to the problem of lost and mislaid luggage. Only security checks and passport control would still involve the human touch.

Airline industry executives admitted that the new techniques would slash their costs. By 2007, every ticket was expected to be an 'e-ticket' issued either by computer or through self-service kiosks – a measure that would cut checking-in costs by 90 per cent. Worldwide, that alone would cut airline costs by £1.5 billion a year. But there were risks with the self-service airport. The International Air Transport

Association, the largest of the industry bodies, admitted that airlines would have to prepare for a computer collapse or massive technical failure that could leave thousands of passengers stranded. Some things never changed.

16. Past, present – and future

WHAT A DIFFERENCE a decade makes. It was in 1995 that Stelios hatched the idea of easyJet, shocking the world with his concept of selling flights for the same price as a pair of jeans. At the time, most people stared, laughed or dismissed the fledgling carrier as ridiculous. Weren't those prices too good to be true? EasyJet surely couldn't survive more than a few months, they told each other, joking that the airline catapulted its aircraft and passengers into the skies using a giant elastic band. And the whole idea of a flight without free food or drink was outrageous, never mind the notion of booking your own flight using the Internet, which in 1995 most people had not even heard of.

Even as easyJet's approach became more familiar, travellers speculated that the low-cost carrier didn't have enough planes and assumed that it wouldn't last long. They assumed that British Airways would soon quash the upstart; until, that is, BA copied easyJet's no-frills idea by setting up Go. The ultimate irony being, of course, that easyJet eventually bought Go.

The world of travel has been reinvented during the past ten years. In 1980, the cheapest return fare on what was then the world's busiest international air route – London to Paris – was around £70, which then represented a week's wages for the average British employee. Nowadays, if you book in advance on easyJet, the fare has fallen to as low as £50, while wages have risen to the point where Mr or Ms Average need work for barely half a day to earn enough for a trip to the French capital.

Today, few people laugh at the idea of easyJet. They are more likely to thank the airline for allowing them to explore Europe on the cheap, visit Auntie Mavis in Edinburgh, and meet regularly with that important new business client in Paris.

Stelios Haji-Ioannou and Michael O'Leary have transformed Europe's airline industry. 'What easyJet and Ryanair did was identify a niche,' said David Bryon, managing director of bmibaby. 'They took out ticket restrictions, kept their cost bases low and reduced their fares, undercutting the prices offered by the major airlines. The pair of them went out there with the message of price, price and price. They stimulated the marketplace and created incremental growth.'

Low costs were essential to their business model. 'The root to being a low-cost airline is to start with a new or renewed focus on operating costs,' said Tim Jeans, managing director of Monarch Scheduled. 'You need to look from the top to bottom at an airline's costs. You need to cut out anything that you don't need that costs you money. Basically you need to be as close to a train as possible.'

The budget airlines' route structures marked a further change in the short-haul market. Most major airlines like British Airways operated a hub-and-spoke system with a major centre like London Heathrow acting as its principal hub from which all flights radiated. The problem was that this could lead to multiple changes and longer journeys for passengers. EasyJet, by contrast, described its route map as looking more like a spider's web, operating routes from a network of central airports in cities including Luton, Liverpool, Amsterdam and Geneva. This enabled passengers to make more direct journeys.

Of course, easyJet did not only have to compete against the traditional airlines. 'One of easyJet's strategic challenges is how to deal with Ryanair,' said Andrew Lobbenberg, airlines analyst at ABN Amro. 'The Dublin-based carrier is more aggressive in its business approach and how it deals with consumers and it delivers better on business reliability and punctuality. Basically easyJet doesn't know how to react to Ryanair. First of all it took the high moral ground, claiming that it offered better service. EasyJet then launched routes into Ireland and Ryanair came back with extra capacity, which brought down easyJet's stock price. EasyJet says it doesn't compete with Ryanair but everyone does compete with everyone else in the airline industry.'

EasyJet differs from Ryanair by competing head-on with the legacy carriers such as British Airways, and often operating to larger established airports such as Nice and Athens – then trying to capture a third or more of that market, said industry expert Professor Rigas Doganis. Ryanair's approach, meanwhile, is modelled on Southwest Airlines, which flies to secondary airports in major cities to take advantage of lower landing charges. It also flies on routes that would not interest a larger carrier, such as Trieste in Italy and Esbjerg in Denmark, and blurs the borders of Europe by describing the Swedish city of Malmo as Copenhagen, and Perpignan in France as Barcelona. 'Ryanair generally tends to fly on thinner, underserved routes and aims to become the dominant carrier on those routes and develop new markets,' explained Doganis. 'Where it competes head-on with the legacy airlines it is normally by serving second-ary airports, such as Hahn (Frankfurt) or Torp (Oslo), very distant from the major centres Ryanair claims to be serving.'

Like Ryanair, easyJet has excelled in getting its brand well established, assisted by its in-your-face marketing campaigns and spectacular publicity stunts, such as Stelios and his easyJet crew turning up at Go's launch dressed in orange boiler suits. Nowadays, consumers immediately associate the neon orange shade with easyJet or the other easyGroup companies. 'EasyJet has two real strengths that its peers admire it for,' Tim Jeans admitted. 'The first is its brand, its styling, culture and tone of voice and that's been self-sustaining. The yield management system, thanks to Webster, is its other strength. EasyJet manages to extract the maximum revenue per flight by being very aggressive on pricing, meaning that it has very strong revenues per flight. EasyJet was set up to win, as was Ryanair.'

The carrier is often praised for looking after its customers better than Ryanair and other no-frills airlines. 'I would rather fly with easyJet than Ryanair any day and I'm an Irishman!' said regular easyJet user Ray Hanley. 'EasyJet employees are not as abrupt as those at Ryanair and have always been helpful if I asked about something such as extra luggage. Ryanair staff are always on the offensive – they always expect you to make a complaint, I guess.'

On the other hand, easyJet's costs aren't as low as Ryanair's. There is a 15 to 20 per cent cost differential between the two carriers, according to Doganis. 'Ryanair is much more disciplined about costs than easyJet,' said Jeans. 'If you cut a Ryanair person down the middle, like a stick of rock, you would see cost control written all the way through.'

EasyJet had other failings. Industry experts criticised the company for spending too much time and effort trying to sort out DBA, the BA subsidiary it tried to buy in 2003, instead of backing out at an earlier stage when it was clear that the proposed takeover wasn't going to work.

Furthermore, easyJet's record of communicating with the financial markets has not been always perfect. The City was outraged after easyJet gave two profit warnings within four weeks in May and June 2004, and did not forgive the company lightly. But the company learned its lesson and resolved to communicate more openly in future. Added to that, the airline has had a tendency to be too inward-looking. 'It took easyJet a long time to realise that it doesn't totally control its own destiny,' Lobbenberg commented, 'and that its revenues can be badly affected by what happens to other low-cost airlines and the market.'

One thing easyJet did recognise from the start was the importance of an impeccable safety record. The airline sought to impress on people's minds that low cost didn't equal low safety. EasyJet wasn't the only no-frills carrier to come to the same conclusion. Low-cost airlines agreed on hardly anything but the one topic on which they were unanimous was safety. Southwest, which had flown over 10 million flights without losing an aircraft in a fatal accident, saw 'safety as its most important priority every day', said the American airline's head of PR, Linda Rutherford. 'You can't be successful if you're not safe. Southwest has a better safety record than Qantas.'

EasyJet's emphasis on cost control was legendary but there could be no compromises on safety. As it strove to point out, easyJet invested in an even younger fleet than those flown by its full-service rivals. The airline was aware that less than perfect maintenance would be its most costly mistake. To quote one of Stelios's maxims: 'If you think safety is expensive, try an accident.' Avoiding crashes was even more crucial for no-frills operators than for traditional airlines. An accident could obliterate a carrier's reputation in an instant. Low-cost airlines only had to look at the example of ValuJet, which destroyed the lives of all passengers on-board, as well as its reputation, when one of its planes crashed in May 1996.

Fatal accident rates among airlines in Europe and North America ran at one in every million or two departures. Most accidents occurred during the take-off, climb, descent and landing phases of flight. Most other forms of transport are more dangerous per mile and even per trip than flying.

Engineers and safety inspectors scrupulously monitored the construction of an aircraft, checking every nut and bolt.

EasyJet is meticulous about what can or cannot be allowed safely on-board an aircraft, sometimes to passengers' annoyance. Donna Marie Parks was due to travel with her two young sons on an easyJet flight from Glasgow to London in June 2005. Desk staff and the cabin crew told her the baby seat was fine to carry her four-month-old son Daniel. But the captain disagreed and ordered the family off the plane. Her husband Gordon turned up two hours later with an alternative car seat, but she was again refused permission to fly. The family was only permitted to travel more than five hours later after an easyJet desk worker loaned a different car seat for Daniel.

'Although the car seat appeared to have the standard requirements, there was no way that this particular seat could be attached to an aircraft seat in a safe and secure manner,' an easyJet spokeswoman explained. 'Therefore, it was deemed inappropriate for travel. Once she had obtained a seat that was appropriate for travel, easyJet transferred them free of charge on to the next available flight.'

EasyJet's safety regulations caused Parks inconvenience. But before the advent of easyJet, she would no doubt have been making the journey by train or car, or not at all. No one could deny that easyJet had changed the world of travel and made flying easy. 'Stelios and Michael O'Leary are responsible for changing the whole travel culture in this country,' said Ian Briggs, press secretary at Luton Airport. 'You would never have thought of flying from London to Edinburgh before the days of easyJet. You would have taken the train or the car instead. Flying was just for wealthier people. Nowadays flying is the first thing people think of. They feel hard done by if they have to take the car or the train and that's purely because of the nuisance value and regardless of the costs involved.'

Before easyJet, who would have dreamed that you could jet out to the South of France for less than £37 return? Cheap fares changed every aspect of people's lives. 'My love life was hanging by a thread until you started flying from Liverpool to the South of France,' said one happy easyJet passenger whose fiancé lived in Nice. She could barely afford to see him before easyJet's arrival.

Flavia Collins, mother of a toddler and pregnant with her second child, was another who appreciated easyJet for allowing her to spend time with a loved one. Collins used easyJet to commute regularly between London and Amsterdam to visit her husband, Shaun, who was working in the Netherlands capital to set up an Internet business for an Anglo-Dutch company. Collins even found commuting with a toddler easy. 'The air stewardesses were very helpful with my son, Toby. Also, refreshments are more hassle than it's worth on a forty-five-minute flight with a toddler. They just get in the way, so I much prefer it when you don't get them automatically included.'

EasyJet changed working as well as flying habits. Cheap and easy flights meant that employees could work overseas and travel home for the weekend. Ray Hanley, an engineer for BMW, was one customer who used easyJet to travel to work. 'I was based in the UK for three years and worked over in Germany so I used to commute back and forth every couple of weeks,' he explained. 'Since then I've moved to Munich to work for BMW full-time, so in a way, easyJet has helped me get the job!'

The advent of easyJet flights encouraged executives to strengthen their links overseas and set up offices abroad. Clive France, business director of Internetics, a London-based Internet and new media design agency, often flew with easyJet between London and Barcelona after setting up an office in the Spanish city. 'When easyJet opened its route from Gatwick to Barcelona, we didn't think twice about making Barcelona our choice of city to expand our design team abroad,' he said. 'Barcelona is a creative city and the cost of living is relatively low, compared with London. I probably wouldn't have considered setting up an office in Barcelona otherwise but the reasonably priced flights out there have made it all possible. We've now set up a second office in Barcelona and taken on employees there. I fly out there regularly with easyJet. Low-cost travel combined with video conferencing and remote working tools have meant that we have been able to expand confidently and cheaply and the operation has been a huge success.'

France didn't just use easyJet for work. The airline and its low fares also encouraged him to fly around Europe for pleasure. 'EasyJet changed the life of my generation,' he declared. 'For a while there, I was jetting off every weekend to cities such as Venice, Barcelona, Nice and Athens. I was the boy about Europe.'

It was clear that the 'easyJet generation' was turning their backs on the traditional Mediterranean package holiday in favour of independent travel. The sun was setting on the package holiday, which traditionally comprised a charter airline's flight and a fortnight's pre-paid accommodation. Holidaymakers increasingly opted for DIY holidays, booking their own flights over the Internet and sorting out their own accommodation. The giant tour operator First Choice abandoned seat-only sales amid rising competition from the likes of easyJet while other operators tried to copy no-frills airlines by offering low-fare scheduled flights in a bid to survive.

'I guess I'm the typical easyJet customer,' France continued. 'I barely travelled apart from on package holidays before budget airlines came along. I used to work as a tour rep for Thomson Holidays and it was always easier and more convenient to take a package tour. Nowadays I wouldn't even consider going on a package holiday. EasyJet and budget travel has given me the confidence to take a flight and wing it when I get there. People like me can do their own thing and take off at any moment. The price is so low for flights that it almost forces people into taking a gamble, even if they would never have flown before.'

EasyJet attracts impulse flyers. People might see that the airline flew to Bratislava, decide that sounded interesting and fly to the city for the weekend. Europe was suddenly an exciting place to explore, full of intriguing cities just one or two hours' flight away. The British jetted off to Nice and Toulouse and the French landed in Liverpool. EasyJet helped join the dots between the various European cities and open up countries to their neighbours. Indeed, *The Economist* went so far as to suggest that easyJet and Ryanair had 'done more to integrate Europe than any numbers of diplomats or ministers'.

In addition, easyJet's cheap and easy flights encouraged the concept of the weekend break at a time when getting away from the office had never been harder. A survey by the Chartered Management Institute found that of more than 3,000 managers surveyed, only 53 per cent found time to use their holiday entitlement. As work pressures made it hard for many to get away for a full two weeks, more people took shorter breaks to Europe on a frequent basis.

Some people even decided to escape abroad just for the day. Before easyJet moved into Britain's airports, a day trip used to mean a quick jaunt to the seaside, equipped with bucket, spade and a picnic. An exotic day trip, meanwhile, usually meant catching a ferry to the Isle of Man. But thanks to the extraordinary expansion of our travel horizons courtesy of easyJet and its pals, sun worshippers could get a blast of sunshine with a day on the beach. Keen skiers were sloping off to the ski slopes for the day for a quick fix of the white stuff. The DIY sector of the ski market grew by some 50 per cent in 2002 as some snow fanatics took advantage of easyJet's early ski flights. These included the 6.30 a.m. flight from Luton which landed at 9.10 a.m. at Geneva, close to several excellent ski areas including Chamonix.

'The effect of the no-frills airlines? Huge – it has transformed this town,' said Simon Norris of the Hotel Eden in Chamonix. 'At least 50 per cent of our British clientele comes through easyJet.' Other popular day trips included the Venice

Carnival and playing roulette at the casino tables in Monte Carlo.

The popularity of low-fare flights helped the airline industry recover after a dramatic dip in sales following the terrorist attacks in the US in 2001. After two turbulent years in 2002 and 2003, the world's airlines clawed their way back to pre-11 September levels in 2004, with China and the low-cost carriers leading the overall recovery. EasyJet's Toby Nicol described 11 September as a 'watershed' in the global aviation world. 'Since then, the traditional airlines have been smaller, and low-cost airlines have mushroomed. After the terrorist attacks, we ran very major seat promotions and cut prices while traditional carriers put prices up due to extra security costs.' He added that until the attacks, the 'low-cost phenomenon' had not been truly accepted in Europe.

Now that they were established in Europe, how long would low-cost carriers survive? From high fuel costs and over-capacity to the threat of development aid taxes and likely eventual inclusion in climate-change emission controls, the challenges for the airline industry kept on mounting. In May 2005, European Union finance ministers agreed to impose a tax on plane tickets to fund development aid programmes in Africa. According to a document drawn up for the ministers' meeting, a tax of €10 on airline tickets for flights within the EU and €30 on flights outside the EU would generate about €6 billion for development spending. The tax would be compulsory in some countries, such as Belgium, France and Germany, while other countries would make it optional.

The move was seen as a major blow by airlines, particularly cut-price carriers such as easyJet. A spokesman for easyJet said the proposal was 'confused'. 'Why only target airline passengers, why not bus passengers?' he asked, arguing that there would be no side-benefit for the environment as the tax would not give any incentive to people to alter their behaviour. 'Aviation could put hundreds of millions of pounds into the Treasury and it would have no impact on the environment.'

But environmental groups were delighted by the news, seeing it as the first step towards making people pay the true cost of plane travel. Environmentalists pointed out that politicians such as Tony Blair denounced global warming as the greatest threat to the mankind while encouraging the development of a fifth terminal at London Heathrow, and as more passengers take to the skies green issues can only become more important. Environmentalists were cheered when a coalition of airlines formed a 'sustainable aviation group' in June 2005, claiming to take green issues seriously. EasyJet was one of the airlines who joined the green fold. One airline was notable by its absence: Ryanair. O'Leary announced cheerfully that Ryanair intended to increase its emissions of carbon dioxide, adding that if his customers were worried about the environment they should sell their car and walk.

The first wave of consolidation had already tightened up the market and many low-cost ventures had fallen by the wayside. EasyJet had taken over Go and Ryanair had bought Buzz. Another low-cost casualty, euJet, was laid to rest in July 2005. EuJet owner Planestation also went into administration, as did Kent International Airport, home for the airline, which flew from Kent and Shannon to more than twenty locations, including Ibiza, Malaga and Nice. EasyJet offered passengers stranded at their European destinations a rescue fee of £25 to return home to the UK. And it was certain that consolidation in the sector would continue at the expense of many more no-frills carriers. 'I see a lot of low-cost airlines in Europe disappearing,' Lobbenberg warned. 'The market simply won't support them all.'

But easyJet and Ryanair were clearly slated to survive. 'EasyJet and Ryanair have first mover advantages,' added Lobbenberg. 'They became established in and outside the UK as pan-European brands, unlike say the German low-cost carrier Air Berlin. Indeed, the majority of low-cost airlines have unknown brands outside the UK. Air Polonia even launched flights to the UK without initially having a website in

English. By being based in the UK and Ireland, easyJet and Ryanair also benefit from the country's low labour costs and flexibility.'

Most industry experts expected only one or two low-cost airlines, apart from easyJet and Ryanair, to stay alive. 'It is certain that many new entrants are not going to survive beyond two to three years,' said Doganis. 'SAS's no-frills subsidiary, Snowflake, is already being phased down. Duo, Volare and Air Polonia all collapsed during 2004. The market simply can't absorb so many low-cost carriers. There will be consolidation around two to three carriers, namely easyJet, Ryanair and possibly one further carrier based in mainland Europe.'

Other industry members, such as bmibaby's David Bryon, were more optimistic. 'I think it will be more like ten no-frills airlines that are doing okay, with a core of five to six major low-cost players in Europe and three to four just starting up,' the airline CEO said.

Monarch Scheduled's Tim Jeans insisted that there was room for some new entrants to squeeze into the market. 'While Ryanair competes on secondary or tertiary routes, it always leaves room for people to compete against flag carriers on primary routes. The French, Spanish and Italian markets have hardly been touched compared with Germany and the UK. I'm more bullish than most. Monarch is taking on three new aircraft this year. The people most at threat here are the legacy flag carriers, who are still in denial and wishing that the whole low-cost thing will go away,' Jeans continued. 'These include carriers such as Iberia and Alitalia who are seeing their yields in freefall.'

Alitalia was still being bailed out. In early June 2005 the European Commission gave its conditional approval to the debt-ridden Italian carrier's restructuring plan, which included a €1.2 billion recapitalisation of its new subsidiary AZ Fly. Despite three government bail-outs since 1997, Alitalia was still losing money; it lost €620 million in the first half of 2004 and cut-throat competition was forcing its market share downwards.

Meanwhile, consolidation was continuing among national carriers. In 2003, Air France, Europe's second largest carrier, bought KLM, Europe's fourth largest, in a deal that created the biggest European carrier and the number one worldwide in terms of sales. Air France held 81 per cent of the group, led by Air France chairman Jean-Cyril Spinetta, with KLM owning the remainder. EasyJet, by now the second biggest operator in the French market after Air France in terms of traffic, opposed the takeover on the grounds that it damaged competition.

But the no-frills market share in Europe had yet to reach anything close to US levels. The US low-fares market is 'probably in its adolescence or maturity whereas the European market is still in its childhood', said Southwest's Linda Rutherford. 'There is a tremendous amount of growth in Europe in the cities that can be served and the number of passengers that can be carried.' Nevertheless, low-cost carriers' rate of growth would inevitably slow down; otherwise, they were in danger of overheating by expanding too rapidly, concluded Doganis. 'Low-cost carriers will grow faster than scheduled airlines but their growth rates will settle down to a rate of 15 per cent to 20 per cent per year, not the 40 to 60 per cent of recent years.'

There was no doubt that the key driver of growth in the budget airline market was the airlines' rock-bottom prices, as they slashed fares to win passengers. The battle for European skies was in full swing, and the big winner was the consumer. Ryanair, for example, continuously grabbed the headlines with its offer of 99 pence one-way flights and offered some routes for free, claiming to undercut traditional carriers by an average 70 to 80 per cent. At easyJet, the model was 'the earlier you book the lower the price': a one-way trip to Palma from London might start at £30 several months in advance, but could rise to £200 the day before travel. This compared with British Airways' efforts to compete with a limited number of seats at £80 to £160 return on routes such as London to Paris.

The good news for the consumer and the bad news for the airlines is that low fares at their current levels seem here to stay. Gone were the days when airlines set the fares. Nowadays, Ryanair even pays people to fly on its aircraft, offering total fares for less than the combined taxes and charges. 'The market is setting the fares for us and we have to manage our costs to tie in with the available revenues per flight,' said Jeans.

Future fares will, of course, be influenced by external factors, such as fuel prices, taxes, US dollar exchange rates and government regulations. Airlines such as easyJet will also be forced to maintain their low fares by cutting out any remaining excess costs in their operations. And they will endeavour to make money by additional revenues such as the food, drink and goods sold on-board and by re-introducing traditional 'frills' such as in-flight entertainment and business lounges, which passengers will have to pay for. 'Airlines will almost become retailers, with the flight viewed as a classic loss leader and the value of the customer becoming highest,' Bryon prophesied.

EasyJet maintained that in the next ten to fifteen years the vast majority of short-haul traffic in Europe would be on low-cost airlines, though if you flew long-haul you would still travel with a traditional airline. But many passengers, pleased with their cheap flights to Malaga, were beginning to ask when they would be able to buy a no-frills flight to Florida or another long-haul destination. If low fares worked so well within Europe, why couldn't the formula be transferred on to long-haul routes? The hypothesis seems simple enough but aviation history is littered with airlines that went bust applying no-frills principles to long-haul: PeopleXpress of the US, Wardair of Canada, Civair, whose secondhand Boeing 747 never got off the ground from South Africa to Stansted, and of course, Laker's Skytrain. Like many others in the industry, Stelios believed that his short-haul model did not adapt to longer flights. 'The controllable costs where you can make a difference are swamped by uncontrollable costs like fuel and air-traffic control charges,' he argued.

In any case, it seemed that Stelios had enough to keep him busy within Europe. According to a publication of the European Commission, air transport was the fastest growing transport mode and was expected to account for 10.8 per cent of passenger transport activity by 2030, compared with 5.4 per cent in 2000. According to the same study, the volume of passenger traffic using air transport should be twice that of the railways by 2030, reaching the level of 923 billion passenger kilometres.

And whether as a result of the bad weather or because the UK had given birth to a nation of would-be explorers, Great Britain remains at the epicentre of the budget airline explosion. The UK might be only the world's twentieth-biggest nation in terms of population but it accounts for 14 per cent of all international air travel – more than any other country in the world. The number of Britons who fly has increased more than six-fold over the last thirty-five years, from 32 million journeys a year in 1970 to 217 million in 2004, and is expected to increase to about 400 million by 2020. Half the population now fly at least once a year and a substantial percentage five times or more. And mostly for pure pleasure. Only one-sixth of the trips made by UK residents are for business purposes. Thanks to easyJet, the British have become a plane-crazy nation of holidaymakers. We fly because we can afford to and because it is as 'easy as travelling on a bus', once you remembered that buses didn't offer you anything to eat, simply got you from A to B and were subject to delays.

In 2005, the British public, as well as many Europeans, can fly cheaply to most corners of Europe – a prospect that would have seemed like pie in the sky just a decade ago when easyJet was born. 'By 2008, no one will be flying on traditional airlines in Europe,' promised Stelios. It certainly looks as if planeloads of passengers will continue to head cheaply into the sun with easyJet. No doubt, you, I and other members of the easyJet generation will all be cursing our neon-orange friend under our breath the next time we get caught in a stampede for a window seat or traipse home in dejection after being refused on a flight for not checking in early enough or forgetting our passport.

But meanwhile, property owners will visit their holiday homes in Spain and France. Stag weekenders will stagger drunkenly around the medieval cobbled streets of Eastern Europe. Businessmen will continue to commute between cities and jet back home for the weekend from their overseas offices. And lovers, friends and families will continue to be reunited courtesy of the bright orange British airline that no one took seriously ten years ago.

17. New man at the helm

IN JANUARY 2006, easyJet appointed investment bank Goldman Sachs as its financial advisor, replacing CSFB. EasyJet hoped that Goldman, known for its aggressive defence strategies, would head off any potential takeover by FL Group, the owners of Icelandair.

Two years had passed since FL had first invested in easyJet. The Icelandic investor had upped its stake in easyJet on several occasions, fuelling interest in its intentions towards the carrier. EasyJet was growing increasingly nervous following the Viking investor's recent purchase of Sterling Airways, Europe's fourth-largest budget airline, for £136.7 million. The deal brought 30 aircraft and a network of 46 destinations, which served 5.2 million passengers each year. EasyJet would provide a perfect addition to Sterling and would create a network spanning from Malaga in the south to Helsinki in the north. FL had also recently added to its aviation interests by increasing its stake in Finnair, Finland's national airline, to 10 per cent. EasyJet didn't want to be the next airline to be swallowed by the aggressive investment group.

It was a tough start for Andrew Harrison, easyJet's new chief executive, who had taken over from Ray Webster on 1 December 2005. He had barely had enough time to get to know the business let alone draw up a defence strategy against a potential takeover bid.

Until then, Harrison's career had focused on cars, not planes. He had joined Lex Services as chief executive in 1996. Two years later he had rebranded the company under the RAC brand. He had agreed to leave the group after Aviva, the UK insurance giant, had bought it out in March 2005.

EasyJet looked beyond the 48-year-old's lack of airline experience to concentrate on the growth in RAC's profits under his stewardship. Harrison was credited with transforming RAC's business into a strongly branded, consumer-friendly services company with 6.5 million members. During his time at the helm, the share price more than trebled.

Sir Colin Chandler, easyJet's chairman, said: 'We had a number of criteria that our new CEO had to meet; in particular, he or she needed to have had senior management experience in a large and well-recognised consumer-facing plc. In addition, Andrew has delivered strong top and bottom line growth, improved cash generation, introduced cost efficiencies and inspired employees in a service industry.'

Harrison's fears of an Icelandic raid at easyJet turned out to be misplaced. On 5 April 2006, FL sold its 16.9 per cent stake in the carrier, making a profit of £98 million in the process. JP Morgan, the sole book runner, masterminded the sale.

FL denied that the withdrawal from easyJet stemmed from problems in the Icelandic economy, which had led to higher interest rates; the devaluation of the Icelandic krona to its lowest level since December 2003; and the credit-rating agency Moody's downgrading the outlook for its ratings on two of the country's biggest banks to negative.

Instead, the Icelandic group claimed that it sold the easyJet stake to free up funds to diversify into industries outside of aviation, adding that it was working on 'several investment projects'.

A major reason behind the sale appeared to be the difficulty in winning over Stelios. Around 40 per cent of the airline remained in the hands of the founder and former chairman, and any takeover would need his blessing.

Meanwhile, Stelios, frequently touted as a hero of the masses for bringing cheap air travel to millions, was about to gain a more distinguished title. In June 2006, only eleven years after setting up his budget airline and introducing an intriguing range of other 'easy' services, Stelios was rewarded for his efforts by being awarded a knighthood in the Queen's Birthday Honours List. The flamboyant entrepreneur joined entertainer and artist Rolf Harris, ChildLine founder Esther Rantzen and TV chef Gary Rhodes on the honours list marking the Queen's eightieth birthday.

Sir Stelios declared that receiving the knighthood was a 'joy' and a 'great honour'.

'It came as a surprise to me and I'm not sure at this stage that I deserve an honour which is usually reserved for those with a lifetime of business achievement,' said the thirty-nine-year-old.

Sir Stelios said he wanted to accept the award in the spirit of entrepreneurship.

'I have always said that in order to make an economy more entrepreneurial we need to learn to celebrate business success and tolerate business failure,' he said.

He dedicated the award to the more than 10,000 staff in the businesses he created, who he said worked to make a difference to the lives of millions of consumers every day.

'On reflection, I am always pleasantly surprised when ordinary members of the public stop me on the street to say "thank you", I guess for making travel and other goods and services available to them.

'To get the same endorsement now from the top echelons

of British society is a joy to me and a great reward for the efforts that I have made,' he said.

Sir Stelios had by now expanded his 'easy' empire into personal finance, online recruitment, pizza delivery, music downloads, mobile telephony, male toiletries and wrist-watches. The serial entrepreneur, with an estimated fortune of £727 million, now preferred to describe himself as the manager of the 'easy' *brand* rather than the *companies*. Perhaps this represented a tactical distancing from some of his more bizarre 'easy' innovations? After all, few of the fifteen 'easy' businesses were doing anywhere as well as easyJet. Sir Stelios scaled back his easyBus discount service to a single route between London and Luton Airport. He also downsized Easy4men, which offered toiletries.

Sir Stelios was reluctant to shut struggling businesses. He insisted that the more firms there were, the more he could raise awareness about him and the group. So it must have been a significant setback when he brought down the curtain on easyCinema in May. Sir Stelios blamed the failure on high rents.

'Now that Odeon, who have become our landlords as well as our competitors, are demanding a totally unrealistic rent, we have decided to let them operate the cinema themselves,' he said.

Gone were plans to create a bright orange national cinema chain, with tickets for as little as 20p. In their place was simply a nationwide cinema-booking site, which allowed customers to view cinema listings and book films, as well as rent DVDs.

Sir Stelios, the first to think of an orange cruise ship with windowless cabins, then admitted he might also be the last. He decided to open up more portholes in the tiny cabins to ease passengers' claustrophobia. In addition, the entrepreneur toned down the amount of vibrant orange on board and introduced a predominant colour scheme of 'sophisticated graphite grey'.

Thankfully, the tycoon's next business idea died a quiet

death. A concept for cheap funerals, no doubt replete with orange coffins, was quietly dropped.

Even if the going wasn't so easy for the easyGroup, Sir Stelios's enthusiasm refused to be dampened. He declared that the future of the easyGroup 'belonged to the franchising principle'. He added in an interview with the German magazine *Der Spiegel*, 'In five years, I would like to have some 20 to 25 firms. Around a third will run well, a third will be okay, the last third will need me as a fireman. It is exciting.'

While Sir Stelios was defining easyGroup's future, easyJet was pursuing a rapid course of expansion. And this time the airline was venturing outside of the European Union. The airline introduced flights to Marrakech, Morocco, and to Istanbul, Turkey, in its summer timetable, with one-way fares starting at just under £40. It also introduced flights to the Croatian cities of Split and Rijeka.

EasyJet wasn't the only low-cost airline to spread its network outside the EU. Ryanair announced that it would fly to the Moroccan destinations of Marrakech and Fez, as well as the Croatian town of Pula. Thomsonfly planned to introduce Marrakech to its timetable.

'Historically, low-cost airlines have expanded only in the EU because it's a lot simpler, as the countries share the same regulations and legislation,' said Samantha Day, easyJet's public relations manager. 'But people are getting more adventurous and the potential of places like Istanbul make the added complications worth it.'

New EU routes in easyJet's summer schedule included Bordeaux, La Rochelle, Rimini and the Corsican capital, Ajaccio. At the same time, the airline announced plans to grow its operations at Gatwick by 10 per cent, particularly to business destinations. This included the addition of a three-times daily service to Glasgow International Airport and an increased number of flights to Madrid, Milan, Cologne, Athens, Berlin and Amsterdam.

Gatwick had become easyJet's biggest base. The carrier

accounted for 18 per cent of the London airport's capacity, flying as many as half a million passengers from the airport during each summer month.

In August, easyJet pursued continental growth with the launch of a new base at Madrid's Barajas airport, marking the carrier's seventeenth base and its first in Spain. Operations started in February 2007. The airline served nine international routes from Madrid, including London, Bristol and Liverpool, and offered a total of seventy-two routes to eleven Spanish airports. Spain was the airline's second largest market after the UK.

Meanwhile, easyJet and Ryanair continued to look east to maintain their expansion targets. The number of flights to and from the Czech Republic, already familiar to Prague-bound groups of British stag and hen parties, was growing by 12 per cent. Prague even opened a new terminal to handle the soaring numbers as inbound tourists jostled at airport terminals with outbound migrants: the budget carriers provided a convenient exit route for millions of eastern Europeans in pursuit of work. After all, flights with the new generation of low-cost airlines cost less than a day's wages and no more than a bus ride.

Poland's unemployment rate was among the highest in Europe and the country also expected to see the steepest growth in air travel, forecast at 176 per cent in 2006. EasyJet and Ryanair were also battling it out in the hyper-growth market of Hungary, with an expansion of 112 per cent predicted for 2006.

But easyJet appeared to have forgotten to add more staff as it increased its network. The airline was embarrassed into admitting that unprecedented demand from the British public to take to the air had left it short-staffed and unable to put its own crew on all the services it had committed to that summer.

Out of easyJet's 2,200 cabin crew across Europe, 250 were grounded: 150 of these were awaiting upgraded security clearance and another 100 were being retrained to fly the airline's newly delivered Airbus aircraft. The humiliating staff

shortage meant flight misery for hundreds of passengers, w
were informed that their flights were cancelled just fourteen
days in advance. Passengers were offered either a re-route with
easyJet on an alternative flight or a full refund. This meant that
easyJet had to fork out £8 million over the summer to hire
other airlines' cabin crew and aircraft to get easyJet passengers
to their destinations.

Desperate times called for desperate measures. EasyJet
resorted to hunting for new staff among its passengers, the
Guardian newspaper reported. Flight attendants shocked
passengers on-board by adding a recruitment advert to the
end of their in-flight announcement. Cabin crew were ordered
to inform passengers that 'due to the rapid expansion in our
network, we are currently recruiting for Luton/Gatwick/
Bristol-based crew. If you are up for the challenge or know
someone who is, then please visit easyJet.com to complete an
online application. The crew on board today would also be
happy to answer any questions.'

'It is just a new way of recruiting staff,' explained an easyJet
spokeswoman. 'We are a low-cost airline – it saves money on
advertising.' In addition to providing a new avenue for cheap
promotion, it gave passengers the opportunity to 'go up and
ask the crew what it is like,' she maintained.

Fare rises at the carrier succeeded in boosting revenues and
the bottom line even amid flight cancellations. In July, easyJet
announced that booming business would send its profits for
2006 soaring up 50 per cent to £124 million – past £100 million
for the first time. Harrison set a target of doubling easyJet's
profit per passenger to £4 within three years.

Bad news followed in August 2006. The world held its
breath in fear of a repeat of 11 September 2001 after UK police
foiled an alleged terror plot to blow up transatlantic airliners
in mid-air. Terrorists targeted three US airlines, namely
United, American and Continental, and planned to hit flights
from Britain to New York, Washington and California.

The news of the failed terrorist attack prompted UK

airlines to delay and cancel flights and triggered a fresh round of increased security measures. Industry experts predicted that airlines could lose £300 million as a result of the tighter security introduced immediately after the alert, which included body searches for all passengers leaving British airports. It was feared that the extra costs would have to be passed on to passengers in the form of increased ticket prices.

Ryanair urged the British government to revise the 'heavy-handed' security measures. 'The goal of these terrorists and extremists is not just to kill but also to disrupt the economic life of Britain. The UK government, by insisting on these heavy-handed security measures, is allowing the extremists to achieve many of their objectives. It is vital that the government works with the UK airports and airlines to prevent the collapse of the London airports.'

Airport congestion prompted passengers to seek alternatives to the scheduled carriers. Executive jet brokers reported that all private jets for hire had been snapped up. Eurostar, whose new high-speed links to the Channel Tunnel already made it faster to get to central Paris than by plane, said it was running at full capacity as it registered an extra 5,500 bookings in the weekend following the terror alert.

Luggage restrictions were relaxed after the terror threat was downgraded from 'critical' to 'severe'. A new regime introduced by the government limited passengers' hand luggage to one small cabin bag no bigger than 45 cm by 35 cm by 16 cm – the size of a small laptop case and less than half the size travellers had been able to take on board before the terror plot. All liquids and aerosols, including toothpaste, shaving foam and deodorant, were banned indefinitely from all hand luggage.

Analysts were concerned that continuing restrictions on hand luggage would mean more baggage shifting to the hold and hence higher ground-handling costs and extended turnaround times. Over the previous couple of years easyJet and Ryanair had been encouraging passengers to carry more hand luggage so that they could make savings on baggage-handling charges and reduce aircraft turnarounds to just twenty-five minutes. Ryanair discouraged passengers from checking in baggage for the hold by introducing a fee of £3.50 per bag if booked in advance on its website, or £7 per bag if presented unbooked at the airport. EasyJet had resisted introducing charges for checked-in baggage but was understood to be considering it.

But easyJet and its rivals shrugged off the baggage rules threat. 'All the same people who predicted the death knell of low-cost airlines after 11 September are predicting the death knell of low-cost airlines now, purely because we can't take such big handbags on board,' noted easyJet's Toby Nicol. 'The low-cost airline model is significantly more robust than that.'

Airlines wanted BAA, the operator of seven UK airports, including Heathrow, Gatwick and Stansted, and the government to make a contribution to the costs of the disruption, which occurred at the height of the holiday season. British Airways estimated losses for cancelled flights from the security alert at £40 million. Ryanair sued the British government for £3 million in compensation for losses suffered from the disruption. Ryanair and BA criticised BAA for failing to have adequate contingency plans in place even though some sort of security alert had been widely anticipated.

EasyJet estimated it lost £4 million as a result of the security alert, which caused it to cancel 469 departures. The carrier cancelled 290 flights on the day of the initial disruption on 10 August, before cancelling 112 flights the next day and another 67 flights in the ensuing days. Added to that were accommodation costs for the majority of affected customers, who could also change any bookings in the period, free of charge, or receive a refund.

Despite the losses, easyJet insisted it was on course to increase profits for the year ending 30 September 2006 by between 40 per cent and 50 per cent, following a profit of £68 million in the previous year.

By October, our friendly no-frills airline had upgraded its forecast for annual profits following a better-than-expected boost in passenger numbers. EasyJet believed it was 'slightly ahead' of profit expectations after September passenger numbers increased by 9.8 per cent to just over 3 million. Total revenues per seat were also rising, this time by 7.8 per cent on the previous year.

Meanwhile, Ryanair was also making the headlines. On 5 October, the Irish carrier launched an audacious and hostile £1.48 billion takeover bid for Aer Lingus, the former Irish state airline that had floated on the Stock Exchange only the previous week. Ryanair had recently bought a 16 per cent stake in Aer Lingus and it now offered to buy the remainder for £2.80 a share in cash, a 27 per cent premium to its float price.

'This offer represents an unique opportunity to form one strong airline group for Ireland and for European consumers,' Ryanair's chief executive Michael O'Leary said.

The move raised competition concerns, with fears that Ryanair would gobble up Aer Lingus and create a near-monopoly on air travel in Ireland.

O'Leary planned to cut Aer Lingus' short-haul fares by an average of 2.5 per cent a year for four years at least. After coming close to bankruptcy in 2002 because of a bloated payroll and lost business following the 11 September attacks, Aer Lingus had managed a turnaround. The airline had essentially emulated Ryanair's successful formula by slashing staff and moving to a low-cost model focusing on European routes.

Aer Lingus dismissed the bid, calling the offer 'derisory' as well as 'ill-conceived, contradictory and anticompetitive'.

In November, Ryanair raised its stake in its fellow Irish carrier to 25 per cent, in effect blocking anyone else from making a bid for the company. By December, however, Ryanair had withdrawn its ambitious bid after the European Commission announced an 'in-depth investigation' into its plans. A statement issued by Brussels said the proposed acquisition 'could reduce choice for consumers and could give rise to higher fares than would be likely if the two carriers remained separate.'

But Ryanair said that if the EC cleared the way for the proposed takeover in the future, it would make a further offer.

Low-cost carriers were growing at a rapid rate, even without takeovers. EasyJet now carried more than 32 million passengers a year – a boon for the airline but not for the Green lobby, which pointed out that airplane emissions were now the fastest rising source of greenhouse gases. It was becoming clear that future generations would possibly pay the real price of cheap flights. Emissions from air traffic had doubled since 1990 and were projected to quintuple by 2050 as more people took advantage of low fares. Environmentalists pointed out that aviation accounted for between 7 and 11 per cent of Britain's harmful carbon dioxide emissions.

Jeff Gazzard, a spokesman for the Green Skies Alliance, estimated the environmental costs of flying at around 3.6p per kilometre. Carbon dioxide emissions from one return flight from London to Florida are equivalent to those produced by a year's motoring. Fly from London to Edinburgh for the weekend and you produce 193kg of CO_2, eight times the amount you would produce by taking the train. Moreover, pollution is released at an altitude where its effect on climate change is more than double that on the ground.

The UK government claimed to act to reduce the environmental impact of flights when it controversially imposed a hike in air passenger duty. Chancellor Gordon Brown doubled the tax to £10 from £5 for economy short-haul flights and to £40 from £20 for long-haul flights.

The travelling public were infuriated to learn that the tax was retrospective, applying to when passengers flew, not to when they paid for their fare. This meant that an estimated four million pre-booked holiday flights cost more than expected, as did many pre-planned business trips.

British Airways said it would absorb the increases on flights bought before the government made the announcement in December 2006 and charge the extra duty on tickets bought thereafter. Meanwhile, no-frills carriers such as Ryanair and easyJet simply asked passengers to pay the extra duty. EasyJet officials dressed as tax inspectors approached passengers arriving at Luton Airport to pay the tax, if they had not already done so, on 1 February 2007, the first day of the tax increase.

Airlines scoffed at Brown's claims that the extra tax was designed to combat global warming, alleging that the levy was just another way of filling Treasury coffers.

'The Chancellor has come up with a tax that will do nothing for the environment while penalising the travelling public opinion even more,' said easyJet's chief executive, Andy Harrison. He claimed it didn't provide any incentive for airlines to run the cleanest aircraft and pointed out that its proceeds were not allocated to any scheme to improve the environment.

'Airlines could significantly reduce CO_2 emissions if Europe's governments would reform our medieval air traffic management systems and would stamp out the illegal subsidies that are still given to ailing national airlines that fly old, half-empty airplanes,' he said.

The chief executive insisted that he operated an 'environmentally friendly' airline, comparing easyJet's network of seventy-four airports in twenty-one countries to public transport. Harrison said its low-cost model of fuller planes, direct flights and newer aircraft were greener than the traditional 'hub and spoke' system of connecting flights operated by other airlines.

The airline has introduced a new environmental code in its corporate and social responsibility report as part of its mission to be seen as 'green'. The code includes pledges to improve the environmental efficiency of its ground suppliers at airports and to participate in the introduction of 'meaningful' European emissions-trading arrangements.

EasyJet pointed out that the average age of its fleet fell from three years to 2.2 years in September 2006. The airline's carbon dioxide emissions per passenger kilometre fell by 18 per cent since 2000, while its A319 aircraft fleet carried 26 per cent more seats and 57 per cent more passengers than the European norm, according to the report. The airline was working with manufacturers to help create more environmentally friendly aircraft, although the next generation of short-haul aircraft is not expected to reach the market until 2015.

No doubt easyJet will become more aware of the environmental impact of travel and will have to battle with a new set of challenges over the next ten years. But at the start of 2007, the once-fledgling carrier is now a heavyweight contender in the world of aviation, respected by those who previously laughed at its no-frills ideas, and taken seriously by those who dismissed it as destined for failure. The airline's garish choice of orange is as well known as its low-cost philosophy – after all, easyJet is now a household name. One thing seems certain, whatever hurdles it faces in the future: easyJet is here to stay.

Index